MINESWEEPER
The Role of the
Motor Minesweeper in
World War II

SHIP ON THE SHORE

What derelict is there,
Lifeless, stranded
Upon the muddy shore,
Like a whale landed
Last night from some remote
Lost land, surely to be
Too old and battered to float
Again on the sea?

Will it lie, old and gaunt,
To rot as the harsh winds ride
Through the torn rigging, haunt
The shore with its broken pride,
Where gulls and the children play
Or secretly, unseen, slide
Strange as it came, away
On a darkening tide?

Anon

Campaign Honours Home and Abroad, 1939–1945

MINESWEEPER

The Role of the
Motor Minesweeper in
World War II

*Especially for you
Dad.
July 1992*

Michael J. Melvin BEM

A Square One Publication

Published in 1992 by
Square One Publications
Saga House, Sansome Place, Worcester WR1 1UA

© Michael J. Melvin 1992

British Library Cataloguing in Publication Data
A catalogue record for this book is available from the British Library
ISBN: 1 872017 57 6

Typeset in 10/11 Bembo and Printed by Severnside Printers Ltd.,
Upton-upon-Severn, Worcs.

Dedication

The wooden Minesweeper was designed and built by numerous yards both at home and overseas as a counter-measure for the dreaded menace of the enemy's acoustic and magnetic mines of World War II, which threatened to send all our ships, Naval and Mercantile, as well as those of the allied forces, to Davy Jones' Locker. That this did not in effect happen is due to the bravery and expertise of the valiant crews who were taken from their civilian professions and thrown in, as it were, at the deep end, overcoming by the skin of their teeth what had become frightening and horrifying odds.

   This book has been written to help to place their achievements on record for all time and it is to those men, and in particular to those who failed to return from the conflict, that *Minesweeper* is dedicated.

Acknowledgements

To the writers of PAD, Lt/Cdr J.A.B. Harrison DSC, RNVR, and Lt/Cdr H.J. Galsworthy RNVR, for the verse at the close of the book: Salute To The Wavy Navy.

To the ex-officers and ratings of the various ships who have taken the time to write with information about their experiences, and to supply material and photographs for inclusion in this book. I can only apologise that I have not been able to include it all. Also for their continued encouragement to put pen to paper.

To the late Lt/Cdr Henry Ceulemans RNVR for his Foreword and expert critique of my original transcript.

Public Records Office, Kew.

Naval Historical Library, London.

The Imperial War Museum and
to many others whose help has been most appreciated, especially my wife Jean who has had to put up with my endless hours in front of a word processor over the last twelve years.

Contents

Foreword

This book provides a comprehensive, exciting, and a much needed history of the role played by the Motor Minesweeper in World WarII.

By the nature of the subject, it carries unavoidably a considerable amount of statistics, but the author has managed very skilfully to blend these with an interesting, realistic and very often humorous narrative.

I paid special attention to the minesweeping operations in which I, as an officer commanding one of these ships, was involved. I found them described in a very accurate and professional manner. They gave me, and I am sure will the readers, a precise and detailed insight of the intricate components of the art of mine warfare.

However, I consider that the two outstanding features of this book are:

(a) the tremendous and inexhaustable amount of research that has gone into its production;
(b) The robust way it tackles – to my knowledge for the first time – firmly and squarely the fact that we were totally unprepared to deal in an effective way with the German mine threat.

The author brings out most vividly, that during the long period in which attempts were made to redress this situation, fundamental errors of judgement were made, coupled with inefficiency and unacceptable delays.

Despite our efforts, the Germans were able to keep up their initiative and as the author puts it "were always a step ahead."

The question can then be asked it we ever did close the gap. My understanding is that the author believes we did not. I agree with him.

At the end of hostilities, however, we were all firmly convinced that we had beaten the German mine. But did we in reality? I don't think so.

The German magnetic mine and the combinations that followed, were all very sophisticated weapons fitted with precise and sensitive circuits and manufactured with non-magnetic materials. By adopting the dip-needle variety, these mines had to be very accurately compensated to the earth's magnetic environment in which they were earmarked to be planted, and this should remind us that this environment varied considerably over the length and breadth of the British Isles.

Considering very carefully all the factors and arguments outlined above, there can be but little doubt that they must have appreciably curtailed the flexibility of the German mining operations. I believe that this prevented them from carrying out a sustained and saturated mining operation in British waters. Deprived of this capability, as I believe they were, there was no chance of bringing the entire Allied shipping movement around these islands to a complete halt, as no doubt was the German intention.

The American mining operations against the Japanese at the close of the war in the Far East, further substantiates this argument, where induction type mines, cheap and easy to manufacture, were used with great success, not only destroying enemy shipping, but leaving a trail of inconvenient wrecks, and bringing the Japanese shipping to a complete standstill.

In conclusion, the type of mine utilised by Germany, which, on the one hand undoubtedly acted as a brake on their operations, and on the other, the considerable skill and courage displayed by all classes of sweepers, allowed us to keep abreast of the situation and avoided being overwhelmed by it.

Of course all this does not in any way distract from the importance of the contribution made by the Motor Minesweepers. Their officers and crews blissfully unaware of what was happening in the corridors of power, displayed, despite the odds, skill, professionalism, and above all courage of the highest degree. For them there were no heroics, only a never ending day in and day out slog to keep the sea lanes open to shipping. The contribution made by these gallant little ships can never be over-rated. This book gives them the place they so rightly deserve.

Lt/Cmdr Henry Ceulemans RNR (Rtd.)
Officer Commanding MMS 191
1942–1945
7th November 1989.

Henry Ceulemans died in June 1990

Introduction

Only part of the story concerning the minesweeping activities of World War II can be told, but Minesweeper does try to explain in a way not done before, the trials, tribulations, errors and indeed the frustrations, together with the successes and some of the lighter moments which came as a result of seeking to combat and equally to eliminate, not only the magnetic mine so cunningly developed prior to and during the early years of the war, but also the other types of mine utilised by the enemy, whose aim was to demoralise and subsequently defeat the allies.

Neither is it claimed that the Motor Minesweepers did all the work. That would be tantamount to showing a great deal of disrespect for the many other vessels and their crews who were called upon to aid in what was to become one of the most difficult, harrassing and dangerous tasks of the war.

The Mickey Mouse (with apologies to Walt Disney) as these vessels came to be affectionately called, formed the largest percentage of inshore craft designed specifically to deal with the magnetic menace and particularly to operate within the five fathom line of the coast, seeking out the enemy which constantly threatened the shipping lanes and the estuaries leading, not only to our British ports and harbours but also to those of our allies in Europe and beyond.

It is only right therefore, that the work done by these worthy craft and their crews should be recognised for what it was...a truly remarkable endurance test, carried out under the most difficult conditions imaginable.

It also needs bearing in mind that without these vessels and their valiant crews, much of what was accomplished would never have taken place, and whatever might be said of the 'big ships', the truth will always remain that, wherever they were destined to sail, the sweepers had already been.

It is then with the deepest admiration and respect for the ships' companies involved that I pen these words, not because I happened to be among them, but because they set out on a task completely alien to anything they had done before, and from which they were never sure they would return.

It has also been my humble privilege to have been associated with many of the officers and men since those hectic days, and sadly on occasions I have had the honour to officiate at their passing and sometimes to commit their remains to the sea where they spent so many anxious days and nights.

I write then conscious always of the many omissions and mistakes I am likely to make in presenting such a record, and indeed my inability to do justice to the task, but it is a record that must be made, before all of those who played any part in this particular aspect of the war have quietly slipped their cables. I hope that whatever follows will prove its worth to historians and indeed to those whom I salute within its pages.

Michael Melvin

Chapter One

A mystery resolved, a deficiency revealed, and a job to be done.

The scene is an aircrew adrift in a dinghy, their aircraft having been shot down in the sea. On the fifth day while trying to keep themselves alive by creating some kind of competition, the crew decided to see who could keep their head longest under the water.

The navigator was the first to have a go. As he brought his head out of the water he shouted, "There's a bloody great mine down there."

They all had a look and there it was, covered with barnacles...one of those gigantic circular affairs with knobs on.

That was only the tip of the iceberg. For when the war broke out in September 1939, public records show that at least 200,000 moored mines had been laid in the North Sea alone. German cruisers, destroyers, torpedo boats and submarines, to say nothing of aircraft, had been deployed to lay all of these and many more between the third and sixth of September off Flamborough Head, Orfordness, Hartlepool and Dover.

This news alone ought to have been sufficient to prompt any nation to take urgent measures to deal with this menace, particularly in view of the fact that Britain, more than any other nation, had to keep her sea lanes open in order to survive. She was however totally unprepared to deal in any effective way with what was to become a growing headache and an almost unsurmountable task.

Our complement of minesweeping vessels at the outbreak of war was, to say the least, totally inadequate, even for the relatively simple task of maintaining free shipping lanes around the coast, which were essential for the safe passage of our merchant and naval craft. The truth is that there was nowhere that could be considered safe. Our one and only minesweeping flotilla consisting of 23 improved Hunt Class ships, was operating in Middle and Far Eastern waters. The only other vessels available were four trawlers designed for this work, plus 17 Halcyon Class Fleet sweepers...far too few to cope with any degree of efficiency and satisfaction which would give mariners some kind of assurance that they would not be continually running into underwater dangers.

Recommendations had been made by the Admiralty as far back as 1936, to the

Magnetic Mine

Magnetic Mine - Spezia run

Enemy mineladen Barges

The interior of the magnetic mine. The scale marked Gauss proved that the mine was magnetic.

The basic arrangement of the actuator of a magnetic mine. The contacts were wired to an electrical firing mechanism.

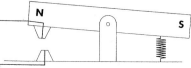

effect that 68 vessels should be built over five years. Further proposals came in July of 1939, asking that as many shallow draught minesweeping craft should be laid down as soon as possible, and utilising as many shipbuilding yards as was possible.

Nothing however transpired to supplement the existing few vessels we had, although there were 14 trawlers, four of which were ex-Russian, the *Dee, Garry, Kennet* and *Luffey*, plus 10 bought in 1935, the *Lilac, Sycamore, Magnolia, Cypress, Hawthorn, Syringa, Willow, Cedar, Holly* and *Laurel* used for minesweeping training.

In addition there were 47 sweepers planned for the Far East and 21 for Home waters. One would have thought that the reverse would have been the order of the day in view of the pending hostilities, but the fact that mine-warfare was not even considered as a possibility, led the government of the day to be satisfied with 21 ships deployed as follows:

Firth of Forth 5: Portsmouth/ Southampton 5: Dover 2: Scapa Flow 2: Liverpool 2: Plymouth 3.

London, together with all the East coast harbours was for reasons unknown, left without any protection in the early arrangements, which in many respects was strange because of its proximity to the European coast. However the first few months of the war were to reveal that the estimates given fell far below the number of craft really required for the task.

So, to meet the emergency in 1939, (and it is interesting to note at this point the strength of the minesweeping fleet of the first world war after requisitioning had taken place...1025 ships in 1918) 150 trawlers were requisitioned from the fishing fleets, and these together with the 17 Halcyon Class fleet sweepers of 815 tons, plus 30 commandeered paddle steamers, constituted the minesweeping line of defence.

There was a great deal of discussion regarding the possible return of the 23 Hunt Class from abroad, but no decision was taken. 30 Bangor Class sweepers at a cost of £140,000 each were in the process of being built, but the first seven of these would not be available till January 1941, that is 17 months later. Approval had also been sought for the purchase of 12 Bord Class vessels, but the Bangor Class were especially urgent in order so it was claimed, that the 23 Hunt Class could be phased out, having been built during the emergency programme of the first World War. It was felt that they were too old for the task, but it would seem that any old ship would certainly have been better than none at all.

The fact that the Navy had taken the view quite wrongly, that the mine was essentially the weapon of lesser Naval powers, deflected attention away from the study of mines and their use in times of conflict, and this may have influenced the view that the vessels available would be more than able to cope with anything the enemy was likely to arrange in the development of underwater warfare. There was a belief at that time, that mines laid on the sea bed i.e. magnetic or otherwise

3

would be too far away from the ship to do any serious damage even if they were detonated, and this view led to an interest mainly in the buoyant mine, and this in spite of the fact that magnetic mines were devised for the Admiralty during the 1914-1918 war by Sir Frank Smith the then Secretary of the Department of Scientific and Industrial Research. Some of these had, during those earlier days, been laid in the North Sea.

Against what was to prove to be the most effective weapon the Germans had produced at that stage, all the ships we had, were seen to be totally ineffective. It was R.V. Jones in his book 'The Most Secret War', who stated that "had magnetic mines been used in sufficient numbers and with sufficient ingenuity, they could have brought our economy to a standstill."

They nearly did, and this was borne out on the 10th September, seven days after hostilities had begun when the steam vessel *Magdepur* was sunk off the east coast of England, following a great deal of effort by the few sweepers we had to keep the lanes in that area clear of mines. In November of 1939, HMS *Gipsy* went down off Harwich with the loss of 40 personnel. Added to that, in the same week, the Dutch liner *Simon Bolivar*, carrying more than 380 passengers met her fate. 130 lives were lost. The Harwich and Manningtree Standard reported, "Maimed and injured passengers were carried ashore and orphaned babies coated in oil looked like bundles of cotton waste."

The Japanese liner *Terukuni Maru* was sent to Davey Jones's locker on the same day as HMS *Gipsy*.

Following the sinking of these vessels, three of the five paddle sweepers of the 12th. Minesweeping Flotilla based at Harwich – the *Queen Empress, Duchess Rothsay* and the *Lorna Doone* were sent out to clear the area and after hours of sweeping no mines were detonated or cut loose. These ships were fitted with Oropesa sweeping gear designed to cut away moored or contact mines. No thought was given at that time to the fact that magnetic mines might be the cause of all the havoc.

As a matter of general interest the other 25 paddle sweepers were dispersed around the British coast:

The 7th. Minesweeping Flotilla at Rosyth with seven ships

the 8th. MSF at North Shields with five

the 10th. at Dover with eight vessels and five at Greenock on the west coast of Scotland making up the 11th.MSF.

The *Magdepur* was the first victim of many mysterious explosions in the same channel in the North Sea and which left the Admiralty completely baffled as to the cause of the losses. Fortunately for the government of the day, a German aircraft inadvertently dropped its load of mines too close to the shore line and on the morning of the 20th. November 1939, just about 24 hours later, as the tide receded, one of the mines was uncovered, all seven feet of it, in the mud off Shoeburyness.

The story of its recovery is now legend, but well worth repeating if only to

4

commend the bravery of the four men who were involved in what can only be regarded as a very dangerous business, dealing with an underwater weapon they knew virtually nothing about and which was likely to explode at any second.

The mine was defused by Lieut. Commander Ouvery of the Royal Naval Torpedo and Mining School HMS *Vernon*, assisted by Lieutenant Commander Lewis, Chief Petty Officer Baldwin and Able Seaman Vearnecombe. The intricate mechanism of the mine was unravelled by the chief scientist of the Mine Design Department.

On the 24th November the secret of the magnetic mine was laid bare and the sinking of the *Magdepur* and other unfortunate and indefensible craft was resolved. The mines it was revealed, were being detonated by the "magnetic signature" acquired during the construction of the vessel and generated by the steel hull of the ships passing overhead.

This resulted in extensive efforts being made to find an effective solution to this growing problem, for there was no telling where these monsters of the deep were likely to rear their ugly heads or to use a more appropriate expression 'blow their tops.'

The four Naval personnel were suitably rewarded for their bravery, the officers receiving the Distiguished Service Order and the ratings the Distiguished Service Medal. Someone was heard to mention that the award was well earned, "after all, they might have been drowned."

It became obvious that some kind of effective plan had to be devised and implemented if the shipping lanes were to be kept clear for the 10,000 invariably unescorted ships which made up the merchant fleet, that is, clear of both moored and magnetic mines, even though it was recognised as early as July 1939 that there was nowhere near the number of ships suitably fitted out to carry out the job. Certainly there were no minesweepers available for the disposal of magnetic mines, for nothing had at this stage been invented to deal with this unknown quantity. Because of the fatalities in the North Sea there was a need to concentrate all available craft in that area. Trawlers were the obvious choice, primarily because of their availability and ease of conversion, but they could not deal with the magnetic problem, because of their metal structure and their deep draught of 18 feet. Magnetic mines were generally most effective in shallow waters, that is in river estuaries up to a depth of 20 fathoms and often in depths of less than three fathoms.

Another difficulty which faced the Navy in those days was the acute shortage of trained personnel required to man the vessels which were rapidly being converted to deal with the minesweeping task of keeping the lanes clear, for the 200,000 mines already laid were being added to daily.

Plans to increase the number of ships were subsequently made and this was to take effect in two stages. Firstly to include the conversion of 230 fishing trawlers, and secondly as equipment became available, another 346 would be added to the fleet bringing the total number of operational vessels up to 576.

The plan unfortunately never materialised in spite of the urgency of the task, due to a disagreement between the Admiralty and the Ministry of Food, the latter claiming that fish was more important or just as important as any commodity which might be lost due to any active mining policy of the enemy.

It was pointed out that there were only two marked secret channels which might be considered free for any kind of movement along the coast line, and that unless trawlers wanted to remain unscathed, they would do well to stick to the one lane for fishing purposes. This was emphasised by the Director of Navigation, but the Ministry of Food won the day, and 375 earmarked vessels were duly returned to the fishing grounds.

It would seem that this may have been due to the intervention of the First Sea Lord who states in a minute to the Controller and Third Sea Lord dated 18th. October 1939:

"It is vital to keep the fish trade going, and we must fight for this part of our food supply as hard as we do against the U Boats."

It did not seem to occur to him that without the sweepers they stood in marked danger not only of losing many vessels, but equally of losing precious fishing grounds because of mine infestation. In fact the records show that up until the end of 1941, a total of 219 trawlers had been lost.

The return of the trawlers to the fishing fleets created an immediate deficiency and it was suggested that this might be made up by purchasing vessels from abroad and bringing home the 23 ships from the Mediterranean belonging to the 3rd Minesweeping Flotilla.

Added to this, directives were issued to the effect that all steps should be taken to hinder the enemy in his minelaying activities, using anti-submarine and patrol vessels of whatever shape or form to harrass and prevent as far as they were able, the extensive minelaying operations that were taking place in certain restricted areas of the east coast. This was to include the combined efforts of air and surface craft.

The few anti-submarine ships we had then had been allocated to the Thames, Bristol Channel and Liverpool areas. The rest of the coastline was barren of any kind of assistance.

It was also arranged that there should be a minimum of two approach channels to each port, keeping them as far apart as possible before converging on the entrance, thereby giving access via one channel while the other was being swept. It was recognised however that there would be times when passage was not possible, necessitating the introduction of early morning and night sweeping procedures which presented their own problems. Night sweeping was an unknown quantity and is discussed in another chapter of this book.

Ships were routed outside the 20 fathom line as far as that could be achieved, but they inevitably had to traverse the shallow waters of the estuaries where the danger from magnetic mines was highest.

Meanwhile there were frantic efforts to convert the existing Borde Class mercantile craft into minesweepers.

There were ten of these ships requisitioned primarily because, having a large forward hold, they were able to accommodate one of the 300 ton magnets which had been designed at short notice as a counter measure for the new underwater menace.

The magnet consisted of a bundle of steel rails each 200 feet long and wrapped with yards of wire, then stowed in the bow of the ship.

The idea was to create a magnetic field in front of the vessel, and in so doing destroy the offending mines. Three of their number, HMS *Corburn*, HMS *Corfield* and HMS *Queenworth* were lost in quick succession primarily because they worked too well. The bow of the ship was blown off.

Their use therefore when they finally became operational, was to say the least limited, certainly for minesweeping purposes, but it was one of the early attempts to deal with the problem.

They were quickly transferred to another role as Minesweeping Maintenance Vessels. There is little known of these craft except to say that their displacement was about 2000 tons gross. The writer has never met anyone who served on any of them.

Others methods in an attempt to deal with the magnetic mine are described in another chapter.

Many endeavours were made at stopping the incursion of mine-laying craft into British waters, including the laying of a mine barrage across the Dover Straits (3000 mines), together with another barrage across the North Sea, using five converted merchantmen of the 1st. Minelaying Squadron.

This effort was switched from the North Sea to the waters dividing Scotland and Ireland, involving the laying of 100,000 mines, all of which had some measured success, but did not prevent the loss of 78 merchant ships of over a quarter of a million tons during November and December of 1939.

It is important at this stage to explain something of the development of the magnetic sweep and how it was finally brought into operation.

Late in October 1939 an extemporised form of magnetic sweep was devised, but only after a great deal of trial, tribulation and effort. The sweep consisted of twin copper cables 750 feet long and fitted with electrodes at the tail end. It was known as the double longtitudinal sweep or for short the Double 'L'. The cables were waterproofed, buoyed and towed astern of the minesweeping vessel.

The development and manufacture of these cables is a story worth relating, and starts with two companies who probably never envisaged that they were ever likely to work in such close cooperation, for their products were as unlike as chalk is to cheese.

The two companies involved were British Insulated Callendar's Cables Limited, and Henley's Tyre and Rubber Company. They were entrusted with the task of producing as fast as was humanly possible, some kind of device as a countermeasure for the magnetic mine.

MMS 189 in operation – 1944/45

MMS 191 in operation off the East Coast – 1944

Cross-section Double L Sweep

MMS 30 in action

On the 22nd. of November 1939, following the discovery of that first magnetic mine off Shoeburyness, a proposal was made by B.I.C.C. that the use of electricity might just solve the problem, the idea being to create a magnetic field astern of those ships chosen for the minesweeping task. The cable was invented by a Mr. P.V. Hunter B.B.E., M.I.E.E., and the principle submitted to the Admiralty on December 23rd. 1939. (The photograph shows a section of the sweeping cable as it was later developed).

Both companies (and there were few in Britain in a position to take on such an assignment) mobilised their resources and the double 'L' sweep became a reality after overcoming a great deal of production problems. The main difficulty was that the cable, all 750 feet of it, had to be able to float, thus the need for Henley's cylindrical rubber balls. This idea was introduced by Dr. Percy Dunsheath O.B.E., Director and Chief Engineer at Henley's, after experiments had been made with ebonite (an early form of plastic) expanded cylinders, and special low density cork.

During the course of the war one million yards of cable and 23 million rubber balls were provided from the works at Erith and Gravesend, and a repair and maintenance service was provided in Europe long after hostilities had ceased, primarily because the clearance of minefields proved to be a problem long after the end of the war.

Through these twin cables, electricity, provided by two 54 KVA generators was passed at 3000 amps. This was done at predetermined intervals and in conjunction with two other sweepers, thus creating a magnetic field over the surface of the water astern of the ships, enabling the mines to be detonated. At least that was the theory, and it worked up to a point for some of the time, but not all of the time as the months ahead clearly began to show.

On the Motor Minesweeper, which did not appear on the scene until 1941, the sweep was stored on a gigantic steel drum fitted on the quarter deck just aft of the galley and toilets, and in the early days turned by handles port and starboard and manned by eight members of the crew, four on either side. Prior to the introduction of the drum, the sweep on the earlier type vessels such as the requisitioned trawlers, was manhandled and festooned around the deck as illustrated in the drawing by Mr. Cook of Paignton in Devon, who served aboard such vessels as well as others.

It proved to be quite a formidable task, especially in heavy weather conditions. There were records broken every day.

Later, some of the more inventive crews devised contraptions which would have put Heath Robinson to shame, involving the use of blocks and shackles and ropes...indeed anything that would save the crew from winding those 'bloody handles'. This was in fact a blessing, for the task was made that much easier in spite of the many bleeding fingers and knuckles suffered by those such as the engineroom branch who were unfamiliar with the handling of ropes and tackle.

The first trial of the double 'L' was made in December 1939, although the first

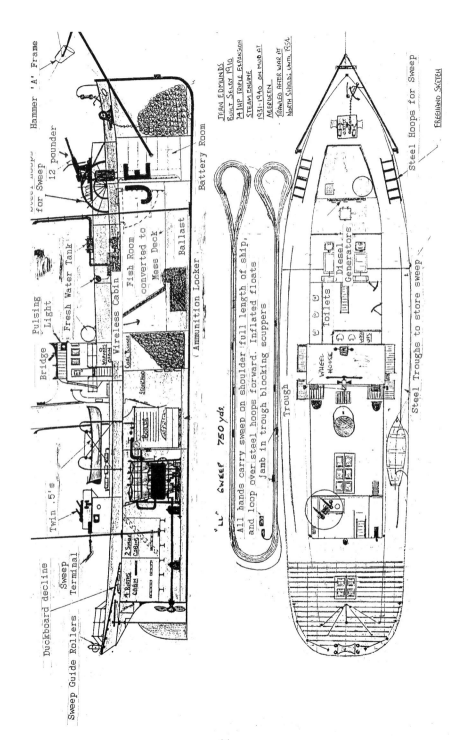

Sweep Guide Rollers
Duckboard decline
Sweep Terminal
Twin 5's

Bridge
Pulsing Light
Fresh Water Tank
12 pounder
Hammer 'A' Frame
Steel Hoops for Sweep

W/T Wireless Cabin
Fish Room converted to Mess Deck
Ballast
Ammunition Locker
Battery Room

JEAN EDMUNDS
BUILT SELBY 1910
74 HP TRIPLE EXPANSION
STEAM ENGINE
1931-1940 ON MUD AT
ABERDEEN
TRAWLED AFTER WAR AT
NORTH SHIELDS UNTIL 1954

Steel Hoops for Sweep
FREEHAND SKETCH

Diesel Generators
Toilets
WHEEL HOUSE

Steel Troughs to store sweep

'LL' SWEEP 750 yds.

All hands carry sweep on shoulder full length of ship,
and loop over steel hoops forward. Inflated floats
jamb in trough blocking scuppers

Trough

reel of floating cable was not delivered until May 1940. Out sweep was an easy matter, but until the introduction of electrically powered sweep drums toward the latter end of the war, 'in sweep' was an exercise which nobody really enjoyed, even though it invariably meant the end of a long session at sea.

The ship would be heading for her home port with the hope of a night or two ashore, or indeed the possibility of all night leave and an opportunity for some to slip off home for an hour or two. That invariably meant, as few lived near the harbour, getting up at some unearthly hour of the morning to catch a train back to base, where sailing orders might have been delivered for slipping at 0800 hours. Many a matelot has nearly missed the boat on such an occasion, one of the worst crimes so we were told in the Navy.

But of course most of the personnel were Patrol Service and were not altogether aware of what the Royal Navy was all about, although some of the more 'pusser' skippers of the Wavy Navy were quick to remind their crews about Standing Orders and the like, with the inevitable threats of 'chokey' for those who were wont to misbehave.

It has already been mentioned that extemporised forms of magnetic sweep were tried out. The fiasco with the railway lines in the bows of the Borde Class sweepers was one of many attempted failures.

Not to be outdone, however, the same 300-ton magnets were utilised on large wooden skids, which were towed behind an adapted tug fitted with a pulsing electric generator. With a cable slung from tug to raft to energise the 16-foot diameter magnet, the magnetic field was created and was largely successful, except that following the explosion it was not unusual to have to return to base to collect another raft, but not before marking the spot where the magnet had been sunk, with the hope of a recovery exercise at a later time. Again, that was the theory, but as time went on, it was one that became increasingly difficult to maintain. It was an expensive business, but nothing compared with the loss of a merchant ship.

Two types of these towed skids were produced, and manufactured in a great hurry to meet the critical situation which developed following the discovery that the enemy was laying magnetic mines all over the place.

The Mark 1, the total weight of which was 21.6 tons, was designed to sweep on a 300-foot tow line up to speeds of five knots, and the Mark II with a well formed hull was capable of being towed at about 25 knots. Details of these skids are as follows:

MARK I

This must have been a strange looking device for it consisted of a 24 square foot platform to support the electro-magnet and this in turn was carried on two wooden pontoons, square in section, length 41 feet and beam 18 feet. The sides were six feet high. They were built from rough stage deals with seam strips inboard, and fitted with a number of watertight bulkheads spaced about four feet apart. With a swim end bow and a square cut transom, they took anything between a week and a fortnight to produce.

They were however subject to leaks making it necessary for a number of large pumps to get rid of the excess water every time they returned to base, that is if they were lucky enough to make it home. Leaky skids were a menace for they were likely to capsize, primarily due to the 300-ton magnet carried on board, making them top heavy.

How many were lost in this manner is not known, but if it was true that they were unstable in smooth waters one can only imagine the problems when it became a bit choppy. A sunken skip was likely to take the tug with it and no doubt there are still those who could tell some hairy tales of their antics at sea.

In the later Mark I skids, the compartments were filled with empty herring barrels to keep the skid afloat and operational when leaks occurred.

MARK II
This was a little more sophisticated and a better built craft. Constructed of double diagonal larch or any other clean timber, and with double diagonal bulkheads, they were quite successful from the design point of view. It was reckoned to produce these in about three weeks, given that the builder was a craftsman. They had an overall length of 52ft.6in., a beam of 16 ft 3 in, and a draught of 5 ft. 6 in.

Altogether these contraptions, for such they were, proved to be very useful at a critical period of the war when there was nothing else available, but were soon superseded with the advance of the technique in the sweeping of magnetic mines in deeper waters. The skids continued to be used throughout the war for, however Heath Robinson they appeared to be, they still had some advantages over the double 'L', especially in manoeuverability in narrow waters, where ships did not have the space to turn around.

The first ships to use the double 'L' sweep were seven small requisitioned tugs operating in the River Thames; *Salvo; Scythe; Solitaire; Souvenir; Servitor; Shako* and *Slogan*, and while ships began to be fitted out gradually with the new equipment as it came off stream, additional measures were taken to see that ships were demagnetised, especially those made of steel.

This exercise was known as 'wiping', when vessels were literally draped with wire cables through which an electric current was passed to remove the magnetic signature from the ships hull, then fitted with degaussing equipment consisting of twin cables permanently attached to the inside hull of the ship and activated by one of the ship's generators when at sea. This would keep the magnetic signature down to a minimum, thereby reducing the ship's mine target area.

It also did a great deal for the morale of those whose task it was to deal with the mines, and who at that time had almost become persuaded that there was little hope of ever finding any answer to these devils of the sea.

There were at that time 10,000 ships on Lloyd's Register, so it was no mean

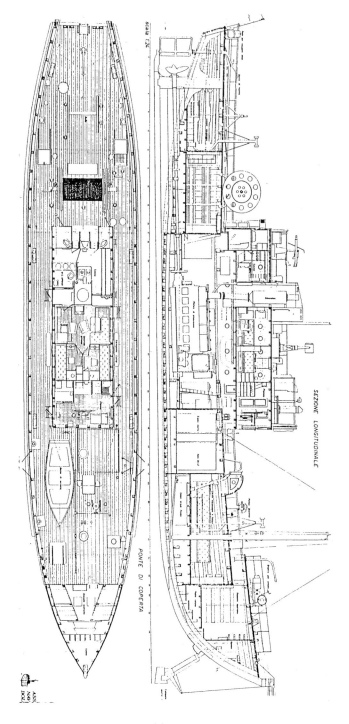

SCALE: 12 FEET TO 1 INCH

scala 1/24

SEZIONE LONGITUDINALE

PONTE DI COPERTA

14

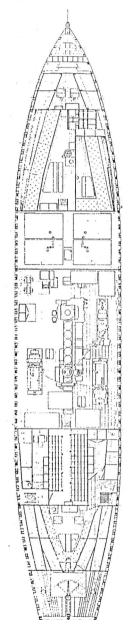

PLAN OF LOWER DECK

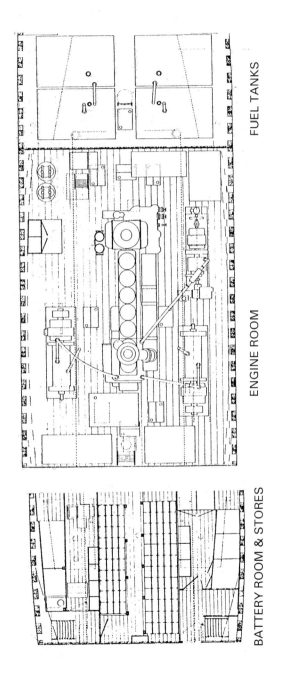

FUEL TANKS

ENGINE ROOM

BATTERY ROOM & STORES

15

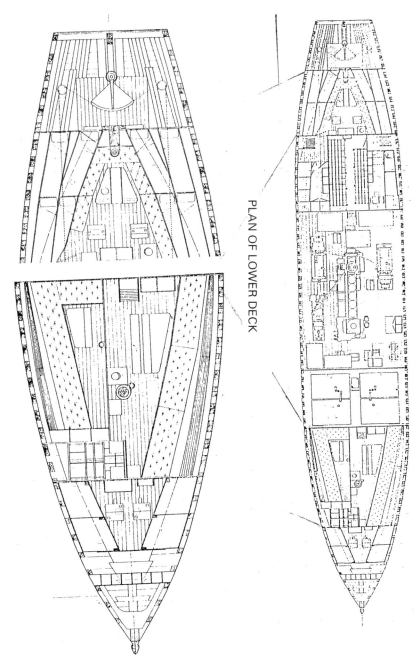

AFTER MESS

PLAN OF LOWER DECK

FORWARD MESS/STORES/AMMUNITION LOCKER
CHAIN LOCKER

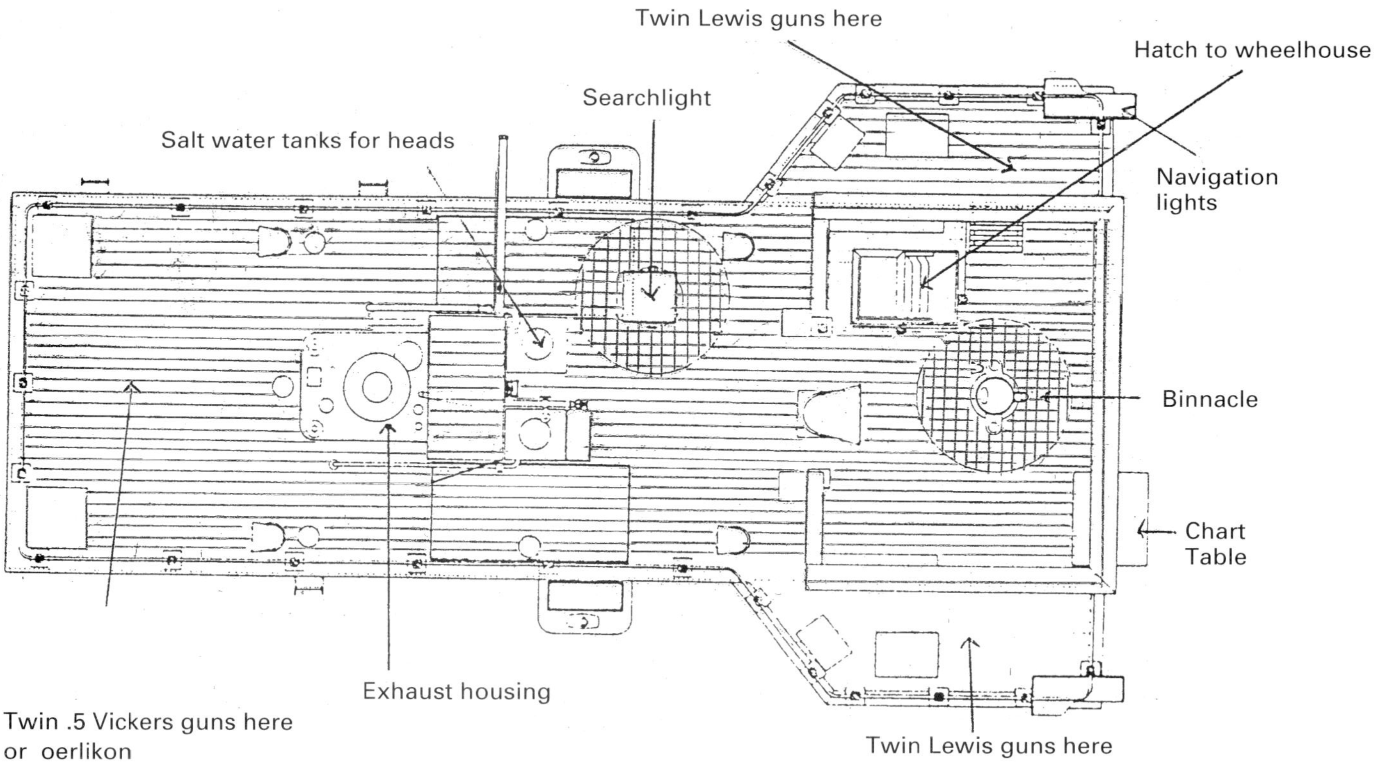

Hatch to wheelhouse

Navigation
lights

Binnacle

Chart
Table

Twin Lewis guns here

Twin Lewis guns here

Searchlight

Salt water tanks for heads

Exhaust housing

Twin .5 Vickers guns here
or oerlikon

PLAN OF OPEN BRIDGE

17

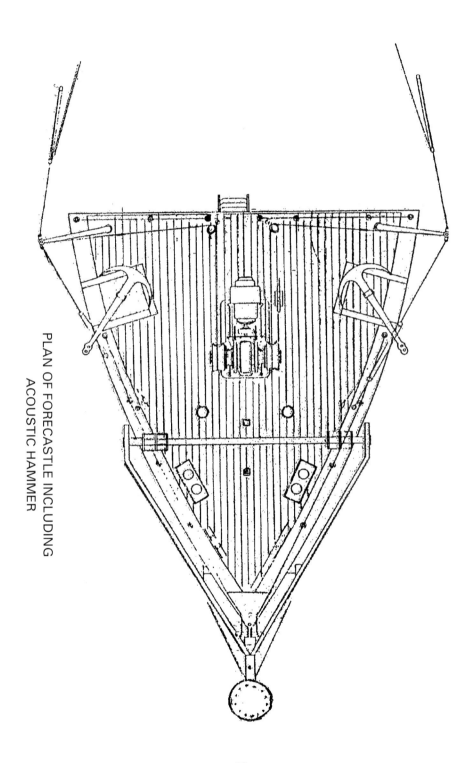

PLAN OF FORECASTLE INCLUDING
ACOUSTIC HAMMER

task to fit them out with such defensive methods as were available in order to minimise the risk of being sunk.

There was a simple formula to follow, and that was that the length of the coil around the ship should approximate to 28 times the ship's height.

The requirement then was for huge quantities of copper cable and other materials, presenting part of the major struggle against the magnetic mine.

This effort was spearheaded by such officers as Rear Admiral Wake-Walker and Commanders O. Bellasis and J. Hext Lewis. In spite of their outstanding work in this field, these measures proved to be very limited for they did nothing but prompt the enemy to greater efforts, making him produce far more sophisticated and sensitive weaponry against which at that time there was no known means of defence.

The new degaussing system brought a major headache to our allies across the Atlantic. Admiral Laud, who was then in the process of producing what came to be known as the Liberty Ships, was none too pleased with the idea of fitting gyro compasses to these cheap craft. They were having an austerity drive and gyros were expensive pieces of equipment.

No sir, we will stick with the old magnetic compasses and to ensure that the ships get to their destination we will avoid any electrical interference from these new-fangled degaussing devices.

He was right of course, for magnetic compasses were vulnerable to giving false readings, and many ships, on their way across the Atlantic with much needed equipment for the war effort, never made it. Many were sunk while others got lost, or ended up stranded in a minefield with no protection whatsoever. The United States Navy was none too pleased.

It is interesting to note that a total of 10,000 Liberty Ships were launched for use across the Atlantic waters. They did remarkably well, especially in the face of perils which awaited them due to the activity of the enemy's submarine fleet. Each of the ships took about two months to build, from keel laying to delivery, and the British government of the day took it upon itself to hire 229 of these at a cost of half a million pounds per month.

It was during the early discussions relating to the minesweeping require-ments of the war, that the Director of Minesweeping made the following comment; 'It would seem to me that what we need today are WOODEN MINESWEEPERS.'

As a result of this, and no doubt because there were, during these early days, an increasing number of ships resting on the bottom of the sea, plus the fact that the minesweeping record for the first three months of the war was, to say the least, pathetic (4 ground and 81 moored), two meetings were held, the first of which produced five proposals as follows:

1. All inroads into the existing minesweeping fleet must be resisted, meaning that they were not to be diverted to any task other than the clearance of shipping lanes.

2. The order for the 30 Bangor Class ships should be accelerated.
3. The highest priority to be given to the 12 Borde Class magnetic sweepers at present on order.
4. 400 extra magnetic sweeps to be given top priority.
5. 50 cheap type sweepers were to be built by private yards if necessary.

It is with the fifth proposal that this book is primarily concerned, the 50 cheap wooden craft and the 200 others which came after them, specially designed for the arduous task of clearing the waters surrounding our shores, and which were finally ordered (after a great deal of hoo-haa), from 50 shipyards situated all over the world. The mine clearance turned out eventually to include everybody else's shores as well as our own.

At a subsequent meeting held on the 7th. November 1939, deliberations ensued to decide what type of craft would best be suited for the task and how many would be needed to be built. HMS *Vernon* was commissioned to design the vessel and this (see drawing) was adopted in January 1940. The actual commencement of the building programme involved a great deal of arguement which began in January 1940 and finally came to a close in the following September which suggest the kind of urgency with which this particular matter was dealt. Set out below is a copy of File Reference A 110172 which has to do with Navy Contracts:

From: Director of Navy Contracts
Title: Building of 105 foot Motor Minesweepers
Date: 15th. January 1940.
No trace of any Treasury approval being obtained for these ships. A special approach to the Treasury will therefore be necessary. Would the D.N.C. give an estimate of the cost of this type of vessel?

18.1.40 DNC writes:

It is understood that the Ministry of Finance has already informed the Treasury that the total cost of each vessel would be £23.000 (this is already an increase of £5,000 on the first estimates) ex-armaments. Treasury agreement to construct fifty vessels was obtained on the 3rd. January 1940. It is understood that five vessels have already been ordered from Messrs. Curtis of Looe. (The Treasury were obviously unaware that Frank Curtis at that time had neither the manpower nor the yards to cope with this kind of order). Early orders are to be placed for 45 more.

26.1.40 Fifty five engines have been ordered.

Letter same file:

Financial authority given for only fifty vessels. Request for authority necessary before machinery can be ordered for a greater number than this, and signed by the Head of Ministry of Finance. New machinery will be ordered when authority is given for additional craft.

8.3.40 The order is placed. The question of design of further craft is now under consideration, with 12 knot double 'L' sweepers now under development. Requirements for vessels to sweep ahead of convoys will arise with a maximum speed of 12 knots. It is proposed that the speed requirement can be satisfied with two 500 horse power engines. (Only one engine had been specified).

15.3.40 Director of Minesweeping Minute;

The situation regarding further double 'L' vessels has been reviewed. The over-riding requirement is to obtain more of these vessels in the shortest possible time. The urgency of this has been stressed by the recent re-commencement of magnetic mine activities on the part of the enemy. Any changeover from the 105 foot vessel to larger and faster types will presumably entail delay in the availability of ships (this would necessitate the redesigning of the engine room and hull) since the engines for the 105 footers are already in production at the rate of 15 per month.

Further, by the replacing of repeat orders for a similar type of craft with companies who already have this kind of experience in building this kind of vessel and commencing another as soon as the present one comes of the slips, production should be hastened.

It is desired therefore to order fifty more 105 foot vessels now, similar to those already being built except that they may have to be made of steel instead of wood and degaussed [presumably because of the acute shortage of timber].

Reply June 1940;

Approved. Place order for additional forty vessels. This is the maximum for the programme at a cost of £10,000,000. The Director of Naval Contracts to report. This approval was duly noted in the minutes. In spite of the lack of potential capacity (this might mean the shortage of yards), everything possible is at 'GO' and in general, orders must be of the nature of 'follow on' orders. The first of the second batch of forty vessels could be laid down in about three months, that is about September.

August 1940; D.T.M.5 Hope to complete forty of Group F by the end of 1941. Engines are available in February 1941. Owing to the fact that the fishing industry as a source of supply of minesweeping vessels has been bled to the full extent, it is of the greatest importance that the order for the further forty motor minesweepers be placed in this country as soon as possible. Orders for ships placed in Canada must be regarded as additional for requirements abroad. Investigation of the capacity of firms building the MMS to take additional orders, reveals that many firms are anxious to receive such orders as soon as possible, so that they can obtain and prepare the necessary materials as the berths fall vacant. List of names for the whole of the production and allocation, to be made on the progress of existing orders, [*meaning, one must suppose, that those with ships first off the slips would be given fresh orders*]. Rapid reconstruction is the order of the day, with preference given to the kind of construction the builders prefer. [It turned out that there was one basic design, and depending upon the builders interpretation, many variations in the detail].

Final Note: September 1940.

Ships are on the way.

From the Director of Navy Contracts dated September 1940.

Ships are under construction and rapid production is the important factor. The machinery is already on order, but there is a scarcity of timber supplies. Could you please advise absolute timber requirements.

It can be seen from this paper conversation, that it took six months to place the order for the second batch of MMS's, and known as the 1940 War Programme Phase II.

Chapter Two

The Initial Stages

The general layout of the particular craft required had the dimensions of 105 feet by 22 feet beam and with a draught of 8 feet. Displacement was 220 tons fully laden. The ship had to be constructed entirely of wood with accommodation for two officers and eighteen ratings. Power came from a single 500 horse power diesel engine making a maximum of 11 knots. It was known that some managed to squeeze a little more speed out of these vessels, primarily by unscrewing the throttle stops, but it could never be much.

One skipper boasted 13 knots, but these claims were always taken with a pinch of salt, especially by the engine room staff who knew the engines capabilities without blowing a gasket or two.

The ships were in any case designed for towing a standard double 'L' sweep at about eight knots, this being the effective sweeping speed, and as already mentioned approval was sought to lay down the first 50 at a cost of £18,000 each.

Par Harbour Devon (F. Curtis) – 1990

It was envisaged that following this initial step to augment the already depleted minesweeping force, the strength would soon be brought up to about 400 vessels.

Requests were then made regarding the supply of marine engines, and it was estimated that none could be supplied before January of 1940. The first delivery was in fact made in the May of 1940, three months late, when the hope had been to provide five sets, meaning one main and three auxiliary engines per month.

When they did arrive, many of them were converted generating plant engines of all shapes and sizes. Ruston, Crossley, Harland and Wolfe, Atlas, Mirlees and Fairbanks Morse (from Canada) were some of the types.

The National Gas and Oil engine was a gas machine converted to run on diesel, and most of them took up half the space below decks. (See chart). There was in fact little need for all the rush, for following the approval of the building of the ships, the first one did not come off the slips until May 1941. Some of the engines are believed to have been installed in pieces after the ship had been completed; all of this delay in spite of the urgent nature and constant reminders of the desperate need for these particular craft.

The United Kingdom builders covered the length and breadth of Britain, 19 yards in England and 11 in Scotland. By far the largest number of the early 105 footers were built by Frank Curtis of Looe, Par, and Totnes.

If one visits these places today there are no signs of any ship building of this kind in evidence although Curtis still has a yard upstream in Looe. His company managed to produce 49 sweepers of this type. Reports by some of the present residents of Par claim that during the war no-one could get near the docks without being challenged by Military Police and Naval Security officers.

Thirty three ships were launched at Par but no facilities existed for fitting them out. A visit to Looe revealed that sweepers of this displacement could not have been built there, for the Curtis yard lies about a quarter of a mile up stream beyond the Looe multi-arched stone bridge built in the 19th century.

While it is known that some vessels were actually lifted over the bridge, this was not possible with ships around the 200-ton mark and over one hundred feet overall.

The practice would seem to have been that that the hulls were prepared at Par and towed to Looe for fitting out. Curtis had the use of all the quay south of the bridge on the east side of the river. Photographs held by Curtis show Motor Minesweepers and Motor Fishing Vessels having the finishing touches before commissioning.

As already mentioned engines were fitted here in bits and pieces, giving some idea of the problems which faced many of the smaller shipyards as they endeavoured to meet their targets.

Richards Iron Works of Lowestoft (still building sweepers of a different construction today), managed 18 ships. Wivenhoe Shipbuilders launched 14, while John Morris of Gosport came up with a total of 12.

J.W. Upham of Brixham came next with 10, Husband's Yacht Yard 9.

J. Bolson of Poole 8, and Doig of Grimsby, Clapson of Barton on Humber, Harris of Appledore and Philips of Dartmouth with 6 each. The runners up in England were Humphrey and Smith of Grimsby, and East Anglian Constructions with 3 apiece, Camper and Nicholson of Gosport and Rowhedge Ironworks with 2.

In Scotland the Noble Brothers W & J of Frazerborough built 16 vessels, George Forbes and R. Irvine both of Peterhead, McDuff Engineering, Herd and McKenzie of Buckie managed 8 each, with Walter Reekie at his St. Monance and Anstruther yards completing 7 and 2 respectively. W.Weatherhead of Cockenzie and Thompson and Balfour of Bo'ness made the running with one ship each, bringing the total to 221 vessels of this class launched, fitted out, and commissioned in the British Isles.

In addition to the U.K. yards, orders were placed with twenty two builders overseas...a total of 91 vessels of the same type from Canada, Newfoundland, Rangoon, Beirut, Tel Aviv,Cochin, Kingston Jamaica, Nassar, Hong Kong, Singapore and Colombo, the largest suppliers being Clare Shipbuilding Company from Metaghan in Canada and Brunton Engineering Company from Cochin in India, who still have a model of a Motor Minesweeper in their head office. These companies built 15 and 13 craft respectively.

Building in many instances was slow, the first 50 ships not being completed until September 1941, two years late. Some of those ships included in the second batch of fifty ordered i.e. the 1940 War Programme Phase 2, were completed before some of those in the first order.

For instance MMS's, 59 and 79 built by Forbes took thirteen months each to complete, while MMS 113 from the Wivenhoe Yard was operational in a little over ten months. MMS 46, ordered at the beginning of 1940 was commissioned twenty two months after the keel was laid in November 1941. Philips and Son actually managed to complete one vessel MMS 18 in nine months and had others followed suit we might have had a minesweeping fleet at a much earlier date. But that was not to be.

The unfortunate thing however was that some of these vessels were still on the slips when the war came to its close, many of them taking as long as twenty eight months before putting to sea.

There are many factors which could have contributed to this delay. Shortage of materials and manpower was always a problem as the war steadily made more demands on men and women for the front line.

The wood required for this production line would probably have to be imported, Canadian pine on oak timbers with mahogany and teak fittings.

Brass and copper, being anti-magnetic was a must to manufacture most of the metal fittings and equipment, and was in short supply.

But that was not all. There were other spanners which appeared from time to time in the works, adding to the delay in production.

There are records of a signal sent on the 15th. January 1940, claiming that no trace could be found of Treasury approval to build the first 50 ships.

MacDuff Shipyard 1989

Wivenhoe Shipyard Essex 1990

25

The Launch

Fitting Out   *Active 1942*

Husband's Yard Southampton 1942

26

Subsequently a special approach had to be made to the Treasury asking for the sum of £1,150,000 to be spent on this urgent requirement. Approval however, had already been obtained on the 3rd. January and the first order placed with Frank Curtis of Looe.

There is also evidence on file to suggest that in spite of assurances given as early as December 1939, the machinery for these craft was in short supply.

Five sets of engines per month, already promised, would have perhaps seen 60 ships operational by the end of 1940, but that target was never reached.

By May of 1941 we had managed 21. It was not until September of that year that the other 29 were commissioned, a further example of the blundering and confusion which existed at that time, in spite of a message from the Prime Minister in January 1940 that:

"We were facing numerical odds",
and a similar message on the 27th. of the same month,

"Come let us to the task..to the battle and to the toil..each to our parts..each to our station. Fill the armies, rule the air, pour out the munitions, strangle the 'U' boats, sweep the mines, plough the land, build the ships, guard the streets, succour the wounded, uplift the downcast, and honour the brave. As far as the sea is concerned we may cherish good hopes that all will be well."

As far as the sweeping of the mines was concerned, Mr. Churchill, certainly at that time according to the records, was living, it would appear, in 'cloud cuckoo land', for all was not well with the sea.

The Navy suffered her greatest losses during the opening phases of the war. 14000 tons of shipping in the first month, 74000 tons in the second month with a quarter of a million tons of cargo, all of which was an urgent reminder of the need to get the minesweeping flotillas operational.

By this time the Admiralty had another problem to face. The enemy had in August 1940, introduced the acoustic mine, another British invention of World War I.

This was a device of equal destructive power to the magnetic, which was detonated by the sound waves of passing ships. Again we had no equipment available to cope with this new weapon. The first encounter with an acoustic mine was in the Firth of Forth in Scotland on August 31st. 1940, at the expense of a motor torpedo boat. The cruiser *Galatea* reported mines exploding ahead of her, while similar explosions were taking place half a mile in front of destroyers.

At first it was suggested that these might be unexploded bombs, so frantic experiments began and the first attempt to counter the acoustic mine was made in the Minesweeping Sloop *Harwich*.

It was a type of vessel with an empty front compartment in the bow, which was filled with water and a road drill utilised to produce a powerful battering noise. The measure proved, as had the Borde Class sweepers before, very effective except that the bow was invariably blown off the ship.

There was a particular type of coaster that was virtually self annihilating in the

UNITED KINGDOM SHIPBUILDERS (MMS PRODUCTION)

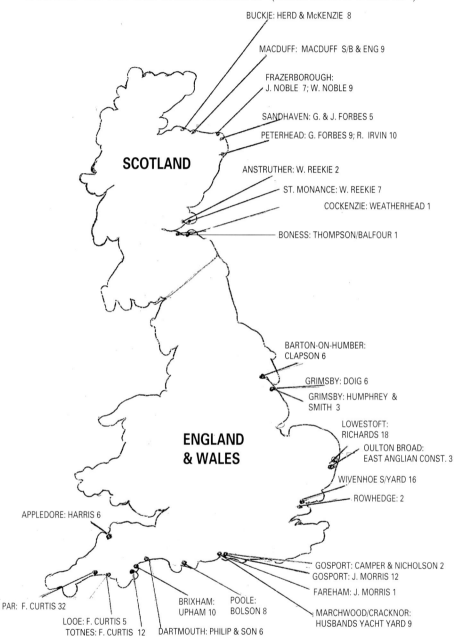

BUCKIE: HERD & McKENZIE 8

MACDUFF: MACDUFF S/B & ENG 9

FRAZERBOROUGH:
J. NOBLE 7; W. NOBLE 9

SANDHAVEN: G. & J. FORBES 5

PETERHEAD: G. FORBES 9; R. IRVIN 10

SCOTLAND

ANSTRUTHER: W. REEKIE 2

ST. MONANCE: W. REEKIE 7

COCKENZIE: WEATHERHEAD 1

BONESS: THOMPSON/BALFOUR 1

BARTON-ON-HUMBER:
CLAPSON 6

GRIMSBY: DOIG 6

GRIMSBY: HUMPHREY &
SMITH 3

LOWESTOFT:
RICHARDS 18

**ENGLAND
& WALES**

OULTON BROAD:
EAST ANGLIAN CONST. 3

WIVENHOE S/YARD 16

ROWHEDGE: 2

APPLEDORE: HARRIS 6

GOSPORT: CAMPER & NICHOLSON 2
GOSPORT: J. MORRIS 12

FAREHAM: J. MORRIS 1

PAR: F. CURTIS 32

BRIXHAM:
UPHAM 10

POOLE:
BOLSON 8

MARCHWOOD/CRACKNOR:
HUSBANDS YACHT YARD 9

LOOE: F. CURTIS 5

TOTNES: F. CURTIS 12

DARTMOUTH: PHILIP & SON 6

BRITISH YARDS

presence of acoustic mines. Twenty five out of the thirty of that class were sunk.

The need now was to find the appropriate gear to counteract this new menace, and a contraption which looked remarkably like a large steel bell on the end of a moving arm was devised. This arm was extended on an 'A' frame fitted on the forepeak of the ship, and the bell lowered over the bows in a position about six feet under the water.

Inside the bell was fitted a 'Kango Hammer' (very much like a pneumatic drill) which acted on a diaphragm, causing sound waves to be emitted ahead of the ship to detonate the mines. The major trouble with this equipment was that there was only one company in the United Kingdom who manufactured the hammer.

As before the need was urgent, but output was limited and many ships had to ply the seas without any protection whatsoever during the earlier years of the war. Even when they were fitted out, there was no guarantee that the hammer would do the job effectively. As long as they kept making a noise it was assumed that the device was in working order.

Early efforts all had a touch of the Heath Robinson about them, and this is highlighted in a secret signal from the Commander-in-Chief Portsmouth containing the following recommendations:

> It is safest to go as slow as possible, and to make the least noise practicable [has one ever come across an engine without noise?] or alternatively to go fast and hope to explode the mines at a distance. The variations in the sensitivity of the mines is so great and the output of sound from ships so variable, that no security can be guaranteed. Motor Torpedo boats at speed, have fired mines at all distances, and Motor Launches seem particularly vulnerable. By measure they can fire an acoustic mine at five fathoms and at 7 knots. The only real security is to keep the channels swept as far as we are able.

Words of wisdom indeed. In other words, you have to take your chances and with a bit of luck you might just make it. It was all a bit of a hit and miss affair, and the Motor Minesweepers or Mickey Mice as they came to be affectionately called were designed and built to follow the last line of that signal . . . to keep the channels swept . . .

In later boats, a towed box was substituted for the 'hammer' and 'A' frame, the arrangement being that the tow, after being slung over the side, would be taken from an eye on the port side of the stem. A derrick was used for streaming and recovering the box. Iron sheeting protected the bottom and side of the ship, to avoid scoring of the wooden hull.

Later forms of acoustic mines contained counters which operated like a telephone exchange. The mine would not detonate until it was, so to speak, called up, meaning that there was no telling when the thing was likely to go off. Four or five ships might pass overhead before an explosion occurred. Clocks were fitted which would keep the mine inactive for days.

Other mines were set to go off in response to very low vibrations, that is below the minimum range of audibility, and to counteract this, a piston displacement mechanism was devised, housed in a casing of about four feet diameter and operated by an eight horsepower electric motor which delivered rhythmic pushes by means of a cam.

It was operated by a lever something like that used on the old type tram cars or on modern diesel trains, with the driver, as it were, watching the revolutions or the pulses translated on to a dial, rating from zero to 300. The ship, on maximum pulse rate, behaved like a kangaroo with hiccups, but because this type of mine was introduced only in the last stages of the war, the apparatus was hardly used. It was never really known whether or not it was an effective measure, but some like to think that we had at last managed to get one step ahead of the enemy.

During the early months of the war, especially in the area of requisition, availability, fitting out and deployment of the existing minesweeping craft, events can only be described judging from the records, as somewhat chaotic, and while all this was going on the enemy was having a heyday sowing mines by every possible means.

Cruisers – destroyers – torpedo boats – minelayers – submarines and aircraft were utilised to the full, all were in use, and in every possible channel and port in the U.K.

Between October and November 1939, the 'U' Boats were busy in Dover, Inner Dowsing, the Firth of Forth, Hartlepool and Cromarty.

In November and December the Thames, Lowestoft, Orfordness, Neward Lightship, the Bristol Channel, the Humber and the North Atlantic had their share.

Mines were dropped by seaplane, 41 in the North Sea on the 20th. November, and in addition, places such as Dundee, Blyth, Cross Sands, Newcastle, Ailsa Craig, Liverpool, the Clyde, Portsmouth, Newport, Penzance, Plymouth, Southampton, Falmouth, Belfast, Middlesborough, Scapa Flow and the Isle of Wight had not been neglected.

There was virtually nowhere that had not had a visit in the first few months of the war.

A report entitled 'Analysis of Enemy Action in the Thames Estuary' and dated as late as November 1942, is a reflection, three years after hostilities had commenced, of the kind of confusion that existed.

The Director of Minesweeping makes the following comment:

> It is observed that the attached interesting and important report is dated 24.12.41, but not forwarded to the Admiralty till 7.1 42, and it is accordingly proposed that the Air Ministry be invited to explain this delay.
>
> Second, it was not received in the Division until 26.2.42, and M Branch is requested why the additional delay in its distribution.

A total of two months delay in the passing of important reports, and concerning crucial information regarding the pattern of enemy minelaying as the following extract shows.

Out of 125 raids plotted in the Estuary on the light nights between the 6th. and 28th. November 1941, there were 25 appearances of bombers and 100 of minelayers. Fighter Command Intelligence estimated 200 minelayers operating over the whole period.

Such reports would seem to emphasise not only the inefficiency of those in command, but equally the constant need for an active minesweeping role by the existing ships in the Thames area and also the importance of supplementing them from other M/S depots where enemy activity was not quite so intensive.

On the positive side, in July 1941, reports contained information that 486 mines had been detonated in the Humber area – 123 magnetics, 233 acoustics, 9 contact and 126 unidentified explosions, with a loss of four trawlers.

In spite of this success story, if it can be called that, it was Vice Admiral Ramsay who commented on the vulnerability of the approach channels by aircraft minelayers, and the dilapidated state of the trawlers being used for sweeping duties.

Chapter 3

Some difficulties involved.

As has already been intimated the process of building was extremely slow, and the following charts show the rate of production after the first order for the Motor Minesweeper was placed in January 1940.

Early Disposition of MMS's

As the ships were commissioned they were allocated in the first instance to five commands as per the following chart 'A', then later re- allocated to the bases listed in chart 'B'.

CHART 'A' 1941

Nore Command

	Jan	Feb	Mar	Apr	May	Jne	Jly	Aug	Sep	Oct	Nov	Dec
Sheerness	1	19				40	41	39	44	45		68
	8								59	56		
									79			
									113			
Port Edgar										53		
Wivenhoe											82	
Peterhead												54
101 MSF			14					16				
					15							
					17							
	2	1	1		2	1	1	2	4	3	1	2
Prog/Total	2	3	4		6	7	8	10	14	17	18	20

Minesweeping Base HMS Wildfire with Depot Ship HMS St. Tudno based at Queenborough Pier, near Sheerness Kent.

Western Approaches 1941

	Jan	Feb	Mar	Apr	May	Jne	Jly	Aug	Sep	Oct	Nov	Dec
Liverpool			4			20	34	2				
					13	33		3				
								50				
Cardiff			9				25	26	28	27		
								38		48		
								47				
Swansea Capt.M/S M.L. 327											80	116
Belfast					10	21		32				
								35				
Londonderry								12			60	61
		2			2	3	2	10	1	2	2	2
Prog/Totals		2			4	7	9	19	20	22	24	26

Portsmouth Command 1941

	Jan	Feb	Mar	Apr	May	Jne	Jly	Aug	Sep	Oct	Nov	Dec
					5	6	29	11	55		22	
							30	7			46	
					1	1	2	2	1		2	
Prog/Totals						2	4	6	7		10	

Plymouth Command 1940/41

	Dec	Jan	Feb	Mar	Apr	May	Jne	Jly	Aug	Sep	Oct	Nov	Dec
	18						24	42		43			78
	1						1	1		1			1
Prog/Totals							2	3		4			5

Rosyth Command 1941

	Jan	Feb	Mar	Apr	May	Jne	Jly	Aug	Sep	Oct	Nov	Dec
						31	36	37		74	75	
Prog/Totals						1	2	3		4	5	

Harwich

The 12th. Minesweeping Flotilla consisting of the Paddle Steamers:
Queen Empress, Duchess Rothsay and *Lorna Doon*, Capt. M/S M.L. 216
Lowestoft Paddle Steamer *Princess Elizabeth.*

There is little need to emphasise the rate of production. The allocation of vessels to Commands speaks for itself with 65 ships by the end of 1941, over two years after war was declared. It says a great deal for the urgency of the situation and would seem to suggest that we were well and truly caught with our pants in the lowered position.

As these ships came off the slips and were subsequently commissioned, it was not a matter of surprise that some of them began to give signs of trouble soon after going into service. A statement of some of the problems is well worth documenting for the record.

(Below) Cylinder heads and scavenging air pump of the eight-cylinder Crossley two-stroke main engine.

(Above) View showing the back of the engine.

(Above) Front of the main engine.

(Left) Control station, showing the reversing wheel and the engine speed regulating wheel.
The chain is extended to a duplicate wheel on the bridge.

(1) Use of Green Timber.

There was no large stock of seasoned timber available at the outset of hostilities, and the heavy beams of nine inches square could not be artificially seasoned.

As time went on and builders received their orders for ships well in advance of laying the keel and starting work on the hull, it was possible to buy in stocks of timber in anticipation and this would have a slight chance of being dried out before use, but the use of green timber as often was the case resulted in changes in the shape of the vessels as they settled down in service.

In the main the changes were not too serious, but it did mean that shaft alignment was necessary more often than need be during the early life of the ship. There was many a leak via the stern gland due to the warping of the timber.

Another effect was that the beams tended to split if green timber was used. This occurred as the wood began to dry out, making the vessel unsightly, rather than unserviceable. Splitting was most marked in those vessels which were dispatched for service in foreign waters in the Mediterranean and beyond. After a period of service in the hot climate, beams were often heard to crack as though an explosive charge had been placed in their centre, necessitating the use of steel strapping to hold the beams together.

(2) Unsuitable Fitting Out Berths.

Some of the yards had to make use of tidal berths for fitting out, where the hulls grounded at low tide. With soft mud berths there was no problem, but in some places, particularly in Looe, where Frank Curtis did all his fitting out, the berths consisted of hard sand, which was, because of the tides, seldom level.

Ships fitted out in Looe usually went into service with a wavy keel, which tended after some time at sea to straighten out, again affecting the alignment of the shaft. Immediate steps to rectify the fault were called for, otherwise serious trouble developed in the stern tube.

(3) Alignment Troubles.

Two sources of alignment troubles have been intimated in (1) and (2) above, but they were not all.

The main engine was generally fitted more or less in the centre of the hull, and requiring a drive of thirty feet to the propellor. There were no flexible couplings fitted, and the steel shaft was borne by Plummer Blocks.

The lack of straightness in the shaft produced a pumping action up and down or from side to side at the front end of the long stern tube. Consequently the bearings ran hot and gradually the stern tube worked loose in the shaft log, resulting in excessive leaks. The writer recalls his first experience as a stoker on MMS 19, when setting foot for the first time in the engine room, with an eight cylinder Crossley two-stroke main and two six cylinder Gardiner bus engines as sweeping generators, plus a Crossley twin cylinder donkey engine.

He was presented with a battered old oil can and told that he would be involved in the most important job on the ship.

"There are three Plummer Blocks on this shaft young fellow, and they will be oiled on the hour every hour. No fancy automatic oilfeeds for us."

One soon realised the importance of that oilcan, when on one unfortunate occasion, having dozed off, the stern tube went on fire. The chief engineer was indeed a kind man. There was no court martial . . . no being shot at dawn.

But the problem persisted, requiring constant attention to alignment. This was carried out while the vessel was afloat, because if placed in dock the wooden keel would take up the shape of the docking blocks which were never exactly level, creating more problems and the need to withdraw the bolts in the shaft couplings to prevent unnecessary straining of the shaft.

(4) Dilution of Labour

Some of the troubles with the early boats were traceable to the use of unskilled labour, general rashness, and over eagerness in building.

As the task was urgent there is little wonder at the enthusiasm to complete each vessel, but as a result of a progressive improvement of skills, this trouble faded away, and in the main, those hulls which were produced in yards where a great deal of unskilled labour was utilised, were reasonably good examples of wooden shipbuilding at that time.

Any major criticism of the hulls would have been in respect of the materials used, rather than the quality of the workmanship. With an urgent need for a large number of wooden minesweepers at the earliest possible date, the material used was dictated by the circumstances in which the Britain found herself at the time. There was little choice.

The Admiralty also had to find appropriately trained crews and allocate each ship to the minesweeping bases which were in the process of being established all around the coast of Britain.

These were finally set up at Great Yarmouth, Harwich, Lowestoft (which became the Royal Naval Patrol Service training depot) Granton, Rosyth, Grimsby, Scapa Flow, and the Nore Command with Captain Minesweeping at Sheerness with sectors at the Humber, Yarmouth, Lowesoft, Harwich, Sheerness, Flamborough, and Margate.

On the south coast Portsmouth, Dover, Plymouth, Newhaven, together with Belfast, Londonderry, Liverpool, and the Clyde, on the west.

The crew of each Motor Minesweeper consisted of two officers, usually a Lieutenant and sub-Lieutenant, Coxswain. Chief Engineer with three staff (stokers), a Signalman (Bunts), Wireless Operator (Sparks), Cook, Steward, Electrician (Wires), plus eight seamen some of whom doubled up as gunners to man the twin .5 Vickers machine guns mounted on the after deck of the bridge and the twin Lewis guns on the port and starboard wings.

As time went by most of the crew had three day gunnery courses at Whale

Island Gunnery School. This was in preparation for Operation 'Overlord', when it may have been found necessary for anyone who was able, to man the guns. Many of the ships were fitted with Oerlikons in the latter years of the war and as they became available.

The first thousand men were hastily produced from the ranks of the Royal Naval Reserve and mainly ex-trawler skippers and fishermen. Other came from the Royal Naval Volunteer Reserve, the Wavy Navy as they were dubbed, and generally inshore yachtsmen with some knowledge of navigation and how to control a ship.

Few of them however had ever handled anything like 260 tons of wood and machinery before, and some of the escapades are quite comical to relate. Try picking up a dan-buoy in a heavy swell. Many skippers would have more than a dozen runs at the same buoy, before being able to get a hook on it. It was no easy task.

The coxswain and the chief engineer were invariably those with most sea time to their credit. The rest were, in essence, rookies, called up for the duration of hostilities,(H.O's).

Some ships were lucky to have a Royal Naval wireless operator, a few of whom were known to eventually skipper their own vessel. They knew the ropes, and had been at the game for some years. He and the signalman were the key men aboard, having access to all the information which came via radio or aldis lamp. Many an hour was spent trying to pump information out of these characters, but like the proverbial monkeys, they said "nowt".

Training for most of the crew consisted of six weeks square bashing (for the uninitiated, endless marching up and down with a rifle on the parade ground) at one of H.M. Training Establishments, such as HMS *Duke* at Malvern or *Royal Arthur* at Skegness, learning the rudiments of seamanship, which included boat-handling and the art of lashing a hammock, plus rifle drill, marching and general discipline.

They were a tough six weeks especially for those who were not used to that kind of life, which meant all of us, away from home for the first time in our lives.

The 'Jaunty' didn't make it any easier – but all were better men for the exercise. They were certainly changed in a dramatically short time from schoolboys to sailors. Stokers went to St. Lukes in Lowestoft, part of HMS *Europa*, the other half (meaning the seamen) being accommodated at the Sparrows Nest, at the North end of the town.

HMS St. Lukes was a converted holiday hotel, built on the summit of Kirkley Cliffs by Messrs. Spiers and Pond and opened in the June of 1900 at a cost of £150,000 and requisitioned for wartime use, housing anything from 600 to 1000 ratings. Here they were taught among other things which need not be mentioned here (the art of skiving, or the ability to become Captain of the Heads), would you believe it, to shovel coal, that is those who were destined to join the trawler fraternity – the coal burners.

But even shovelling coal is an art, especially when trying to aim it into an orifice which was only just bigger than the shovel. It was worse while attempting the exercise in a force nine gale. The usual comment from the instructor was that one would no doubt do much better if there was hair around the hole, but most of the youngsters there wouldn't have a clue what he was on about, although they were soon to learn.

Internal combustion engines were of course another kettle of fish. We had to learn how these things functioned (it was a three week course), and more than that how to repair them if, as frequently happened, they broke down at sea.

They were quite different from anything the so-called stokers had ever been acquainted with, being large and cumbersome affairs. Most were air started which was an easy matter if the engine had more than five cylinders. If not, the engine had to be turned over by slotting a long steel bar into a hole in the flywheel and turning the engine over so that one of the pistons was in the right position to take the sudden rush of air from the 500 psi bottles in which it was stored.

Stories are told of stokers and enginemen forgetting to remove the steel bar, with drastic results. If the donkey engine which drove the air compressor broke down, there was little use thinking about getting the starting handle out. It did not take long to empty both of the air bottles especially if the engine was a bit dicky.

Some, born and bred within the family of the steam trawler, never learned the difference or perhaps never had the inclination to find out. They had been engineers all their lives and nobody was going to tell them how an engine worked or indeed how it should be treated.

One chief was known to fill the diesel generators with oil right up to the filler cap. Dipsticks had no significance whatsoever.

"Plenty of oil and you can't go wrong," was the principle behind all good maintenance. It might have been O.K. for the steam jobs, but exhaust pipes were known to go on fire as a result of this 'over oiling' process.

Not all the stokers were housed in St. Lukes however. Some of the more fortunate (so they said) had billets in the town, among whom was The Right Honourable James Callaghan, one time Prime Minister, who served, not as a stoker, but as a seaman on a minesweeper.

While St. Luke's no longer exists, the Sparrows Nest now houses the Royal Naval Patrol Service Association's museum, and is visited annually by many of the officers and ratings who attend the memorial reunion in October of each year.

In Belvue Park, there stands a memorial to those who never returned. 40 feet high and mounted with a golden bronze sailing ship.

It has inscribed on bronze plaques on its circular base the names of 2385 sailors including 49 from New Zealand. It was was erected in 1953, and indeed it is a fine monument, but one often wonders why the Minesweeping Silver Badge (the unique symbol of the minesweeping and anti-submarine fraternity) was not incorporated in the design.

38

R.N. Patrol Service Memorial,
Belvue Park, Lowestoft.

HMS Europa *Sparrows Nest Lowestoft*

Following training there was the long wait for a draft to a ship which could be anywhere in the UK or overseas. Waiting seemed like an eternity, and for the 'Barrack Stanchions'(and there were a few of those around) that is, those who never left the land-based ships, and whose task it was to train and employ, most of the day must have been a pain in the neck. They were probably glad to get home every night. And home it was, for some were known to have joined the Navy and never been more than a couple of miles from their own doorstep.

If that was true of Lowestoft, how many more matelots spent the war years in such cushy numbers? Naval periodicals are littered with names of those who never left the shore.

Sailors in the communications branch took a little longer to train, for learning the intricacies of morse and semaphore was quite an achievement. To send a message was one thing, but to read it and get it right was something entirely different.

Most of the ship's company had never been to sea in their lives apart from the odd sail at holiday times. Many skippers had never left sight of the shore, and certainly few had ever commanded a vessel of the minesweeping variety before. This is evident from the number of collisions recorded and especially those which occurred while coming alongside in tidal waters and making way through harbour bars. The records list numerous incidents which caused a great deal of damage to the ships.

There is of course need to make allowances in all these cases for the only time given for 'practice' was on the job. Skill may not have been their main attribute in those early days, but skippers need to be applauded for their courage and sheer guts. In the end crews were found rough and ready perhaps, but nevertheless keen to do their bit to win the war.

Harry Tate's Navy indeed, but some would say Hurrah for Harry Tate, whoever he was, for indeed without them and others just like them, the war might just have taken a little longer to draw to an end.

Daytime sweeping with the possibility of attack from the air at any time was difficult enough, but night sweeping when it was introduced in October 1940, became something of a nightmare until all the problems had been ironed out.

It was found necessary to do a great deal of the lane clearances at night, or rather very early in the morning, usually between the hours of 0200 and daybreak, but the following report submitted by the Officer in Charge Minesweeping Sheerness, gives some indication of the difficulties which faced the early poineers of the night sweep.

" The main problem was not with the sweeps, difficult though that was from time to time, but with navigation.

It was essential to work completely in the dark. Oropesa, Double L, and Acoustic sweepers were most effective working together, especially leading convoys out to sea, but the problem lay in the fact that there were no lights available either on the channel centre line buoys or indeed on any of the lightships.

Ships had to maintain their distance as well as keep the proper sweeping speed, with the convoy keeping station on the leader.

Buoys and lightships were four miles apart, and even in good visibility it was difficult to see them. (Ships' radar as we know it now was non-existent).

It was a case, as indeed many of the activities were, of trial and error. Sometimes the buoys were spotted by Aldis lamp after they had been passed. It was absolutely vital to pass close to the buoys so as to ensure that there were no 'holidays' left in the sweeping pattern.

It was finally suggested that the buoys be lit and covered with shades to prevent enemy aircraft from spotting them. This seemed to resolve the problem, and accurate navigation was ensured.

Ships fitted with Double L sweeps could not suddenly go astern, nor put the helm over at quick notice to avoid an obstruction such as a wreck. Once a buoy was fouled, there was little chance of getting the sweep freed, so it had to be destroyed with the result that the whole operation was disrupted and sometimes had to be abandoned."

More sophisticated patterns of minesweeping identified by the letters P.Q.R.S. and U formations were devised as technical advances were made, but in the early days it was a question of trial and error. New lessons were learned from the successes and the failures.

Station keeping was a constant problem, but it was imperative that the required distance between each ship, port and starboard, was maintained. True, sophisticated methods (including synchronising slave control mechanism) were introduced in time, but in the beginning skippers had to revert to makeshift shaded lights extended on bits of wood and coupled to a Bell's Station Finder, a device similar to that used in contemporary cameras for focussing the lense. This proved to do the job quite effectively.

Added to all this was the fact that with the introduction of night sweeping, manpower difficulties became acute. Officers were in short supply. Situations arose where a Group Officer, responsible for a particular section, would take over a formation due to sweep on the day of sailing, take the formation to sea that night, return to harbour in the morning, and ensure that any defects in the ships were rectified.

The task would invariably involve the sweeping of two channels on average about sixty five miles long, constituting at least a twelve hour tour of duty providing there were no snags. On a Motor Minesweeper the tour would be longer than that at eight knots.

Officers were not permitted to leave the bridge except for short intervals for meals etc. and in addition there were often additional special sweeps to complete. This was a full time task in itself but a night watch ashore in the Minesweeping office was an additional requirement.

"In many ways," claimed the Officer I/C Sheerness, " I have found that this war resembles the last in regard to the use of small craft. There are never enough of them. Minesweeping, refitting, repairing, resting. When not refitting and repairing there was very little resting."

In reply to these comments, Admiral Nore Command had this to say in March 1941, as a tribute to those early poineers of the Minesweeping Flotillas.

"Captain M/S Sheerness pioneered the sweeping of narrow channels at night which, besides giving protection to the M/S personnel against enemy attack, ensured that sweeping was completed in time for the convoys to move through the channels in daylight.

He and other officers who are no longer young have had to bear the brunt of the enemy's intensive mining activities, as well as compete with many changes while our counter-measures are being slowly developed.

In addition Captains Hertford, Heaton and Kirby bore the heat and burden of the day, deserving high praise, and this is extended to Captain J. Wootten who started the minesweeping force."

We salute you brethren.

Captain and crew – MMS 27

ALLOCATION OF SHIPS TO BUILDERS (Home)

England.

Bolson J.L	Poole	MMS's	46..58..202..233..234..281..282 304.
Curtis F.	Looe,Par,Totnes	MMS's	24..25..26..27..28..42..43..74 75..139..140..149..150..167..168 169..170..171..172..203..204..205 207..220..221..224..225..226..227 228..265..266..267..268..269..270 271..284..285..286..290..291..292 293..294..295..296..297..298.
Camper/Nicholson	Gosport	MMS's	5..29
Clapson & Son	Barton on Humber	MMS's	50..135..181..263..280..305.
Doig J.S.	Grimsby	MMS's	116..117..118..179..206..229.
East Anglian Const.	Lowestoft	MMS's	71..72..73.
Harris P.K.	Appledore	MMS's	9..38..92..165..183..<u>210.</u>
Husband's Yacht Yard Cracknor/Marchwood		MMS's 309	7..22..23..65..66..67..137..138
Humphrey/Smith	Grimsby	MMS's	180..212..213
Morris J.	Gosport	MMS's	49..89..90..91..109..110..111.. 112..274.287..288..289.
Philip & Son	Dartmouth	MMS's	18..30..88..175..216..300.
Rowhedge Iron Works		MMS's	36(1)..37(1)
Richards Iron Works	Lowestoft	MMS's	1..8..19..39..40..41..44..45.. 68..69..70..76..77..78..176..177 178..262
Upham J.W.& A.	Brixham	MMS's	6..47..48..173..174..218..231.. 272..283..303.
Wivenhoe S/Y Ltd.	Wivenhoe	MMS's	15..16..17..82..83..84..85..86.. 87..113..114..115..236..237.. 36(2)..37(2).

Scotland.

Forbes J.G.	Sandhaven	MMS's	12..33..59..60..190
Forbes G.	Peterhead	MMS's	2..20..79..80..81..184..185..209 230.
Herd & McKenzie	Buckie	MMS's	4..21..53..54..192..193..211.. <u>235</u>
MacDuff Eng.	Macduff	MMS's	13..32..61..191..214..232..275.. 276..<u>299</u>
Irvin R.	Peterhead	MMS's	3..55..136..186..187..261..278. 302..308
Noble J.& W.	Frazerburgh	MMS's	10..11..34..35..56..57..133..134 188..189..<u>208</u>..215..219..277..301 307
Reekie W.	Anstruther	MMS's	31..64
Reekie W.	St. Monance	MMS's	14..63..182..217..260..279..<u>306</u>

Orders for MMS's 264 and 273 were placed with Thomson and Balfour of Boness and W Weatherhead of Cockenzie respectively, but were cancelled. Other ships cancelled were MMS's 208.210.235.299.306 (underlined).

1941	Jan	Feb	Mar	Apr	May	Jne	Jly	Aug	Sep	Oct	Nov	Dec	
Bolson											46		1
Clapson								50					1
Curtis					24	25	26	28	27	75			
						42		43	74				9
East Ang C.													
Harris			9					38					2
Humphrey													
Husbands								7			22		2
Morris													
Philips	18						30						2
Richards	1	19	39			40	41	44	45		68		
	8										78		10–
Upham						6		47	48				3
Wivenhoe		15	16	17			36	37	113		82	83	8
Camper				5			29						2
Doig												116	1
Forbes G				2		20			79	80			4
Forbes J			12		33				59	60			4
Herd/McK			4		21					53		54	4
Irvin			3						55				2
MacDuff				13				32				61	3
Noble J			11				34			56			3
Reekie				14	31								2
Wilson/Noble				10				35					2
Totals	3	1	3	6	5	7	7	8	7	6	6	6	65
Prog/Totals	3	4	7	13	18	25	32	40	47	53	59	65	

1942	Jan	Feb	Mar	Apr	May	Jne	Jly	Aug	Sep	Oct	Nov	Dec	
Bolson			58					202			233		3
Clapson			135				181						2
Curtis	139		140	171	150	172	168	169	204	221	224	225	
			149		167	203	207	205	170	226	228	266	
								220	227		265	268	24
East Ang C.					72	71		73					3
Harris	92					165			183				3
Humphrey	180					212		213					3
Husbands			23				65	66		67			4
Morris	89			49		90			109	91			
											110		6
Philips			88					175					2
Richards	76	69			70			176			177		
	77												6
Upham					173		174			218		231	4
Wivenhoe		84		114			85	115	86	87	236		7
Camper													–
Doig				117		118	179		206	229			5
Forbes G		81			184		185		209			230	5
Forbes J				190									1
Herd/McK					192			193			211		3
Irvin		136			186		187				261		4
MacDuff						62		191			214		3
Noble J		57				188			215				3
Reekie	63			64				217		182			4
Wilson/Noble	133			134				189				219	4
Totals	8	5	5	8	8	9	9	11	9	9	12	6	99
Prog/Totals	8	13	18	26	34	43	52	63	72	81	93	99	

UNITED KINGDOM BUILDERS (Rate of progress) – continued

1943	Jan	Feb	Mar	Apr	May	Jne	Jly	Aug	Sep	Oct	Nov	Dec	
Bolson						234			281	282			3
Clapson	263					280					305		3
Curtis	270	267	269	286	294	293	296	290	298	291			
		271	284	292		295		297					
		285											16
East Ang C.													
Harris													
Humphrey													
Husbands			137		138				309				3
Morris	111		112		274		288		287		289		6
Philips		216											1
Richards	178												1
Upham				272						283			2
Wivenhoe				237									1
Camper													
Doig													
Forbes G													
Forbes J													
Herd/McK													
Irvin			278			302		308					3
MacDuff				232			275				276		3
Noble J													
Reekie				260									1
Wilson/Noble				277				301			307		3
Totals	4	4	5	7	3	5	3	3	5	3	2	2	46
Prog/Totals	4	8	13	20	23	28	31	34	39	42	44	46	

1944 Bolson MMS 304 Aug. Philips MMS 300 Jan. Upham MMS 303 Jne.
Reekie MMS 279 Jan. MMS 208, 210, 235, 262, 264, 273, 299, 308 cancelled.

ENGINE TYPES

Main engines were provided by the following companies. These were not designed specifically as marine engines but were generally, apart from the Canadian Fairbanks Morse, machinery utilised in generating plant and converted for the job in hand.

ATLAS

MMS's 14..15..16..17..24..25..26..27..28..31..36..37..42..43..51
52..74..75..76..77..78..82..83..84..85..86. (26 ships)

BURMEISTER & WAIN

MMS's 151..152..153..154..156 (5 ships)

CROSSLEY

MMS's 1..5..6..7..8..18..19..22..23..29..30..39..46..49..53..54
55..56..57..58..59..60..61..62..63..64..65..66..67..68..69
70..71..72..73..79..87..88..89..90..91..93..94..95..96..97
98..109..110..111..112..113..114..115..119..120..121..122
129..130..131..132..137..138..139..140..149..150..165..176
180..181..202..203..204..205..212..213..217..220..221..224
225..226..227..228..229..230..231..233..234..236..237..261
262..272..274..275..276..277..278..281..282..283..287..288
289..290..291..292..293..294..295..296..297..298..300..301
302..303..304..308..309..310..311..312 (126 ships)

ENTERPRISE

MMS's 145..146..157..158..159..160..194..195..222..223 (10 ships)

FAIRBANKS MORSE

MMS's 99..100..101..102..103..104..105..106..107..108..141..142..
196..197..198..199..200..201..238..239..240..241..242..243..
244..245..246..247..248..249..250..251..252..253..254..255..
256..257..258..259..(40 ships)

HARLAND AND WOLF

MMS's 2..3..4..10..11..12..13..20..21..32..33..34..35..50..133..134
135..136..183..184..185..207..211..214..215..232. (26 Ships)

MIRRLESS

MMS's 9..38..47..48..80..81..92..116..117..118..167..168..169..170
171..172..177..178..179..206..209..218..268.(23 Ships)

NATIONAL SUPERIOR

MMS's 123..124..125..126..127..128..143..144..148..155.(10 Ships)

NATIONAL GAS & OIL

MMS's 182..186..187..188..189..190..191..192..193..219.(10 Ships)

NEWBURY

MMS's 147..173..174..175..216..265..266 (7 Ships)

PETTERS

MMS's 260..263..279..280..284..285..286..305..307 (9 Ships)

RUSTON

MMS's 40..41..44..45..267..269..270..271 (8 Ships).

The following Pennant Numbers are not listed.

MMS's 161..162..163..164..166 were lost on the stocks (Rangoon)
MMS's 208..210..235..264..273 were cancelled in 1942
MMS's 299..306 were cancelled in 1943
MMS 313 built in Beirut was probably fitted with Crossley engines like her sister ship MMS 310.

Total number of ships listed 313 including cancellations and those lost on the stocks, accounting for all Pennant Numbers issued for this type.

VESSEL DISPOSITION BY BASES (Home Waters) 1941

M/S Bases	Jan	Feb	Mar	Apr	May	Jne	Jly	Aug	Sept	Oct	Nov	Dec	Totals
Portsmouth	8		18	11	14	40	30		44		45		
			19		17				27		46		
					5				28				
									113				15
Sheerness	1		15	16			25		26	53	80	54	
				39			41					68	11
Dover						6	29	7	55	56	22	78	
							42		59		82		
									79				11
Plymouth					24								1
Harwich									43				1
Lowestoft			9				38		47	48		116	5
Newhaven												61	1
Belfast				10	21			32					
								35					4
Londonderry											60		1
Liverpool			2		13	20	34						
			3			33	50						
			4										8
Clyde				12									1
Rosyth						31	37			74	75		4
Granton							36					83	2
	2		7	4	5	7	10	3	10	4	7	6	
Prog. Totals	2		9	13	18	25	35	38	48	52	59	65	65

Of the total of 65 completed all those underlined were earmarked for overseas and had left the UK by the end of the year, 44 vessels remained in operation in Home Waters.

VESSEL DISPOSITION BY BASES (Home Waters) 1942

M/S Bases	Jan	Feb	Mar	Apr	May	Jne	Jly	Aug	Sept	Oct	Nov	Dec	Totals
Portsmouth	<u>63</u>		<u>140</u>		186	62	71 181	115 176 189 202	66 182 204 213	219 220 221	110	230	19
Sheerness	<u>92</u>	57 69 <u>81</u>	149	171 <u>114</u> 190	<u>70</u> 173 192		85		175	109	211 265	266	17
Dover	139			<u>49</u>		165	205	183		87 218	91	268	9
Plymouth	76										229		2
Harwich	77			191	188 226	187	193	73				231	8
Lowestoft											224 225 228		3
Swansea	<u>167</u>			117	118 172		<u>169</u> <u>170</u>	206	209	177			9
Newhaven				64							67		2
Belfast	<u>133</u>		<u>88</u>	174									3
Londonderry													
Liverpool		136	<u>135</u>	<u>134</u>	150 <u>184</u>		185 207		215		214 233 236 261		12
Clyde			23	<u>58</u>	72	90	<u>65</u> 168						6
Rosyth		84							86				2
Granton/ Grimsby								119 120 121 122					4
Totals	7	5	5	9	8	7	9	11	10	7	14	4	
Prog/Totals	7	12	17	26	34	41	50	61	71	78	92	96	96

All ships underlined were drafted overseas.
MMS 180 is not listed, having been sunk in a collision four weeks after commissioning 130242.

VESSEL DISPOSITION BY BASES (Home Waters) 1943

M/S Bases	Jan	Feb	Mar	Apr	May	Jne	Jly	Aug	Sept	Oct	Nov	Dec	Totals
Portsmouth	No additional vessels												
Sheerness	267	269		294	295				287	282			
	216	137											8
Dover	No additional vessels												
Plymouth	141★			242★	244★	245★					250★	243★	
	142★				246★								
					254★								
					255★								10
Harwich			112	237	138	234						240★	
				292									6
Lowestoft									281				1
Swansea	178				247★				248★	257★			
					251★				252★				
					256★				253★				8
Newhaven	111		278				297	298					4
Belfast						275							1
Londonderry	No additional vessels												
Liverpool				232	274	293	288	301	308	283	289	276	
				277		302	296			291			13
Clyde									309				1
Rosyth/Leith	263			260		280					305	307	5
Grimsby											238★	241★	
											239★		3
Scapa Flow	270	285	284	272				290					
		271		286									7
Totals	6	4	5	7	4	12	4	3	8	4	5	5	
Prog/Totals	6	10	15	22	26	38	42	45	53	37	62	67	67

Those ships asterisked were built overseas in Canada.

1944	MMS's 249, 279, 300, 303 and 304 were completed in UK..
	MMS's 131, 132, 144, 310, 311, 312, 313 completed abroad.
1945	MMS's 143, 145, 151, 258, 259 completed abroad.
1946	MMS's 97, 98, 148, 154, 222, 223 completed abroad.
Totals	1941, 65; 1942, 96; 1943, 67; 1944, 12; 1945, 5; 1946, 6 + 2 = 253

The following Pennant Numbers are not listed.

MMS's 161, 162, 163, 164, 166 were lost on the stocks (Rangoon).

MMSs 208, 210, 235, 264, 273 were cancelled in 1942.

MMS's 299, 306 were cancelled in 1943.

MMS 313 built in Beirut was probably fitted with Crossley engines like her sister ship MMS 310.

Total number of ships listed 313 including cancellations and those lost on the stocks, accounting for all Pennant Numbers issued for this type.

ALLOCATION OF SHIPS TO BUILDERS (Overseas)

Abdul Wahbad	Beirut	310..313
Arbid Moussali	Beirut	144(2)
Armand Inbeau	Tadoussac	108(1)
Brunton	Cochin	97..98..129..130..131..132
		151(2)..152(2)..154(2)..157
		158..159..160
Bombay/Burma Trading	Rangoon	148(1)
Bailey	Hong Kong	95..96..123..124
Belmont DK Co.	Kingston Jamaica	222..223
Clare Sh.Bldg.Co	Metaghan Canada	104..105..106..107(2)..108(2)
		196..197..198..199..242..243
		244..245..246..247
Chantiers Maritime	St.Laurent	107(1)..254..255
Cargo Bt.Despatch Co.	Colombo	145(1)..146(1)
Irrawadi Flot.Co.	Rangoon	147(2)..151(1)..152(1)..153
Le Blanc Sh.Bldg.	Nova Scotia	252..253
Marine Trust	Tel Aviv	155(2)..311..312
Port Commissioners	Colombo	143(1)..144(1)
Rayal Bodden	Caymen Isls.	258..259
Rangoon Govt.D.Y.	Rangoon	147(1)..154(1)..155(1)..156
		161..162..163..164
Shelburne Co.	Nova Scotia	103..200..248..249..102(2)
Steers	St.Johns N.F.	141..142..238..239..240..241
Stone H.	St.Johns N.F.	119..120..121..122
Scindia	Bombay	145(2)..146(2)..148(2)
Symonetty	Nassau,Bahamas	194..195
United Eng.	Singapore	51..52..93..94..125..126..127
		128..166
Vaughan	St.Andrews N.B.	256..257
Wagstaff & Hatfield	Canada	99..100..101..102(2)..201..
		250..251
Zoghzoghy H	Beirut	143(2)

The figure (1) indicates where building commenced. (2) where the ship was completed. Why there was this chopping and changing is not known, but it could have been that some of the smaller companies were just not able to cope. Many of the ships building abroad, especially those in Singapore were captured by the enemy before completion.

OVERSEAS BUILDERS (Rate of Progress) 41–45

1941	Jan	Feb	Mar	Apr	May	Jne	Jly	Aug	Sep	Oct	Nov	Dec	Totals
Armand													
Clare													
Chantiers													
Le Blanc													
Shelbourne													
Steers													
Stone							119 120	121 122					4
Vaughan													
Wagstaff										99	100		2
Bailey HK	95, 96, 123, 124 lost on slips												4
Belmont													
Burma Tr.													
Brunton	157, 158, 159, 160 Cancelled												4
Cargo Col.													
Col. Port.													
Irrawadi	147, 153, Lost on slips 152 Cancelled												3
Marine Tr.	155 Cancelled												1
Wahbad													
Moussali													
Rangoon Gvt.	156, 161, 162, 163, 164 Lost on slips												5
Cayman Isl.													
Scindia	146 Cancelled												1
Symonetty	194, 195 Cancelled												2
United Eng,	51, 52, 93. 94, 125, 126, 127, 128, 166 Lost on slips												9
													33
Lost and cancelled													29
Totals													4

OVERSEAS BUILDERS (Rate of Progress) continued;

1942	Jan	Feb	Mar	Apr	May	Jne	Jly	Aug	Sep	Oct	Nov	Dec	Totals
Armand	Fitting out MMS 108 only												1
Clare							104					196	2
							105					197	2
							106					198	2
Chantiers								107					1
Le Blanc													
Shelbourne									103	102			2
Steers													
Stone													
Vaughan													
Wagstaff											99	100	2
Brunton													
												Totals	12

OVERSEAS BUILDERS (Rate of Progress) continued;

1943	Jan	Feb	Mar	Apr	May	Jne	Jly	Aug	Sep	Oct	Nov	Dec	Totals
Clare		199			242 243	244 245 246 247							7
Chantiers						254 255							2
Le Blanc									252 253				2
Shelbourne			200						248				2
Steers	141 142										238 239	240 241	6
Vaughan								256		257			2
Wagstaff		101	201			251					250		4
Brunton				129	130								2
Totals	2	2	2		3	8		1	3	1	3	2	27
Prog/Totals	2	4	6		9	17		18	21	22	25	27	

1944	(Jan)	249 Shelbourne;	132 Brunton	2
	(Mar)		131 Brunton;	1
	(Oct)	144 Col. Port;		1
1945	(Jan)	222 Belmont; 311, 312 Marine Trust		3
	(Jan)	223 Belmont		1
	(Apr)	145 Cargo Col;		1
	(Jne)	143 Col. Port;		1
	(Aug)	310 Wahbad;		1
	(Oct)	313 Wahbad		1
	(Dec)	151 Irrawadi		1
1946	(Jan)	154 Rangoon Gvt.		1
	(Mar)	258 Cayman Isl; 97, 98 Brunton		3
	(Apr)	259 Cayman Isl;		1
	(Nov)	148 Scindia		1
		Totals		46

MINESWEEPING BASES (Abroad) 1942

BASES	Jan	Feb	Mar	Apr	May	Jne	Jly	Aug	Sep	Oct	Nov	Dec	Early Arrivals
MSF 103 N.Africa	68	53		114	70		85						MMS 1
MSF 105 Brindisi	32						185						MMS 34
MSF 108	133		135	134	184								MMS 2,3 13,20, 21,33, 50
W.Italy													
MSF 110	92	81		171									MMS 9 47,38 48,80
Madelina													111
MSF 111 Madelina													
MSF 114 Messina	63		88	58			65						MMS 5,
		140		49									46
MSF 120							104	102	103		99	100	
							105						
							106						
Port Said													
MSF 121							107				196		
							108				197		
MSF 122											198		
E.Indies													
Totals	5	2	3	5	2	6	3	1		1	4		16
Prog	5	7	10	15	17	23	26	27		28	32		48

It can be seen from this table that by the close of 1942 there were a total of 48 MMS's in the Mediterranean, all in active roles, but it took a long time to get them there.

MINESWEEPING BASES (Abroad) 1943

Month of Commissioning

M/S Flotillas	Jan	Feb	Mar	Apr	May	Jne	Jly	Aug	Sep	Oct	Nov	Dec
103	No additional vessels											
105			4		10				35			
108	No additional vessels											
110	No additional vessels											
111	167			117	172	168	169					
114	No additional vessels											
120		101										
121	No additional vessels											
122		199	200									
			201									

1944

M/S Flotillas	Jan	Feb	Mar	Apr	May	Jne	Jly	Aug	Sep	Oct	Nov	Dec
146 (Levant)										144		

1945

M/S Flotillas	Jan	Feb	Mar	Apr	May	Jne	Jly	Aug	Sep	Oct	Nov	Dec
146 (Levant)	311						143		310		313	
	312											

Overseas strength 1943–1945

MSF		
103 MMS's 1, 53, 68, 70, 85, 114	6
105 MMS's 4, 10, 32, 34, 35, 50, 185	7
108 MMS's 2, 3, 13, 20, 21, 33, 133, 134, 135, 184	10
110 MMS's 9, 38, 47, 48, 80, 81, 92, 116, 118, 171	10
111 MMS's 117, 167, 168, 169, 170, 172	6
114 MMS's 5, 46, 58, 63, 65, 88, 89, 140	8
120 MMS's 99, 100, 101, 102, 103, 104, 105, 106	8
121 MMS's 107, 108, 196, 197	4
122 MMS's 198, 199, 200, 201	4
146 MMS's 143, 144, 310, 311, 312, 313	6
Tota	169

To India in 1945 MMS's 145..151

To India in 1946 MMS's 148..154

MMS's 258 and 259 were not completed in Canada until 1946. They were sold there.

MMS's 222 and 223 were completed in Jamaica and sold in Bermuda.

MMS's 81 and 92 returned to the UK in 1944

UNITED KINGDOM/ABROAD BUILDERS (Summary)

	Home		Abroad		
1941	65		4		
1942	99		12		
1943	46		27		
1944	4		4		
1945			9		
1946			6		
	214	+	62	=	276
Ships lost on slips					20
Ships cancelled					17
					313

313 was the total number to be built, but it was inevitable
that many would not be actively involved in the conflict.

Those that were however, must be commended for their sterling service, albeit that most of the work was very little more than routine.

MAGNETIC AND ACOUSTIC SWEEPING FORMATIONS

There were a number of basic formations devised for sweeping influence mines. Description of these is very technical and it is not necessary to go into the detail here. Suffice it to say the formations named 'P', 'Q', 'R', 'S' and 'V' were designed for specific purposes.

MMS's generally used the 'P' and 'Q' formations that is

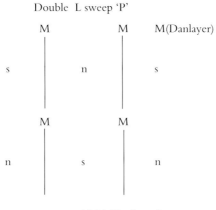

Double L sweep 'P'

M   M   M(Danlayer)

M   M

M M (Danlayers)

n and s indicate North and South polarity of sweep

Normal clearance used two or more vessels sweeping two abreast with half a mile between each pair, and danlayers were stationed another half a mile astern of the last two sweepers.

'Q' Formation was somewhat different and classed as a high percentage searching sweep which covered a wide front and with vessels sweeping two or three abreast as under

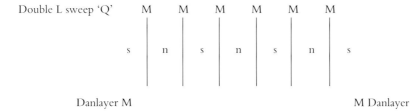

Double L sweep 'Q'

The sweepers maintained a distance of 450 yards from each other.

'R' Formation was used when sweeping ahead of a convoy, or when operating in marked channels as under

Double L sweep 'R'

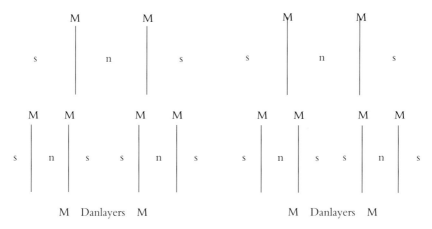

The ships swept in an arrow-head formation in pairs, covering the area twice in single or double pulsing and half a mile apart in line astern, Danlayers were positioned so that there was always an overlap thereby eliminating any 'holidays' which might arise in the sweeping operation.

'S' Formation was used for 100% clearance with mines of both polarities, operating in three pairs position in quarter line to port or starboard depending on which side the minefield lay. Station keeping was half a mile in line astern as under

Double L sweep 'S'

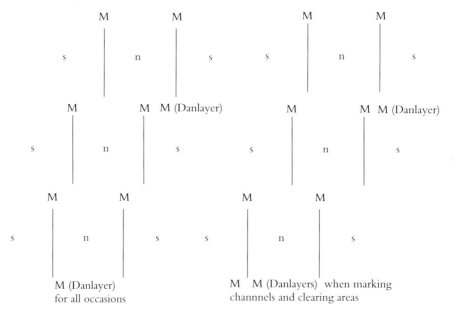

The fifth formation used was 'V' for super sensitive mines and was as under:

Double L sweep 'V' Formation

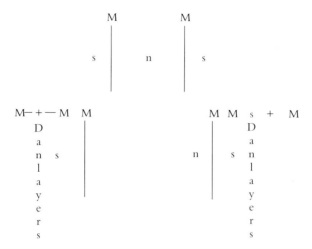

Only four ships were employed on 'V' formations, at half a mile distance fore and aft. The danlayers on the extreme port and starboard positions were employed while sweeping an area on double pulsing. Those on the inboard positions when marking a channel on single pulsing. As has been already mentioned, it was not the sweeping that proved to be difficult but the station keeping which invariably caused a problem as it was essential to the success of the whole operation.

Chapter 4

Vessel Disposition, more problems, and the Minesweeping Badge

There was by the end of 1941, a total of 66 ships completed, of which 22 had been earmarked, or had already departed for foreign waters, leaving a total of 44 less MMS 39 which was lost almost as soon as she was commissioned.

The chart clearly indicates how long some of the established bases had to wait for their quota of the first 50 vessels. May 1941 found the depots at their weakest with only 18 ships capable of dealing in any effective way with the magnetic menace, and if those destined to operate abroad are subtracted (it is not certain whether they had in fact departed), then that made matters even worse.

Nine bases had no ships at all. Sheerness with its responsibilities for the Thames and Medway estuaries, together with Portsmouth as a major naval base had, it would seem, some kind of priority for mineswseeping craft, with Liverpool, probably because of its ability and size, being able to receive urgent imports from abroad, coming a close second.

By the end of the year priorities had drastically altered. Liverpool was then stripped bare of all her Motor Minesweepers until May 1942 when the first ship she was able to call her own MMS 150, was received. Lt. Cdr. Hails tells his own story of the successful completion of a minesweeping course at HMS *Vernon* following the Dunkirk evacuation in 1940.

He volunteered in October 1939 for the Royal Navy, went to HMS King Alfred at Skegness where particular attention was given to instruction in the use of the Double 'L' sweep. As a Sub-Lieutenant at the time, he was attached to a group of trawlers operating out of Portsmouth.

As a peacetime lawyer, he claims that he had a fairly good grounding regarding the working of this new device. To substantiate his claim, he passed out with 100% marks. His first draft was as a watchkeeping officer on a paddle minesweeper *Princess Elizabeth*, belonging to the 10th. Minesweeping Flotilla, on the 10th. July 1940. The 10th. MSF was disbanded soon after and the ships dispersed. The *Princess Elizabeth* was allocated to Great Yarmouth, then a few weeks later to Harwich and the 12th. MSF.

It was during his patrols between Harwich and Lowestoft that Lt.Cdr. Hails saw his first Motor Minesweeper. She was in the process of being built at Richards Iron Works at Lowestoft.

His claim that he had never seen anything like her before was accurate for they had just been ordered. His expression as he saw her progressively take shape with sweep reel and 'A' frame, was that, 'He had fallen in love with the little thing'.

In July 1941, he was recommended for his own command, having been a Lieutenant for six months, and was offered the opportunity of serving aboard a Double 'L' Corvette, but his preference was for the smaller craft and he ended up as the Commanding Officer of MMS 32, built by MacDuff in Scotland, becoming, as he himself so ably puts it, "one of the iron men who manned the wooden ships."

Lt. Cdr. Hails states that he thinks it is fair to say that the Royal Navy had the measure of all German mines for the greater part of the war, but the records clearly show that this was not in fact the case.

The allocation of this particular type of vessel proved to be a difficult task, for the needs were great in every area around the coast.

In spite of the claim that the Thames estuary had never been closed to shipping, except for a few hours during the first twelve months of the war, no sweeping was possible outside the special channels or anchorages because of the acute shortage of specialist craft.

It was Captain Hertford already mentioned, who stated in one report that for every mine dropped in the channel, three or four may have been deposited outside these areas. During this time only 15 magnetic and 38 acoustic had been detonated inside the Thames estuary.

Prior to the completion and allocation of the MMS's, certain measures were taken to keep the channels open and to find out where in fact the mines were being laid. To this end two trawlers were fitted out with Double L sweeps and allocated to each port, together with two drifters and four shallow draught motor boats fitted with Mark 5 magnetic sweeps.

These vessels were utilised in a daily search programme in order to clear the channels before the tide turned, allowing the deep draught ships up the rivers and into the docks.

How were the mines to be detected?

With the use of mine spotters. Minespotting was introduced early on in the war, as the only realistic and dependable method of knowing where the mines actually lay, most of which were dropped in the rivers and estuaries during the hours of darkness by low flying aircraft.

The only way to deal with these explosive death traps, was either to mark them with buoys once their position was known, or sweep them as soon as possible following their sighting.

In order to identify the position of each mine, a system of lookouts was introduced, so that the location of the mine could be accurately reported.

As there was no single organisation available to provide this service, all those people who had riverside interests were called upon to offer their assistance. As an incentive the sum of five pounds (that would be the equivalent of a week's wages in those days) was offered for each mine's accurate position.

Observers were positioned on each side of the river bank at 400 yard intervals during the hours of darkness. They usually worked in pairs, and information regarding the kind of object they were looking for, was provided in the following form;

"The magnetic mine is between six and eight feet long by two feet in diameter. There is no noise created by its falling even at a speed in excess of forty miles an hour, but can easily be identified from the 26' foot diameter parachute on which the mine is suspended, and equally by the 20' high splash when it hits the water and is visible from a long way off. Only these parachute mines are to be reported."

This human minespotting exercise was practised mainly along the banks of the river Thames and proved to be so successful that on April 7th. 1941, a minesweeping base was proposed for the river Thames as opposed to the Thames estuary, using the training ship *Woorster* as a Base Ship and with a force of four Motor Minesweepers (when they finally became available), together with four tugs, four drifters, and one motor drifter.

MMS's 14,15,16, and 17 constituted the 101st. Minesweeping Flotilla. (but see the charts as to where they finally ended up).

Coping with the straight magnetic mine was difficult enough, but the danger increased when it was discovered that the enemy was invariably one step ahead of us, not some of the time, but all of the time.

A paper by a Captain Walton in November 1942 on minesweeping activities reveals that there were various devices introduced by the Germans to delay the activity of mines on the sea bed.

This may sound old hat now, in the light of our present experiences, but at the time it proved to be a very serious setback to the counter-measure operations, which at that time were being devised by our own departments to meet what was becoming an almost unsurmountable task.

The abbreviation MAD stood for multi-action delay and consisted of a device which stopped the mine being active for any given time following its deposit in the water.

This was usually effected either by a spring, a clock or with less accuracy by a chemical plug, or by the motion of the water in which the mine was laid.

There were in addition, other gadgets which allowed the mine to fire after it had been activated a predetermined number of times, the mine lying dormant until the sweeper had passed over it the requisite number of times to start the clock, which might be set to go off at that precise moment or at any other time following its starting, and irrespective of how many times it was swept.

This made the magnetic sweep totally ineffective, but those of us who were called to do the task were quite unaware, certainly those on the lower deck, that we were using obsolete equipment.

In fact the magnetic Double L sweep constituted in itself, where these particular types of mine were sown, an added danger to the ships they were designed to protect.

Both time delay and multi-actuating mechanisms were fitted in certain German mines, which made it almost impossible for the minefield to be swept immediately the information of their position had been received, as was the usual practice.

Mines often became active following a sweeping operation, giving the impression that because there was no explosion the lanes were clear. These were cunning devices as we were to learn as the war progressed, designed to make any efforts to clear the lanes ineffective.

That is exactly what happened in spite of the many reports being circulated in various periodicals at the time, such as War Illustrated which one must suppose for propaganda reasons was telling the population that we were creating havoc with the enemy's minelaying tactics, which was not in fact the case. The truth was that the powers-that-be were extremely worried about the whole sorry business. In October 1942 the Prime Minister sent the following message to the First Sea Lord:

> I am disquieted to learn that the German 'E' boats are getting the upper hand again and that they are becoming a serious danger to the East Coast shipping by the laying of mines. I had the impression that you had overtaken the mosquito fleet menace. Pray let me have a statement showing the position, and also what measures you will take. We cannot possibly allow ourselves to be outmatched in mosquito warfare.

Winston Churchill.

But outmatched we truly were.

Apart from getting more sweepers on the active list which might not be as effective as they should due to the constant modifications being made to the mines, a number of ways and means were suggested to bring about the effective control of these weapons.

One consulting chemist came up with the hair-brained scheme of using patrol boats to drop charged magnetised spheres in the vicinity of the minefields, but it would seem that the cost of producing these bits of equipment made the idea prohibitive, so it was never tried out.

One had visions of a quarter deck full of magnetic cannon balls creating a current which was likely to detonate the mines before they had the opportunity of getting rid of the things over the side.

Ships' microphones dangling over the side of the vessel was another scheme designed to pick up a signal from anything that might be lying below. Efforts were made to put that idea into practice, but there were so many false signals from this primitive detector, that the efforts were abandoned.

It was not unlike the panic stations which ensued at Scapa Flow where microphones were placed across the harbour entrance to detect the approach of enemy submarines. All the warning lights started flashing, action stations were manned but nothing was seen or found. It was discovered later that the panic had been caused by a shoal of shrimps snapping their claws.

Another idea offered as early as November 1939 was that ASDIC (Allied Submarine Detection Investigation Committee) ought to be used, as it was a device to detect underwater obstacles. For reasons unknown this was turned down, but it is ironic and perhaps a little comic to know that ASDIC is the method currently in use in minehunting vessels of the present day fleet.

By the end of 1942 there were over 170 motor minesweepers in operation both at home and overseas. These together with the British Yard sweepers or BYMS as they were called, coming to us through lease and lend from the USA, plus the introduction of the 126 foot Big Mickey, and of course the Royal Naval Flotillas, the task was met with a new determination, in spite of the fact that it was known that the battle was to be a long and weary one.

In the December of 1939 a proposal was made by the Director of Minesweeping, that a badge of some description should be designed and issued to those who had been called to man the sweepers.

A precedent had been established during the first World War, when a badge had been issued to those on mine clearance duties. The proposal recognised that those engaged on this arduous and dangerous routine work, were proud of the fact that they were employed on a job that might result in a watery grave.

The public too had a distinct sympathy with men and women who were subjected to rigour and hardships of any kind.

Decorations were now due to the minesweeping forces and it was therefore suggested that the striking of such a badge be announced at the same time. The idea was referred to the then Director of Anti-submarine Warfare, with a rider expressing the view that it might be appropriate to include his own men who were involved with auxiliary anti-submarine craft and recruited from the same source.

His reply was none too salutary, but it put the cause for the minesweeping personnel in perspective:

"It is not desirous to recommend the introduction of the proposed new non-substantive badge for men serving in anti-submarine trawlers. Their work is considered to be no more hazardous than any other craft, except mine-sweepers."

A further minute from the same document, number 98, which would appear to be more of a directive than a comment, came from the 4th Sea Lord to the First Sea Lord of the Admiralty with copies to ACNS, dated 23rd. December 1939:

I am told that the minesweeping men have no badge. If this is so, it must be remedied at once. I have asked Mr. Bracken to call for designs from Sir Kenneth Clarke within one week, after which production must begin with the greatest of speed and distributed as deliveries come to hand.

Signed: Winston Churchill

Following this, a letter was sent to the Director of Minesweeping and signed by a Mr. Lang, stating that action had been taken by the First Sea Lord vide minute 98.

In spite of this however, protests were still made about the badge's introduction. An unsigned letter, but obviously from someone in the higher echelons, shows a total disagreement with any idea of a minesweeping badge. (and who pray would argue with Winston Churchill one might ask? Only someone of exceptional high rank one would guess.)

Quote:

I feel that at the present rate, this badge is premature, nor is the whole story shown on this paper (referring one assumes to the original proposal)

A suggestion was included in recent papers about the possibility of broadcasting an appeal for fishermen recruits, which was not favourably received by D.P.S. or A.R.C. on the grounds that such a broadcast would be both expensive and superfluous. The cost could not be justified.

I am not clear whether D.M.S. has in mind a cloth badge to be stitched on to the uniform, or a metal badge which would be detachable. If the latter, Treasury sanction would be necessary and in either event the production of such a badge would take some time.

It is presumably not the idea to issue the badge to trawler personnel. The principle objection I have to the scheme is that the danger of the service is relative. There are other services for which the Admiralty has even seen fit to introduce a form of risk money. They are not to have special badges. The precedent of the mine clearance staff in 1919 in so far as the object of the exercise is to persuade men to stay in the service, is not too sound.

It turned out that he did not get his way, even though he may have had it in mind that there were more important things to think about at the time, such as the production of more minesweepers.

The badge was subsequently designed, produced and issued to those personnel who were currently serving on minesweeping or anti-submarine vessels and had been for a minimum of six months.

It was made of silver and worn on the left sleeve of the Naval uniform just above the wrist. The design is as shown on the drawing, and shows an anti-submarine net, two of the moored type of mine, and with a shark representing the enemy which in turn is pierced through with a marlin spike.

The badge was highly treasured by those who were entitled to wear it, and still is, but it caused a great deal of jealousy in the war years especially among the Royal Naval ratings who did not qualify.

It can be seen proudly displayed on many of the Standards at the annual re-union of the Royal Naval Patrol Service Association held in Lowestoft during the first week in October. Some of the Standards seen on parade, which come from branches all over the United Kingdom, have the letters RNPS in place of the M/S-A/S, but this is simply because the insignia has been adopted, and quite rightly so, by the Association.

A close look at some of the lapels of those who in their latter years proudly continue to march past the saluting base, will reveal, set against the colourful display of campaign medals, the silver badge, retained and treasured over the years.

Following the cessation of hostilities, a minesweeping medal was approved and issued. There are still many of the old school who have never heard of it.

The qualifications for wearing what is termed the Naval General Service Medal with clasp 'Minesweeping 45/51' is a minimum of 180 days engaged in actual operational minesweeping after the 8th. May 1945 (time spent steaming to and from the sweeping area or tied up alongside the jetty does not count).

The author failed to qualify in spite of the fact that from the date in question he was employed on M/S duties until December of the same year. In fact it is doubtful if many did.. Given that post war crews would be working a five day week and taking into consideration times for refits, breakdowns, rest periods, leave, and even without the deviations experienced by hostilities, it would be difficult for anyone to qualify inside four years.

Reference to the Log Book of MMS 260, and kindly presented to the MMS Trust by C.H. Andrew of Clevedon, Avon, and one time C.O. of the same ship, shows that between the dates of the 12th. June 1944 and 18th. June 1944, a period of seven days at the height of Operation Overlord, she completed, give or take a minute or two, twenty nine hours sweeping time. That would be, during hostilities, about average, taking into consideration that many of the ships were employed on other duties, such as dan laying and coffin ship, as well as escort duties. As a dan layer one could spend as much time, if not more, than those vessels doing the sweep, for dans had to be picked up following the clearance.

The medal would appear to have been issued to those personnel who extended their time after the war was over, when a great deal of clearance work had to be done, but done nevertheless without the harrassment of the enemy and mostly in daylight.

Neither would they be involved as target towing vessels or as guide ships for our Air Force or any other of the many tasks which could then be done by vessels not employed in wartime activities.

It would be interesting to know just how many of these medals were awarded, for few of them have been seen. It was recently discovered by the author that Lt/Cdr. Jim Bowie (Rtd.) Commanding Officer MMS 81, of Aberdeen, sports one of these elusive awards, but Jim was sweeping many moons after the war had come to its close.

The latest information is that a new minesweeping medal is being struck for those who served in such a capacity both during and after the war.

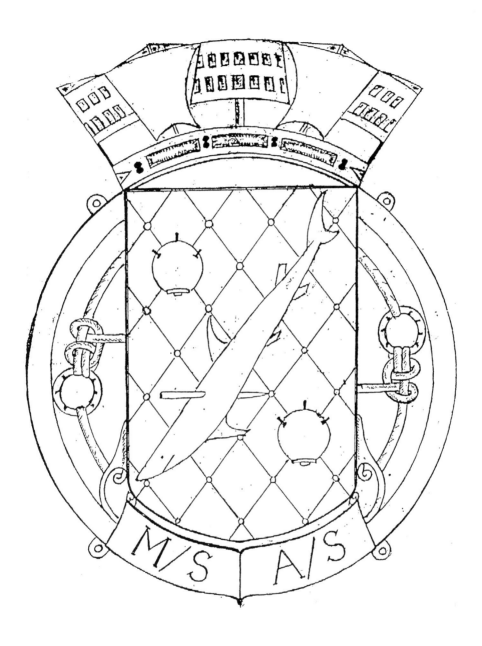

Silver Arm Badge awarded to personnel who served during the Second World War 1939–1945 on minesweeping and anti-submarine vessels of His Majesty's Royal Naval Patrol Service.

Chapter Five

News from Abroad
Activity in the Mediterranean and beyond.

Any operations in the Far East in early 1941, were, as far as minesweeping was concerned, almost negative. The Navy was to all intents and purposes not involved in any war. Fleet sweepers were non existent. Four Bangor Class sweepers were being built in Hong Kong, and while it was the government's intention to provide the first ten Bathurst Class ships off the stocks, to China or some East Indian station in the event of any need for minesweeping activity, there was little chance of that need being met, basically because of the increasing demands for these craft in home waters.

The same was true for the Mediterranean, even though this area was regarded as a greater priority.

New vessels coming off the slips were being commandeered and commissioned for sweeping duties at home. All the existing available craft had been monopolised such was the urgency of the situation.

While there appeared to be no immediate cause for panic, it must have been obvious to the government of the day that with Italy's entry into the war in June of 1940, the minelaying activities of the enemy were bound to intensify along practically every coast line, necessitating the urgent need for sweeping equipment.

One instance will be sufficient to highlight the situation.

Frustration must have been the order of the day when commanders of ships like HMS *Kelly, Jackal* and *Kelvin*, all of the 5th. Destroyer Flotilla, were, between the 4th. and the 9th. of May 1941, blockaded by mines in Malta's Valetta Harbour ...put out of action because there were no craft to sweep the channel.

It is said that there were desperate attempts by the Captain of HMS *Gloxinia*, a Flower Class corvette, to clear a way through the mines, using her depth charges but without much success.

As a result of all this inactivity, and in order to make up the deficiency, three fleet sweepers, the *Aberdare, Harrow* and *Widnes,* were despatched to the area, and 25 minesweeping/anti-submarine corvettes began training for use in Eastern waters.

The fleet sweepers were sent with a great deal of reluctance, primarily because the Navy recognised that the need at home was more urgent.

But time proved that the Mediterranean was going to be just as dangerous as the North Sea and English Channel.

According to German High Command South, there were in the region of 56,000 mines laid in the Mediterranean, the main concentration being in the San Remo-Vechio area on the North Western coast of Italy (12000) and 14000 deposited in the Adriatic.

However, before any advance into Europe could be attempted, the mines had to be cleared, and an effort was made to get the ships now coming off the slips in greater numbers, into action, with the main objective being very similar to that of the U.K., to establish swept channels to the newly captured ports, avoiding where possible the thickly sown minefields. This would ensure, it was hoped, safe passage for unescorted shipping.

It was not until April of 1943 that the waterways between Alexandria and Gibraltar, Sicily and Tunisia were declared open and the first convoy for two years passed through in the May and June of that year.

This was mainly due to the concentrated efforts of the Motor Minesweeping Flotillas which finally arrived on the scene, some of which had set out from the UK late in 1941 and early 1942 and were based as follows:

103 MSF consisting of MMS's	1(41)..53(42)..68(42)..85(42).114(42)..69(42)..70(42)
105 MSF ,, ,, ,,	4(43)..10(41)..32(42)..34(41)..35(43)..50(41)
	185(42)
108 MSF consisting of MMS's	2(41)..13(41)..20(41)..21(41)..33(41).133(42)
	134(42).135(42).184(42)
110 MSF consisting of MMS's	9(41)..38(41)..47(41)..48(41)..80(41)
	81(42)..92(42).116(42).118(42).171(42)
111 MSF ,, ,, ,,	117(42).167(42).168(42).169(42).170(42)
	172(42)
114 MSF ,, ,, ,,	5(41)..46(41)..58(42)..63(42)..65(42)..88(42)

89(42).140(42)

Numbers in brackets denote the year of arrival

These flotillas were based in the first instance and as they became available (see chart) at Brindisi in North Africa, then in turn Madelina, Messina, and Western Italy in Naples, Leghorn and Genoa.

Desmond Jacobs who was First Lieutenant of MMS 133 set out in August 1942, having commissioned the vessel in Frazerburgh following her completion in the January of that year. The passage was via the Caledonian Canal in Scotland to the Mersey.

In company were MMS's 21..134..135..and 184, the rest of the 108th MSF having departed early in 1942. Desmond tells of the 20-25 foot Atlantic swells, and when it is considered that these ships were designed primarily for inshore sweeping, returning to base each night, and not for long distance journeys, it is no wonder that the engine failed from time to time, resulting in the indignities of having a tow to Gibraltar.

The engine room staff were not miracle men, but some might be described as bloody heroes. There was little equipment in the way of spares or indeed the tools to do the job at sea. Some of them barely knew the front end of the engine from the back, but somehow they managed remarkably well.

Following Gibraltar, the next port of call was Bougie in North Africa where they were, as he described it, 'pestered' with Italian bombers. His ship was transferred to Algiers in the Spring of 1943 which offered some light relief with off duty spells. The purchase of an old motorbike for a fiver allowed him to explore some of the surrounding desert views.

September of the same year saw them involved in the Salerno landings with all that meant in the way of routine sweeps and enemy action, about which little has ever been reported.

A glance at the Ship's Log Book for that operation if it were available, would probably read, very much like that of MMS 260 during the 'D' Day landings. 'Routine sweep carried out'.

After a spell in Naples the ship returned to Algiers in July 1944 to be handed over for the use of the French Navy.

Desmond Jacobs commissioned the building of one of the few models of the MMS that are known to exist. The MMS Trust was responsible in large measure for supplying the drawings and the photographs which made the building of the model possible.

MMS 50 was another of those ships which did her stint in the Mediterranean with the 105th. MSF. Mr. Church was the coxswain and he tells about the good news of the arrival of a daughter to his wife in the UK. These bits of joyful information came in the form of a signal, and generally in code.

MMS 50 was involved with her flotilla in the invasion of Sicily, following which the journey was made up the East Coast of Italy to Dubrovnick in Yugoslavia where the signal was received.

A baby born called for celebrations and an occasion to 'splice the mainbrace', a custom no longer enjoyed by the Navy since the issue of 'grog' or the 'tot' was discontinued on 31st. July 1970.

'Sippers all round' was the order of the day, which usually laid the recipient low for a couple of hours – for some it was a couple of days! It has been known for a sailor to down a half pint of 'neaters' which he had unlawfully saved, and ending up out for the count for three days. Those who were used to it, rallied in a little less time.

Such an experience happened to a leading stoker serving aboard MMS 46 in the same Italian waters with the 114th.MSF. A son was born on the 1st. January 1945.

MMS 46 had her own trials and tribulations. The author joined her after a spell in Malta, where having just recovered from a bout of dhoby rash on the troopship Arundel Castle, he immediately fell foul of the female sandfly. The fever did not last too long, but it was bad enough while it lasted.

Reggie Meen the one-time heavy weight champion of Britain was a well known figure in Fort Manoel in Malta, a physical training instructor who spent most of his time relating the stories of his fights to those who were somewhat fed-up waiting for a draft away from the watery grog, the rancid Australian tinned butter, and the over chlorinated drinking water. Tea never tasted like that tea. It was out of this world. . .

With demands for manpower steadily increasing one did not have too long to wait. MMS 46 was at that time operating out of Leghorn, which meant a journey on board one of the captured Italian minelaying cruisers at about 40 knots to Naples and another long wait at HMS *Byrsa* for onward transmission by whatever mode of transport became available.

The stay was for most mateloes a time of light relief. The local Neapolitan palace had been taken over for the troops and together with the young bambinos offering a cheap night with their sister who may only have been about 12 years old,[and this for a bar of chocolate and a tin of sardines .. . with chocolate not easy to come by in those days, nor indeed sardines for that matter] life a little more pleasant.

Not that one dabbled frequently into affairs with these nymph-like senoritas, for there were things you could catch without going fishing, but to get your boots polished outside the palace steps for a few lira was a delight in itself.

The palace, it was said, catered for every need apart from sexual,(some would say that was debatable.) The bromided tea from the NAAFI took care of that, as did the constant lectures from on high. Drama, dancing, theatre. swimming pool, restaurants, one could spend a couple of days and not taste all the delights.

But it was only a brief spell of relaxation, if that is the correct description, before passage was found on an Italian corvette (where were our own ships?) The ship's crew, all Italians, did not seem to like rough weather. In a choppy sea they were found hiding in any nook and cranny available with two life jackets on.

Shelter had to be sought in an Italian harbour, which offered a brief opportunity for a run ashore where the only meal available in the local café, was cooked cat. Of course nobody knew that till after it had been eaten. Food was short in those days.

The journey was completed on a three ton truck with a driver who gave the impression that he had never driven a vehicle before. That would not have been so bad on normal roads, but this journey from Piembino to Leghorn was something not forgetten in a hurry.

Quite a hairy experience in an open backed lorry, more than convinced that at any moment life would come to its close in the sea some hundreds of feet below the bomb-cratered road. One got the distinct feeling that the driver either had a grudge or that he had been indulging in too much of the local brew. Vino could be quite potent as we were to find out as time went by.

During the hostilities in the Mediterranean, the Mickey Mice, were employed in practically every operation from North Africa up through Sicily to the East and West coasts of Italy and extensively throughout the Aegean, following the line of enemy retreat.

MMS 117 was lost in Civita Vechia harbour having just completed what was known as 'fluffing' operations. This name was given to describe the practice of sweeping from a tied up or anchored position, mainly because it was impossible to manoeuvre a 260 ton vessel in narrow channels.

The procedure was to anchor the ship off shore or tie up alongside the quay and tow out the 'Double L' sweep with the use of the small boat. This could be a long and tiring task. The use of an outboard motor was forbidden for obvious reasons. The electrodes were then anchored with a concrete sinker in the shallow water, and sweeping would commence.

Local people who happened to be wandering around or passing over a road bridge which straddled the waterway, were warned by means of signs like

'MINE PERICOLOSO', but they seemed always oblivious of any danger, that is until the first mine went off and somebody was injured.

Following the hostilities in Italy the locals spent a great deal of their time on the sea shore, especially in the summer months. Mines were often detonated within yards of the bathers, who thought in spite of the many warnings given, that the war was over. For the crew of MMS 117 it was. There were but two survivors. MMS 70 (MSF 103) was another casualty in the Aegean, lost in the Gulf of Toronto in September 1943. For the rest it had only just begun.

A similar occurrence happened in Genoa harbour, when MMS 168 was lost while sweeping the shipping lanes within the harbour breakwater.

It was the morning of 25th. June 1945. It was a toss up between the Skippers of the 46 and the 168 to see who would stay in harbour. The 46 won.

The object was to sweep the lanes before any work in the harbour began. The ship was blown to smithereens by the very mine, she had sought to destroy. The funeral took place that same week when 15 members of her crew were laid to rest in Genoa Cemetary, the only British personnel in the place and designated as a British War Grave.

The author, who was one of the firing party, returned to the spot about 20 years ago, when he met a lady at the cemetary who actually witnessed the ceremony. She was able to lead our party to the quiet spot nestling on the side of the hill overlooking the sea. It is doubtful whether the place would ever have been found at such short

Burial of the crew of MMS 168 – Staglione Cemetery, Genoa, Italy, 25th June 1945.

notice if that particular senora had not been around.

The names of those who lost their lives were Skippers Tucker and Watt, Chief Engineman Hughes, Engineman Andrew, Leading Stokers Carter and Ewbank, Leading Seaman Jackson, and Seamen Bennett, Clements and Alexander, Wireman Parish, Cook Harper, Steward Ballantyne, Telegraphist Meenz and Signalman McGroarty.

In the Adriatic during the days of the enemy occupation of Northern Italy , MMS's in concert with a flotilla of BYMS and Motor Launches, which were also fitted out with sweeping equipment, were constantly harrassed by enemy shell fire from the shore batteries situated about 35 miles north of Rimini.

Sweepers of the 114th. MSF spent weeks preparing the channel for the naval bombardment of the port of La Spezia. British and American destroyers were engaged in that operation while the sweepers looked on. The big ships got the pat on the back. That was in 1945.

The inshore sweepers during that operation were constantly shelled, narrowly escaping with their lives because they were sitting ducks with no means of returning the enemy fire and indeed with very little speed to get out of the way. Perhaps their good fortune was that they were small and more difficult to hit. The shells were too close for comfort at times and a great deal of patching up had to be done on return to base.

MMS 170 was sunk so they say by a mine while exercising with the Motor Torpedo squadrons in a target towing role off the coast of Genoa. That was on 12th. October 1944.

That may be the official story, but it was suspected in many circles by those who were there, that the 170 was struck, not by a mine, but by a torpedo – that she was mistaken for the target she was towing and ended up at the bottom of the Med.

However, it is doubtful if the truth would be ever be known.

MMS logbooks are almost non-existent and this is probably because the vessels, following hostilities, were disposed of lock stock and barrel.

One skipper commanded one of the 126' MMS's or a 'Big Mickey', out of Lowestoft for some years after the war had ceased. When the task had been successfully completed, he was told to pack his bags and leave the ship. His vessel together with five others of the same class were taken out to sea, just as they were, and sunk, or as some would put it 'services no longer required'. What a pitiful end to a proud career.

It is, one must suppose one way of dealing with surplus requirements, and sentiments should not come into the picture, but such stories make painful reading to those who lived with these ships for so many years. If they had lived out their useful lives, certainly a fitting end, but some had only recently come off the slips.

Among the many tasks allocated to the minesweepers was the one known as 'Limpeteer Watch'.

Limpeteers were those mean frogmen from the other camp, described so adequately in the book 'Cockleshell Heroes',who came stealing down the coast as far as they dare in an 'E' boat or some other craft, to within comfortable swimming distance of the allied ports, passed through the boom which guarded the entrance against submarine infiltration, and planting what were known as 'limpet mines' on the bottom of unsuspecting ships.

The resulting explosion caused havoc in the dockyard, especially if the damaged vessel happened to be loaded with high octane fuel. A spark, a lighted match carelessly thrown over the side would have set the harbour ablaze.

Ships took it in turn to tie up at the boom and keep a sharp look out for these shady characters. It was like looking for a needle in a haystack. All sorts of mysterious objects were spotted giving excuse to let off a few rounds from the .303, plus getting a ticking off from the officer of the watch for firing at odd lumps of wood and being so bloody stupid.

In all fairness it was difficult in the extreme to know the difference between a lump of wood and a Limpeteer's head, basically because there were few of us (if any) who knew what a Limpeteer's head looked like!

In any event no-one was taking any chances, especially when searchlights were not to be used. Better to have a bollocking from the C.O. than a court-martial for letting the enemy as it were, through the nets. Indeed how could anyone be certain of anything in choppy seas in the middle of the night? But the job had to be done.

Added to this it was not unknown, especially on the occasional stand down, to be called out at any odd time of the day or night, to rescue some ship, often from America, which had managed somehow to miss the buoys clearly marking out those channels which were free from mines. They had become 'lost' in a minefield.

To get them out was always a tricky operation, because the 'lost' vessel might in fact be sitting on top of one of these underwater explosive mixtures.

The object of the exercise, if that is the correct expression, was to sweep up to the ship, which was wallowing in the water like a dead duck, steam past her with the sweep switched off, and ask her skipper to proceed slowly in our wake once given the signal to move.

The dangerous bit was that first two or three hundred yards immediately in front of the ship's bow which could not be swept for fear of detonating any mines in that area which would either damage the ship, or blow her and her crew to hell. The skipper had to take a chance. It was a risky business indeed, and the gamble didn't always come off. The captain however was always grateful, as indeed were the sweeper's crew, when the task had been successfully completed.

One particular operation involved MMS 46 having to tow the 125 ton iron steamer *Lerici* from the Port of La Spezia to Leghorn without degaussing equipment.

The passage was a successful but nail-biting one, as there was no swept channel from the harbour and the course was directly across a known minefield. With a tow in progress sweeping was impossible except on the inward journey, and with many of these multi-action delay mines around, there was no telling what might happen. Successful completion brought many sighs of relief. The photograph shows the 125 ton iron steamer *Lerici*, which was launched at Lerici, Spezia, Northern Italy in 1906. This is the vessel referred to in the text.

She has long been scrapped, but following her 'rescue' in 1945, she was owned by the town of La Spezia, and ran on daily tourist service between Lerici and Porto Venere, regarded now as the Italian Riviera.

The older people there who may be still alive might have cause to remember some of the crews of the minesweepers. Their custom was to row alongside in their small boat while we were at anchor in the harbour or bay, seeking to buy our goods. What goods, one might ask? Well anything that was floggable. Tickler (Naval tobacco which one rolled) or cigarettes, or the odd tin of paint or gallon or two of diesel or engine oil, or perhaps a nice new pair of navy boots, if one was lucky enough to get any from the pusser's store in the Naval Barracks ashore.

They were all at it in one way or another, even some of the higher ranking officers.It all helped to augment one's meager income,(as a leading stoker I was earning the princely sum of 3/6 a day plus my hard laying money of 1/−, making a sum total of 22 new pence) and provided the odd pair or two of silk stockings for a loved one at home, which in spite of the war and shortages, were available on the black market.

There were lots of other things available which will not be mentioned here, in exchange for the odd bar of soap (which was in very short supply abroad), a tin of sardines, or even a slice of bread and jam, but this kind of barter was invariably followed by a trip to the M.O.

The Minesweeping Flotillas mentioned in this chapter were not the only craft of this kind to traverse the Eastern waters.

There is the story of those which came from afar to serve in distant places. The Bay of Fundy may not feature much in the activities of World War II, but to Jim Lowndes and others like him, it presented a somewhat strange and frightening experience.

He was shipped overseas to Nova Scotia where some of these short MMS's were being built, and as a telegraphist was drafted aboard MMS 102. This vessel set sail in company with nine others for the longest voyage ever attempted by any inshore boat of this type.

The 120th. and 121st. MSF's consisted of MMS's ;
99..102..103..104..105..106 and 100..101..107..108.
Their destination was the Far East.
MMS 102 managed to get herself lost in the Bay of Fundy.

That is not surprising, as records show a profusion of ships getting lost. It must always be remembered that most of the officers in command were safe as long as they could see the shore or some kind of marker buoy, but all it needed was a storm with visibility down to zero and that was it. Settle down for the night lads till the skies clear.

Ships were known to steam for hours beyond their port of call until something could be seen and recognised. Navigation was not their best subject. No one seems to know why the 102 was lost, but the claim is that they were adrift, meaning that the main engine had failed. That would be unusual, for Fairbanks Morse were considered to be one of the most reliable among all the various types of engines fitted to these craft.

It could have been that the engine room branch were unfamiliar with this particular type, being Canadian. No one seems to know. Perhaps it was just plain foggy, and it is known that sea fog in that area can last for days.

The Bay of Fundy of course is not like Loch Ness, it is vast and it is more than likely that they were going around in circles.

The story goes that the ship was presumed sunk with all hands, and a memorial service arranged ashore in Buzzards Bay. They were finally found by an aircraft and were guided back to base, and the funeral arrangements turned into a celebration.

Until quite recently the author had assumed that a hulked MMS found on the shores of one of the Falkland Islands was MMS 102, basically because the vessel was owned by a Mr. MacCullum who could have been the First Lieutenant of that ship, a New Zealander with the same name. It was assumed that he had bought the vessel after the war, to use with the whaling fleets in those waters. A nice theory but not correct, for the hulk turned out to be ex-MMS 251 also built

MMS 251 Hulked New Island Falklands 1985

Towed to safety by MMS 46 (Lerici)

MMS 312 (Levant) 1946

MMS 13 en route to Malta 1946

in Canada, but which served in the U.K.

Her story is that following her war service, she became a Fisheries Protection Vessel and was named *Protector III*, but was sold to the South Atlantic Sealing Company.

A Mr.A.B.Monk,OBE, from whom the story comes and who held a deep sea certificate, was invited to sail *Protector III* to the Falkland Islands, with another vessel the *Golden Chance* in tow. With the help of 120 fathoms of 9" coir rope, a successful 5,500 miles was completed. Actual steaming time was 42 days, starting at Colchester, Essex and visiting Lisbon, Las Palmas, St. Vincent, Pernabuco, Rio, Montevideo and Stanley. That was in November 1949. Mr. Monk was in Stanley during the Falklands war in 1982, as a sheep farmer, and now lives in Wales.

These two flotillas voyaged some 15-20,000 miles, calling at Cape Cod, New York, Norfolk Virginia, Jacksonville, arriving in Miami on Christmas Day 1942.

Then it was onward to Trinidad and Sierra Leone with a brief stop up the River Amazon for repairs. (See the chart for the route followed). The ships spent a great deal of their time in various parts of the Mediterranean, losing one of their number MMS 101 in the Agean Sea off the coast of Salonika on the 29th. November 1944.

Ernest Rourke, now resident in Tampa, Florida, was another of those who traversed the oceans of the world to serve his country, joining MMS 101 in Boston following his passage to that port on *Queen Mary*. He still cherishes the original White Ensign which had to be changed after crossing the Atlantic, a bit tattered and torn, but a worthy reminder of those eventful days

MMS's 143,144,145,310,311,312 and 313 were in the process of being built for service in the Mediterranean, the first three at Columbo in Ceylon (now Sri Lanka) and the other four in Tel Aviv and Beirut. At this stage in the war they were still on the slips, and records show that it was there they remained until 1945, although MMS 143 managed to get into operation at the latter end of 1943.

One assumes that these sources are accurate, but there are one or two anomalies in the records. For example, MMS 143 commenced building at Colombo, then was moved to Beirut for completion, a distance of approximately 2500 miles. Then she is listed as having joined the 143rd. Minesweeping Flotilla at Normandy following her commissioning in 1945, returning to serve with the 146th. MSF in the Levant in the same year.

MMS's 144 and 155 were also listed as being completed in Beirut and Tel Aviv, but it is difficult to believe that these three ships were moved all that distance, when similar vessels such as MMS's 145,146 and 148 were completed in Bombay, not too many miles up the Indian coast.

However, there may have been very good reasons for such moves, which will remain unknown unless one of the crew of these ships turns up to put us in the picture. On the other hand these anomalies may very well be the result of simple typing errors. The case of MMS 143 is an interesting one however and raises a great deal of questions which to date remain unanswered.

The record would not be complete without reference to MSF 122 whichconsisted of four ships MMS's 198,199,200 and 201. They too were built in Canada, 198 and 199 by Clare Shipbuilding of Metaghan, 200 by Shelbourne and 201 by Wagstaff and completed in February and March of 1943.

These vessels travelled to Northern Ireland following the North Atlantic route,.a distance of 1700 miles. With an endurance of 2000 miles they only just made it, then it was south to Gibraltar, then on to the Mediterranean where they linked up with the 121st. MSF to serve in the East Indies under the wing of the Royal Canadian Navy.

The Reverend I.H.M. Robertson of Cupar in Fife takes up the story of the crossing.

He was Number One on board MMS 199, and only the Commanding Officer, the coxswain, the chief engineman and himself knew anything about operational sweeping procedures. These ships prior to their departure from Nova Scotia had work to do just outside Halifax harbour where the enemy had been active with magnetic mines. It was, as it were, 'on the job' training.

According to a report from Halifax which the signals reproduced here prove, these crews, raw and untrained as they were, did in 1943 an outstanding job in those waters. Rear Admiral Murray records the fact that such good work and results were achieved before the crews had had the opportunity to work up, reflecting a great deal of credit not only on the officers and ratings, but equally on the staff who were involved in fitting out the vessels.

There was no opportunity for trials to enable them to work closely in formation. As soon as the ships were fitted out they were thrown in at the deep end. The crews had been waiting in Canada for a number of months with no training facilities, so it was all credit to them for a task well done, and in unfamiliar waters.

The seven day journey from Halifax, Nova Scotia to Loch Foyle was not without its difficult moments, although the initial stage of the passage from Halifax to St. Johns, Newfoundland, a distance of approximately 500 miles, took three days, at an average speed of just over six knots. This was due to what Lieutenant Robertson described as a typical 'Grand Banks fog', a danger to shipping at any time.

This was followed by an easterly gale, when the ship did everything but capsize. This would not have bothered the crew too much, but there was all sorts of additional equipment and stores were lashed down on the deck which, had they broken loose, could have caused a great deal of damage.

Among those items were 40-gallon drums of fresh water, not for drinking or washing purposes, (there was a ban on the use of fresh water which forbade washing and shaving), but to ensure that there was sufficient supply to keep the Fairbanks Morse diesel engines cool.

For those who know little about cooling systems, these American and

Canadian engines were fresh and salt water cooled. While the writer had no experience with the Fairbanks Morse, the General Motors engines fitted in many of the lease/lend vessels had the same system, which was very effective while operating in good weather conditions with a flat calm, but they were a 'hell's delight' in rough weather.

The fresh water, used as the primary coolant, was in turn cooled by the salt water which was pumped from the sea. If the intakes were uncovered in a heavy sea, airlocks and overheating became a problem difficult to correct while under way.

The first indication one had of anything untoward occurring, was that the temperature guages started to go haywire; then there were frantic efforts to bleed the system, sometimes without much success. In Fleet Tenders, also American designed, an airlock meant a trip into the bilges.

To ensure that the passage would be free from too many such incidents and that sufficient fresh water would be available for drinking purposes, all the cooking was done in sea water. Apparently the reserves in the drums were not needed, but they had to there 'just in case.'

In spite of the lack of engineering experience, a 'duff' diesel injector was successfully changed in less time than it took to stop the ship.

MSF 122 was the only flotilla to be fitted out with copper bottoms, providing protection from the dreaded Toredo wood borer, which could play havoc with the ship's woodwork. Many of the ships which spent most of their days in the Mediterranean were subject to this kind of 'attack', the worm being an inhabitant of warmer waters, and necessitated the renewal of a great deal of the hull underwater woodwork which was two and a half inches thick throughout. It may have been that the other vessels were not coppered because of the acute shortage of raw materials.

In 1942, a document headed 'Shipbuilding Policy for War', had this to say in paragraph 3:

> It was unwise to forecast that the war would be short. There is evidence to suggest that the war will be long, and this makes it necessary to have overwhelming forces available. There is a need to take the long view, and build a Navy which will be able to meet this responsibility in the most efficient and economical manner, working on the basis of a LONG WAR. There would always be a requirement for minesweeping craft.

It was envisaged however, that by the end of 1946, the major part of the mine clearance operations would be completed. Any reduction of minesweeping forces would naturally prolong the final result of the total mine clearance of the Mediterranean.

It was considered therefore that at least two minesweeping flotillas consisting of three BYMS's and four Motor Launches should be retained, together with all the trawlers and MMS's, until the end was definitely in sight, and that the existing M/S forces be retained until the end of October 1945. If reductions were necessary the MMS's could be withdrawn.

As many 'old hands' will reveal, many of these craft were sweeping long after hostilities had ceased, after they were in 1946 paid off in Malta, and then handed over to the Italian and Greek Navies who were left to finish the task.

The vessels were returned to the UK in 1950 and 51 after taking nearly five years to make the Mediterranean reasonably safe, and after giving ten years admirable service to King and country. Like all the rest in their class however, they were quickly forgotten.

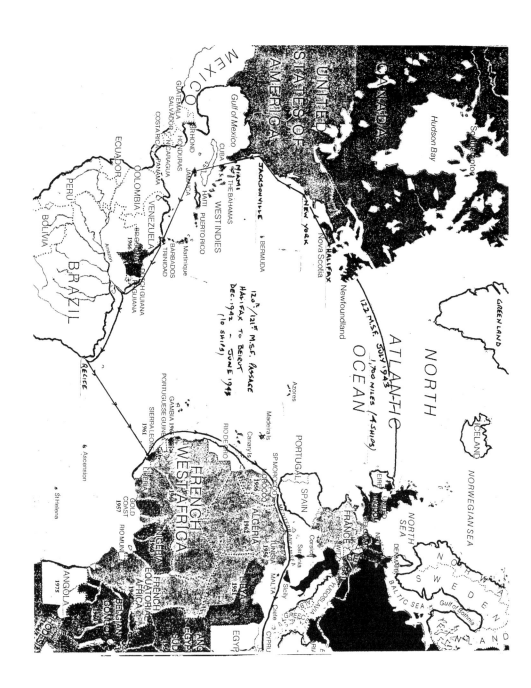

S. 1320H
15,000M-5-42 (4534)
N.S. 815-9-1320H

NAVAL MESSAGE

To: 122 MMS FLOTILLA (R) C IN C CNA   From: C HALIFAX

C IN C CNA
C OF S
SOD
SOJ
C HFX
MMS 196
MMS 197
MMS 198
MMS 199
MMS 200
MMS 201

THE TIMELY ASSISTANCE AND VALUABLE WORK OF THE
WOODEN SHIPS AND IRON MEN OF THE 122 MMS FLOTILLA AT
HALIFAX IS DEEPLY APPRECIATED I WISH YOU A SAFE
RETURN TO ENGLAND HOME AND BEAUTY AND GOOD HUNTING IN
YOUR FUTURE FIELDS OF OPERATIONS GOOD LUCK AND
GODSPEED.

ISD COMMODORE TAYLOR.

031615Z

031616Z   E IM/MS   03/7/43

S. 1320H
15,000M-5-42 (4534)
N.S. 815-9-1320H

NAVAL MESSAGE

To: 122nd MMS FLOTILLA (R) ADMIRALTY, NSHQ,   From: C IN C CNA
C HFX.

ON LEAVING MY COMMAND I WISH TO EXPRESS MY THANKS
TO THE FLOTILLA FOR THE VALUABLE ASSISTANCE RENDERED
IN CLEARING THE HALIFAX APPROACHES.
YOU HAVE ACCOUNTED FOR MORE THAN 1/3 OF THE MINES
DESTROYED . GOOD HUNTING IN THE FUTURE.

MMS 196
MMS 197
MMS 198
MMS 199
MMS 200
MMS 201

031352z

CODE "X" S.H.M.   031405z   NS/MS   3-7-43

SUPREME HEADQUARTERS
ALLIED EXPEDITIONARY FORCE

Soldiers, Sailors and Airmen of the Allied Expeditionary Force!

You are about to embark upon the Great Crusade, toward which we have striven these many months. The eyes of the world are upon you. The hopes and prayers of liberty-loving people everywhere march with you. In company with our brave Allies and brothers-in-arms on other Fronts, you will bring about the destruction of the German war machine, the elimination of Nazi tyranny over the oppressed peoples of Europe, and security for ourselves in a free world.

Your task will not be an easy one. Your enemy is well trained, well equipped and battle-hardened. He will fight savagely.

But this is the year 1944 ! Much has happened since the Nazi triumphs of 1940-41. The United Nations have inflicted upon the Germans great defeats, in open battle, man-to-man. Our air offensive has seriously reduced their strength in the air and their capacity to wage war on the ground. Our Home Fronts have given us an overwhelming superiority in weapons and munitions of war, and placed at our disposal great reserves of trained fighting men. The tide has turned ! The free men of the world are marching together to Victory !

I have full confidence in your courage, devotion to duty and skill in battle. We will accept nothing less than full Victory !

Good Luck ! And let us all beseech the blessing of Almighty God upon this great and noble undertaking.

Dwight D Eisenhower

1944. Letter from General Eisenhower.

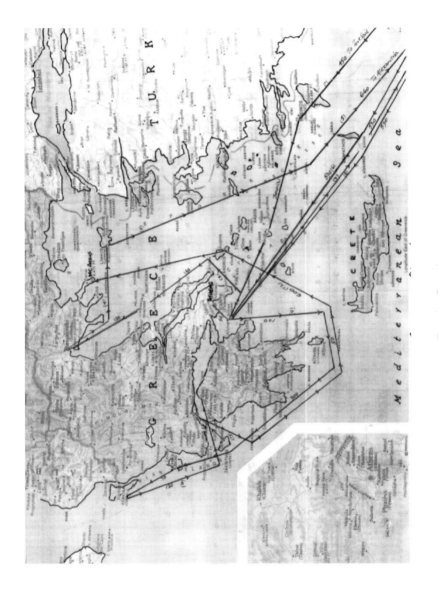

Sweeping Operations
MMS 106 (120th MSF) Oct 7th 1944 – Aug 20th 1945 from Port Said

Chapter Six

Operation Overlord

Operation 'Overlord' was the name given to the whole task covering the invasion of Europe in June of 1944. This brought together 1,213 ships of varying types, from warships to midget submarines, plus hundreds of merchant vessels. Operation 'Neptune' was the code name for the outline order to the Western Task Force's role, i.e. the Navy's role.

Added to that were 4000 vessels of Combined Operations, all of which assembled in the main, in the Solent and Portland Bill on the south coast of England, the waters around the Isle of Wight acquiring the nickname 'Piccadilly Circus'. Those familiar with London will know what is meant. For those uninitiated it means that there was little room for movement amid the large conglomeration of 'traffic' waiting as it were, for the starting gun.

It would be difficult in the extreme to outline all the activities of the the 42 Motor Minesweepers which initially took part in the assault, but without their active participation Operation 'Overlord' could not have taken place. The initial plans for this massive coastal assault were laid as early as 1943, and the minesweeper was destined to play one of the most important roles of the invasion fleet.

The sweeping requirements were listed as follows:

A large concentration of ships will pass through a central corridor to the French beaches. While the passage is in progress, other ships will be passing along the normal channels of our coastal convoy routes and will feed into the convoy. Preliminary examination suggests that it will be necessary to sweep lanes by Oropesa through the central corridor to about latitude 50 degrees North approximately.

There are to be three assault forces and each will require a slow and fast lane, so that the faster craft can overtake the slower vessels ahead, and all reach their destinations at the same time. There are suggestions that the fast lanes be reduced to two, but this is not acceptable due to the fact that ships are also needed for the bombardment of the invasion coast-line.

Six lanes of approximately five to seven cables wide and 50 miles long will be neccessary, and the duration of the sweeping demands that extensive operations should begin before the night of 'D' Day in order to avoid losing all tactical surprise. The requirement is for a large force of fleet sweepers (Fleet sweepers were those larger craft of the Hunt and Algerine variety and regarded as belonging to the pukka Royal Navy where the Mickey Mice were strictly Patrol Service vessels, which classified them in some eyes as quite different from all the rest, [even though the term Patrol Service was prefixed by Royal Naval.]

Landing craft are to proceed by the slow lane and the need will be for these craft to be swept into their destination, then the lanes cleared continually thereafter by use of the Double 'L' sweeping equipment. There will also be a requirement for Motor Launches for operations close inshore(there were about 1400 Motor Launches of various types utilised in many roles during hostilities including inshore minesweeping.) The convoy routes will be in continuous use requiring a commitment to sweep long after the invading forces have passed.

The total number of minesweeping craft required will be 135, comprising of 48 Fleet Sweepers..42 Motor Minesweepers..45 Trawlers..plus an unspecified number of Motor Launches (ML's) with berthing facilities for the MMS's at Newhaven, Portsmouth, Poole, and Dartmouth.

These were the plans but things did not materialise as was envisaged, indeed, nowhere did allied operations proceeded as planned, and the need is to spell out as well as one is able with the information gathered over the years and in the light of the prevailing circumstances of the time, the task which the Motor Mine-sweepers were called upon to do. The object of this book is to look at Overlord as it affected these particular craft.

First it is necessary to say that when the convoys arrived on the appointed hour, there were already lanes of dan buoys marking the way through the German minefields, and covering the 60 miles of assault area. Indeed the Germans had failed to see, never mind to report, that allied minesweepers were already at work long before 'D' Day cutting a passage through the minefields which lay across the path of the Utah/Omaha convoys and within sight of the shore of the Cherbourg Peninsula.

One of the tasks, indeed one of the major roles for the MMS's was to screen the battleships on route to the bombardment area, meaning that the lanes had to be cleared of mines before the ships ventured forth into the English Channel.

The 115th. Minesweeping Flotilla was involved in this kind of work. Officer Commanding MMS 6, Lieutenant T.C. Muir D.S.O.(deceased) was there and tells the story of arriving in Dover from his operating base at Lymington in the Solent, ten days prior to 'D' Day, being Saturday the 27th. May.

There, he recalls, he was supplied with his operating instructions for the landings plus three Naval barrage balloons, setting out from Dover on Sunday the 28th. to Selsey Bill, and finally heading for the beach head early on Tuesday the 6th. June, steaming a mile ahead of HMS *Warspite*.

It would appear that the flotilla was acting as decoy, the balloons being manu-factured with a material which would show up on the enemy radar screens as battleships.

In effect the sweepers were sitting ducks. Lt. Muir states that the enemy shore batteries were firing short of their target, meaning that the shells were coming uncomfortably close to the sweepers. All ended on a distinctly happy note as the *Warspite* effectively eliminated the opposition ashore. Then it was sweeping, sweeping, and still more sweeping, clearing Le Havre and Dieppe, and returning to Portsmouth in August 1945.

MMS 260 of the 104th. MSF left UK, according to her log book, on Monday

5th. June at 0900 hours and arrived on the French coast off Port En Bessin at 1930 hours and commenced sweeping in company with the rest of her flotilla at 0230 hours on the morning of the 6th. Far from there being only 42 motor minesweepers involved, few weeks had passed before there were 22 flotillas carrying out extensive sweeps in all areas of the invasion coast, a total of some 156 vessels.

The Eastern Task Force 'U' and 'O' had six flotillas at the outset , sweeping the Gold, Juno, and Sword areas, under the command of Admiral Kirk, Rear Admiral Moon, and Rear Admiral Hall namely the 132nd. 133rd. 138th. 141st. 147th. and 104th., but they were very soon to be augmented by others as time progressed.

Ships particularly those of the 118th. MSF were charged with the task of escorting the Mulberry Harbours towed from Sheerness for use as wind and sea breakers. The crew of MMS 189 is recorded as having rescued the survivors of a tug which had been sunk as the result of a direct hit from an 'E' Boat torpedo.

Letters from the skipper of MMS 181 of the 132nd. MSF, John Grieve, who is still alive, tells the story of his ship being badly damaged, and having to be beached on 'D' Day. She was subsequently floated and towed back to Rochester in Kent, where he assumed that she had been scrapped.

But Rochester shipyard had done a first class job and sent her back into the fray, serving with the 104th. MSF until the end of hostilities, a fact about which John until recently was unaware, and which came as a total surprise.

While much of the story of these little ships is concerned with the routine task of sweeping the channels day and night, meaning the constant traversing of the same waters because of enemy action, there was a great deal of activity in other areas. The arrangements for the special sweep which have already been mentioned regarding the four approach channels, necessitated what many people seem to forget...the preparatory work which had already taken place in the English Channel long before the actual operation commenced.

MMS's were constantly on the move along the English and French coastlines . . . forever on the search for the 'devils of the deep'.

The 'D' Day operation was to be executed in two phases, the first to be performed in complete darkness with the swept waters being clearly indicated by lighted dan Buoys. Owing to the large number of vessels involved in the clearance, and with sweeping being carried out simultaneously and in a confined area, accuracy was absolutely paramount, and timing essential. Terminating the boat channels at the exact spot on the assault beaches called for expert navigation, and this had to be completed before 'H' hour, that is the time of the assault, which varied between one beach-head and another.

Following the landings, phase two would consist of the sweeping of the inner anchorages, thereby linking up the channels between the assault forces and widening the approach channels. This was to be a daylight activity.

On completion of both phases, 'U' and 'O' forces would combine and operate under Commander Minesweeping West, who had led the assault with American forces on the Utah and Omaha beach heads. All the ships which Commander Minesweeping had worked up and administered in the three months prior to 'D' Day, that is March to May 1944, had been allocated to the Western Task Force, but 48 ships out of the ten flotillas (normally a flotilla had eight ships) involved in the task had no previous practical experience in sweeping, they had yet to sweep their first mine.

This would seem to have been shortsighted in many respects, but many of the ships had only recently been commissioned, some BYMS's in late 1943, so there was little time to get the crews involved in a practical way.

The cross channel route, being a special task, was carried out very much in line with the initial plans for Overlord, which as already mentioned, had been devised in 1943, using initially a total of 42 Motor Minesweepers.

Sweeping commenced on the night of 4th. June, but was abandoned due to adverse weather conditions. As General Eisenhower put it in his initial report of the whole operation, and in his capacity of Supreme Commander:

"June 1944 saw the highest winds and roughest seas experienced in the English Channel in June for 20 years....so heavy were the seas that the craft were compelled to turn about and seek shelter."

Most of the sweepers out of Portland were too far away from base to return when the order came to abort, so they had to weather the stormy seas until sweeping recommenced on the 5th.

The postponement was in a way fortunate, for it would appear that, according to the records and for reasons which have not yet been revealed there was a mix up in the orders for the Western Task Force, and had the assault taken place, there would have been a major catastrophe. As a result of the 'to-ing' and 'fro-ing' of signals, the matter was sorted out in time.

Added to this was the story about a large consignment of minesweeping equipment consisting of mooring sinkers and wire cable required for Operation Neptune, being lost en route to the assembly points. It was finally located after the Training Officer had scoured the countryside for two days. Most of the equipment was found in a United States dump at Falmouth, which had been closed owing to the presence of butterfly bombs dropped in an air raid a few nights previously.

Various other pieces of essential gear were adrift and it was some days before Operation Neptune actually got underway. But it did commence and Force 'U' suffered the first casualties. While steaming in line astern USS *Osprey* hit a mine, was taken in tow, but capsized with a loss of five personnel. Five mines had been detonated in the same channel on the previous day just prior to the postponement.

The 104th. MSF was active in all of this, sweeping within one mile of the Utah and Omaha beaches. The skipper of MMS 74, Lt.Cdr Drake, sighted distress signals from a Walrus aircraft down in the sea. The crew of three plus a pilot from a crashed Typhoon aircraft, was rescued, and the plane on instructions from the pilot was destroyed.

Sweeping up to the first fathom line was a tricky number in which many of the inshore craft were involved from day one, and this meant a 'fluffing' exercise, already described in another chapter.

The MMS's were detailed to carry out this static sweep when weather permitted, but there is no mention in the scheme for obtaining enemy permission. It must have been considered however that such an operation would be extremely hazardous, with the possibility of harrassment not only from enemy aircraft and 'E' boats, and also from the gun batteries ashore, especially in the early days of the assault. To carry out this kind of manoeuvre in the dark was almost suicidal.

The life of MMS 219 of the 101st. MSF was short lived.

Following day and night sweeps in the English Channel prior to the 'D' Day onslaught, she struck an underwater object during the initial stages of the attack, just off the Omaha beach. The ship was beached on a sand bar, and with the assistance of an American LCM (Landing Craft Mechanical for transporting tanks), plus the expertise of a Harry Tate shipwright, and of course 'our friend above' as Guns Logan from Stevenage puts it, the ship was refloated and limped her way back to the U.K.,and her home base at Queenborough.

As she proudly passed the base ship HMS *St. Tudno* a signal read, 'Welcome home 219', a message which, says Mr. Logan, brought a lump to his throat.

This was not however the first MMS casualty of the war, for in August 1941 MMS 39, four months following her commissioning, struck a mine and was sunk.

When Seaman Haddock joined the ship in Lowestoft, he describes her as 'being like a motor yacht'. Others have been known to use more derogatory descriptive language, especially in a heavy sea when the steering has jammed.

MMS 39 operated out of Sheerness before she had actually joined any known flotilla, and Mr. Harrison Haddock relates some of the other difficulties he experienced during hostilities. The war would not have been quite so bad if only he could have understood the coxswain who, being a Hebridean fisherman created something of a language barrier. Haddock could not understand him half of the time. It made life just that bit more difficult. But he had a lucky escape, not from the coxswain, but from death itself.

Seamen normally bunked in the after messdeck, but Haddock had his accommodation forward with the so called intelligencia . . . the engineroom branch, the Sparks, the Buntingtosser and the like. He was on leave when the ship 'caught her packet' as the saying goes, and all in the forward mess died. He was lucky indeed.

Chief Engineman Davidson served on board MMS 31. Her task in the early days with the 104th. MSF constituted a regular upstream/downstream activity in the Firth of Forth, from Granton to the Forth Railway Bridge, and sometimes he claims, with a bit of luck, as far out as the Isle of May.

Big deal, he writes, and he a real sailor, having been at sea a long time. So he asks for a draft to something 'which goes to sea now and again'.

He was another RNPS man who was mildly surprised when he was informed 40 years after the event that his old ship MMS 31 set sail with her sister ships to participate in Operation Overlord. If he had decided to hang on a little longer, he might have had his bellyfull of sea! He left the ship in the March of 1944.

With regard to the actual assault sweep a report issued soon afterwards, had this to say:

" All minesweeping reports negative".

The success of the assault sweep came as a surprise factor, as the waters south of latitude 50 degrees were thought to be heavily mined. Early that afternoon flotillas of sweepers had begun sweeping ten channels from 'Piccadilly Circus' south to the Bay of the Seine. They encountered fewer mines than they expected, though at that time they did not know the reason. The coastal waters from Le Havre to Dunkirk had been heavily mined in the Spring, but the German Navy's plan to lay a special barrage of mines between Cherbourg and Le Havre had been foiled by Allied Naval and air power. The bombing of the French railways had delayed the arrival of the mines, and when at last in the May of 1944 when there were sufficient stocks at Le Havre, and a minelaying flotilla was despatched from Brest to carry out the plan, Coastal Command and the Royal Navy intercepted the ships and only one got through. The barrage was never laid, which was a bit of luck for the Allies.

The timing and location was on schedule, the sweepers being clear of all swept channels and transport areas and carrying out the second phase of the programme, after leaving the swept waters well defined by dan buoys in spite of a strong cross tide and far from smooth sea, which made sweeping difficult especially for the smaller craft. Considering that half the ships' companies had little or no sweeping experience, the result was to say the least, quite remarkable as shown from the following extract from Admiral Moon's observation report:

> The approach channels 1 and 2 were swept and marked all to schedule without losses. Both channels were reported to be as much as one mile wide at the North ends and this contrary to all expectations. The laying of lighted dan buoys was expertly carried out. An excellent performance of the 14/16 MSF (RN) is commendable. The 132nd. MSF consisting of MMS's 84..181..209..211..236..283..301..and 302 performed the difficult task of sweeping and marking the boat lanes from within a mile of the beach.
>
> In view of the fact that this particular flotilla was fitted out for 'LL' sweeping and had trained only for one week with Oropesa gear prior to the assault, it is remarkable that they were able to accomplish such excellent results.

This would seem to suggest that the whole complicated operation was carried out without loss (one presumes to the minesweepers only) and exactly according to plan, but the opposite proved to be the case.

During this particular period many enemy aircraft were active in the dark hours of the early morning, with all ships at action stations for several hours. This put extra strain on the minesweeping craft for it was out-sweeps at break of day.

When the personnel were off duty, and the shifts were generally five hours on and five off, the five off meant manning the action stations, which could be in the ammunition locker up in the bows, or hauling boxes of ammunition on to the top deck for the oerlikon fitted aft, or indeed loading ammunition into the magazines.

Marker flares dropped during the hours of darkness, together with many detonations and huge splashes in the sea meant that intensive minelaying had taken place. Orders passed in the night from the Commander in Chief Minesweeping were to the effect that sweeping would commence by all available vessels so fitted out.

There was very little time to sleep, and the crews in time became exhausted. Everybody on the MMS's had a job to do and sometimes someone else's job as well. Prior to the commencement of the whole operation, stokers were trained to double up for electricians as well as to load and fire a gun.

Seamen had to have some idea what happened in the engine room. There being only one signalman and one wireless operator, they got no respite at all, nor did the cook or steward.

The Commanding Officer and the First Lieutenant were constantly on call. Ships were shelled from the shore as they approached the British/German lines, and many returned to their anchorage full of shrapnel holes.

A signal dated 'D' plus 2 highlights the situation as it was in those early days:

> Enemy creating mine barrier to prevent Northerly deployment of our bombarding ships. If he succeeds, the 7th. Corps will lose the support of Naval gunfire.
>
> 'E' boats have been active and especially around St. Marcouf Island. More magnetic sweepers are required. Commander Minesweeping now in operational control of all minesweepers. Reports to be passed to Commander M/S West and mine drops searched according to their priorities but only after the daily coverage of prepared channels and anchorages.
>
> Keep shipping in swept waters, and treat all suspect areas as dry land until sweepers have covered it.

116 mines were swept in the West assault area during the first three days of Operation Neptune. A quote from "A Bodyguard of Lies" by Anthony Cave Brown would suggest that the whole operation was something of a walkover:

> Because of Operation Fortitude (which was set up to hoodwink the Germans into believing that the assault would come further along the coast) all the new mines available to Admiral Theodore Krancke, the German Naval Commander, had been laid off the coast between Le Havre and Dunkirk.
>
> The Normandy minefields were laid with old-type mines, most of which had been there for years, and were so crusted with barnacles that nothing short of a direct hit with a ship's bow at high speed, would make them explode.

Try telling that to some of the lads who had to do the job!

The St. Marcouf Islands proved to be of special interest to Leading Seaman

John Phillips who relates his experiences on board MMS 288 (132 MSF) and attached to the American fleet.

When the landings were postponed for 24 hours on the night of June 5th., they were stuck out in the channel, and went to shelter among the islands where they could actually hear the Germans talking ashore.

It is somewhat surprising that they were not challenged, with the possibility of giving the game away, but it appears that no-one was expecting anything untoward happening on that particular night, at least they did not show any signs of it.

'D' plus 8 was to all intents and purposes a relatively quiet day with no enemy action, no mines detonated and no casualties, but it was a very special day for Commander M/S.

It was his birthday, and a cake suitably inscribed was presented to him on his return to USS *Chemo*, his H.Q., after a visit ashore.

Chemo of course being a United States naval craft, was unfortunately, as all USS ships were, 'dry'. There is little doubt that a 'tot' of the usual would have been found to enhance the celebrations, otherwise the Royal Navy would have been seen to fail in its duty. Only those who attended the party would know that however, and to date no one has owned up.

In spite of all the effort put into the clearing of these war zones, it did not make a great deal of difference to the task, for the sweepers had then to deal with the dreaded delayed action mine described in an earlier chapter.

These had a nasty habit of detonating under ships when nobody was moving. What in fact happened and was soon discovered, was that the magnetic sweepers were activating what was already a dormant explosive charge. The clocks were set in motion and programmed to go off at any given time. There were many casualties, and the sweepers had no response to this new-fangled device.

Divers were used as an alternative, but that was not a great deal of help. What the enemy desired had been accomplished, meaning everything had to stop, and stop it did. Added to that was the threat not yet encountered, of the pressure or 'oyster' mine.

A signal to M/S staff from the C in C posed the following question:

"Have you experienced spontaneous detonation of mines in your area?"

This was answered in the negative, which was in a sense rather premature for no sooner had the reply been sent, than it was followed by an almighty crash, and *Chemo* shook from stem to stern, reverberating from an explosion 100 yards off her bow, cascading salt water over the forepeak.

Some form of delayed action acoustic mine was suspected, as there were no sweeping activities at the time.

An hour later the 205th. MSF consisting of seven of the 126 foot MMS's observed two other explosions a mile and a half astern of the ships.

Reports had been received from MMS's detailed to carry out minespotting duties when not sweeping, that aircraft had been seen laying mines, but in many cases mines were exploding on unusual bearings quite different from the places where they had been seen to land.

Too frequently these were close enough to ships lying at anchor to cause serious damage to superstructure and machinery, an indication that the mines had been in place for a considerable length of time, but dormant until the appointed moment.

Bad as the weather was on 5th. and 6th. June, there were other days during the early stages of the invasion when heavy seas brought everything to a grinding halt. Lieutenant Muir of MMS 6 writes about surviving the 'great storm'.

He was referring to 'D' plus 13,14, and 15, June 19th.–21st. when heavy north-eastern gales swept the channel. All landings were suspended, beaches were strewn with wreckage, and a geat deal of serious damage was caused to the Mulberry Harbours. Ships were dragging and losing their anchors, and cables were parting due to the ferocity of the winds and waves.

Minesweeping became an impossibility and the beaches were a shambles. It took a month according to official sources, to make up the deficiencies, proving a major set back in the engagement. During the first few weeks of Overlord, it was not unknown for the MMS's to be deployed on strange jobs. Numerous requests were received to despatch a ship to investigate floating objects which were thought to be mines.

When such objects were suspected, everything in the vicinity stopped. It has been said since that all one has to do is to set a 40-gallon drum afloat in the middle of an estuary and ships will neither leave nor enter the river until it has been proved that it unlikely to explode.

Many such objects turned out to be flotsam or jetsam, sometimes discarded aircraft wing fuel tanks, aircraft wreckage or on occasion some poor soul who had not made it. On one occasion three separate reports were received of a torpedo shaped object adrift in the convoy anchorage. MMS 252 of the 143rd. MSF was duly sent to investigate, and after two hours search, took the culprit in tow to Utah beach where it was identified as a glider bomb, complete except for its warhead which accounted for its being afloat.

John McKay, now living in Maidstone Kent, was a midshipman serving as an Electrical Officer at Newhaven in June 1944. He describes the ludicrous use of two MMS's in an experiment to assist Royal Air Force pilots in their battle against the dreaded V-1's or 'doodle bugs' as they became known.

These unsightly and devastating monsters of the sky were introduced in large quantities into the war game after the 'D' Day landings. They were literally unmanned flying bombs which landed all over England in their hundreds, with tragic results. With a ton of explosives in each they were a fiendish weapon, but fiendish or not 'all is fair in love and war' so the saying goes and the Germans used these to great effect, bringing a reign of terror over the countryside for no-one knew exactly where they were likely to land.

They were supposed to have sufficient fuel to take them to a specific target, but very often they were innacurate and caused a great deal of havoc among the civilian population. Of the 10,000 launched, 2,500 hit their target, 71 on London alone.

In order to counteract this menace, aircraft were stacked around a central searchlight beam, set in the English Channel, awaiting the arrival of the 'bugs'. The MMS's were the ships who were privileged to provide this guiding light, and for this purpose were fitted out with searchlights which were made up from dozens of 100 and 150 watt lamps packed tightly together in tiers.

Unfortunately they could never carry enough spare lamps to replace those which were constantly blowing due to being sprayed with sea water coming over the side of the ship.

The experiment did not last very long, because the enemy, having infiltrated the stacking pattern, opted to distinguish the beam with the help of a few rounds of armour piercing shells. The MMS's proceeded to hightail it for home, recognising that they were nothing but sitting ducks.

It would appear however that the powers-that-be would try any Heath Robinson arrangement to help advance the final victory, but it must have been obvious to those who planned such an operation, that there was a strong likelihood of these ships being blown out of the water, giving their position away as soon as the lights were switched on.

If this was not the case in the control centre, it was quite clear to John McKay, and no doubt to the skippers of the two ships involved, who no doubt were relieved when the experiment came to its close, so that they might return to the more peaceful exercise of sweeping mines, and glad because it was an experiment which might have cost them and others their lives.

Mines were still taking their toll of ships as the days rolled on. BYMS 2069 and YMS 167 were severely damaged by acoustic mines.

On 'D' Day plus 13 the first MMS of Overlord was sunk. At the Eastern end of the assault area MMS 229 of the 138th. MSF was the centre ship of three. She sunk in seven minutes, and credit must go to the quick action of her sister ships, whose numbers are not known, but could have been either MMS's 224,225,228,281 or 307, all of whom belonged to the 138th. in 1944, who saved all of the crew except two.

Blockship *Norfolk* was mined and sunk.

Four mines were detonated at the same time in a radius of 300 yards, one directly beneath YMS 304, which sank in two minutes with fatal casualties. YMS 378 had a near miss off the port bow while involved in sweeping operations. MMS 297 was badly damaged on the 17th. June by a near miss detonation.

Cyril Edwards of Morecambe relates some of the history of this particular vessel. He joined her in Fowey in the August of 1943 following her commissioning. She spent her early days operating with the 106th. MSF out of Newhaven (HMS *Aggressive*) where incidentally Sir Peter Scott, then a Naval Officer commanded a Motor Torpedo Boat.

Their main trouble at that time was in the galley, not with the war. The stove, claims Cyril, would not draw. (Stoves were of the cast iron cylindrical coal burning type). Meals were always late and the galley always full of smoke.

It took weeks to get the thing in working order, rectified by simply fitting a longer flue pipe with an 'H' piece on top. (We had excellent ship builders who could not fix a galley stove. They had to get a chimney sweep to do that no doubt.)

The first C.O. and the First Lieutenant left the ship at Newhaven, only to be replaced, according to Cyril Edwards, with a pig's orphan of a skipper, who only spoke to the crew in the course of duty. There was something of a mutiny, and Edwards spent five uncomfortable days in a cell, which was not the best place to be.

If he did his time in Chatham where half of a boys' Borstal had been taken over for likely mutineers, then he had one helluva time, especially if he had the first three days on 'hard tack' (a solid square devilishly difficult to chew kind of ship's cracker) and equally if he had the task of picking 'oakum' used for caulking ships wooden decks.

It usually took from 0600 after scrubbing the cell out, till midnight to unravel two pounds of the stuff (it was tarry rope). Some of the prisoners thought that by disposing of part of their allocation down the toilet, they would have a comparatively 'cushy' number, but they soon discovered that the prison staff were smarter than they.

Each individual's effort was weighed on completion, and any shortfall would be replaced by another pound or two to be completed before morning. After the 'light diet', he would then be upgraded to 'full diet', a jacket spud and a cup of watery cocoa. Such would be his punishment.

Perhaps Edwards was lucky and did his time locally, where he would be treated in a much 'kinder' fashion, such as peeling half a ton of potatoes, not forgetting to take all the eyes out. They were hard times.

Apparently the C.O. of 297 was a cattle auctioneer in civilian life, and the complaint was that he treated his crew very much the same as his poor old cows. He was nicknamed Captain Bligh. Edwards was drafted to BYMS 2080 where he reports that he sighted his old ship operating off shore at Arromanches. It is not known whether 'Captain Bligh' was still in command. MMS 8 of the 102nd. MSF was sunk on the 26th. June while acting as 'coffin ship' during sweeping operations in the Eastern sector, the term given to those ships detailed to follow up the sweeping trio in case of breakdown.

What happened in this particular situation was that MMS 8 had been part of the trio, and had developed engine trouble. She dropped astern with the original 'coffin ship' taking up her station in the sweeping line.

It transpired that the sweepers set off a delayed action mine, which unfortunately went off directly beneath MMS 8. All but two of the crew were lost. The skipper, knocked unconscious by the explosion was drowned by the weight of his duffel coat keeping his head in the water. The wireless operator spoke of a 'rising feeling, then the whole bloody lot fell asunder.' He escaped with a few bumps and bruises, and was picked up as he hung desperately to the upturned lifeboat.

It was immediate 'off sweeps',and rescue attempts made to recover the bodies from the sea. It was seldom that many survived. The Double 'L' sweep, being as it was then, something of a secret weapon, plus of course a hazard to other shipping, had to be cut away and hauled aboard the rescue vessel, and this to be done within enemy shelling distance from the shore.

Mr. Jim Jones of Grays in Essex left MMS 8 on the 16th. June to join BYMS 2284. He still has in his possession a letter received from another member of the crew, a Mr. John Butler who went down with the ship – a letter talking about a get together which never transpired.

On the 5th. July 1944, a conference took place concerning the problem of the constant minelaying activities of the enemy. It was stated with a great deal of emphasis that the build up of Overlord was being seriously hampered by the extensive laying of mines. It was subsequently suggested by a Captain Jennings that the following procedures should be adopted immediately to try and transform the situation:

> As the mines were at present being laid by aircraft, 40 minesweepers should be fitted out with balloons flying at 1000 to 2000 feet at night, and to be close-hauled during the day to 100 feet when aircraft approached to prevent any mines being laid.

It was considered that the number of sweepers available was adequate for this particular exercise, but it was a stop–gap affair and efforts were still required to investigate the best methods to deal with this ever increasing problem.

The truth is that the mines were proving to be unmanageable, and were likely to be so until the end and beyond the close of hostilities as time was to prove, and as the following comment by Admiral Ramsay, who commanded the whole of the Naval operation, made quite clear:

> "The enemy," wrote Ramsay, " introduced two new types of mine, both of which were activated by the reduction of pressure caused by a ship passing over them. One of these could not be swept under any conditions, and the other only in certain weather."

This, he states, was the only German countermeasure during Overlord which caused him any anxiety – the laying of pressure mines in the anchorages. He was surprised that these mines had not been dropped before 'D' Day in the harbours of Southern England, for there they could have and would have wrecked havoc among the closely packed ships waiting as it were at the starting line.

German Commanders had asked that this should be done, but because the new device was to be kept secret, this request had been refused. After all had not the British laid bare the secret of the magnetic mine after one of the German pilots had stupidly dropped the thing in the mud flats of Shoeburyness?

That must not be allowed to happen again, in case the device was discovered and used in a retaliory fashion in the Baltic Sea, which was the only safe training and testing grounds remaining for the new 'U' boats coming off the slips. Pressure mines were not even laid in advance on the German side of the Channel, because they had not been introduced in sufficient numbers to cover all the threatened areas.

When at last a decision was made to rectify the situation, they were dropped in the Bay of the Seine on the third night of the invasion, instead of in the congested waters between the Rivers Orne and Contentin where they would have caused most damage.

The enemy also chose to deposit them between Le Havre and Ostend, an area where because of several decoy arrangements made by the Allies, they thought the invasion was likely to take place. This caused less trouble than was expected, but had the German commanders achieved their own way with their suggestions about the use of this new weaponry, it may very well have won them the war. Those mines which the sweepers had to contend with and against which they had no known countermeasures, in spite of the fact that two of the new pressure mines were found intact on the French shores on June 10th., were enough to keep them busy.

Many acoustic and magnetic mines of devilish ingenuity were sown along the invasion coast and beyond, and the success of Operation Overlord was established and maintained only because, in Admiral Ramsay's own words, "minesweepers and supply craft took risks which were generally unacceptable."

It was envisaged that some effort should be made to liberate the Channel Islands, and in September of 1944 Operation 'Nest Egg' came off the drawing board. The plan however was postponed primarily for two reasons.

First there was a great demand on the minesweeping flotillas and none could be spared for the task. Secondly it seemed a total waste of manpower and time to embark on such a venture, when if the Germans were defeated in Europe, it would only be a matter of weeks before surrender became the order of the day on the islands.

Added to that they were the most heavily defended areas of occupied territory for their size. Any conflict would cause unnecessary loss of life, especially among the civilian population for whom no protection had been provided.

Ultimate victory in Europe effectively blockaded any reinforcements and supplies getting through and capitulation came without a shot being fired.

Two ships of the 142nd. MSF arrived in Guernsey in May 1945, eight months after the production of the plan and following congratulatory messages from Commander M/S in Le Havre for work done in the area of the River Seine.

MMS 244 (Lt.C.H.Greenwood) in company with MMS 245 (Lt/Cdr. Baxter), as part of the Liberation Fleet made exploratory sweeps and cleared the area inside one month, but that was long after the next stage of the minesweeping drama, Operation Kalendar, had commenced.

Time	Log (stating type)	Distance Run		Mean Revns. per Minute	True Course	Gyro Compass Course	Standard Compass Course	Deviation	Variation	Wind		Weather and Visibility	Sea and Swell	Corrected Barometric Pressure in Millibars	Temperature °F	
		Miles	Tenths							Direction (true)	Force (0—12)				Dry Bulb	Wet Bulb
0100	0645 Call Cook Steward 0715 Call Hands 0800 watch dress, complete															
0200	necessary preparations as to stowage of ammunition, dems etc. for the like															
0300	In contact from time to time with S.O. 104 flotilla 22 30 f.fire down															
0400	Guns overhauled.															
0500																
0600																
0700																
0800																
0900																
1000	EXTRACT FROM SHIP'S LOG MMS 260															
1100	AT ANCHOR PORTLAND JUNE 4TH 1944															

Number on Sick List	Distance run through the Water.	Zone Time kept at noon.	Leave Granted to Ship's Company			Anchor Bearings.
			5th June 1944			Operations
1800	0630 Call Cook Steward 0645 Call Hands 0730 hands busy about					
1400	Ship 0815 weighed anchor 0900 proceeded 1315 a/c S40°E					
1500	14.55 LG 9 1540 a/c S.30°E 1930 reached channel marking					
1600	buoys. Continued on course in company with Division I and II					
1700						
1800						
1900						
2000						
2100	Armament tested.					
2200	1200	992	NW	4-5	c	Armament tested, gongs tested
2300	1800	993	NW	5-6	c	
2400	2400	996	NW	5-6	c	

| 19 | . | From | to | , and at | |

6th June 1944   REMARKS Off Port en Bessin

0000 Course continued   0234 started off'n company with MMS 279
+ flotilla. Completed laying 7 dans at 0330 and turned back and
came to anchor at 0430. No incidents recorded except extensive
bombing of craft.   1130 weighed anchor and proceeded with MMS 31
to change sweeps   1320 completed   1335 dropped anchor.
2100 USLCT 639 came into contact with us due to wind + tide +
fouled cable. Damage to forepeak stbd side   2230 pipe down
2200 anchor watch doubled.   2230 weigh anchor to ship's anchorage
(Armament tested) due to possibility of being run down by USLCTs.
2245 anchored.   2330 General alarm, 3 low flying aircraft hostile in
vicinity. Not engaged by us.
        Emergency stores started.

                                                                    P.

	Latitude	Longitude	Depending on	Currents experienced	
0800	° '	° '	.		
1200				7th June 1944 off Port en Bessin.	
2000					

0600 Call Cook Steward 0630 Call hands 0730 hands busy about ship
1110 weigh anchor 1120 proceeded to fresh anchorage near senior ships 1210
anchored. 1950 weighed anchor 2005 proceeded to lay dans in rear of division
Heavy bombardment of coast by our forces. 2245 commenced laying dans.
        Armament tested.

                                                                    P.C.

| 1800 | 995 | NW | 2-3 | C | |
| 2400 | 995 | NW | 2-3 | C | |

		Distance Run		Mean Revns. per Minute	True Course	Gyro Compass Course	Standard Compass Course	Deviation	Variation	Wind		Weather and Visibility	Sea and Swell	Corrected Barometric Pressure in Millibars	Temperature °F		
Time	Log (stating type)	Miles	Tenths							Direction (true)	Force (0—12)				Dry Bulb	Wet Bulb	Sea

H.M.S. Christmas Eve   Le Havre day   of

0100	0700 Call Cook Steward 0730 Call hands 0820 slipped moorings
0200	0845 out sweeps 0907 swicel on 0945 swicel off 18 BL 0947
0300	S 80° E swicel on 1050 swicel off BL 18 1058 swicel on 1136
0400	swicel off 18 BL 1140 swicel on 1239 swicel off 18 BL 1241
0500	swicel on 1325 BL 18 swicel off 1329 swicel on 1346 FIRD
0600	1425 swicel off 1430 in sweeps 1450 proceeded 1515 dropped
0700	anchor 2 shackles 2230 pipe down
0800	Armament tested. NE-3-1010-C
0900	
1000	
1100	
1200	

Number on Sick List	Distance run through the Water.	Zone Time kept at noon.			Anchor Bearings.

25th December 1944   Le Havre

1300	0800 Call Cook Steward 0830 Call hands 0930 hoist down 1100 S.M.
1400	Church Service on MMS 305 Secure, hands to dance and skylark 1300
1500	liberty to four men 2230 pipe down
1600	
1700	
1800	26th December 1944 Le Havre
1900	0700 Call Cook Steward 0730 Call hands 0810 weigh anchor, due to foul anchor
2000	boat hook lost over the side by accident. 0840 passed harbour entrance 0845
2100	out sweeps 0915 swicel on 0945 swicel off 18 BL HV 3 0953 swicel on
2200	1030 swicel off as hammer defective 1035 in sweeps 1100 proceeded 1140 tied up
2300	alongside Empire Cricketer for water 1400 proceeded and tied up alongside MMS 280
2400	1630 liberty men 2230 pipe down
	Armament tested NE 3-4 1005 fog C

The Assault on Normandy
June 6 1944

THE ASSAULT AREA

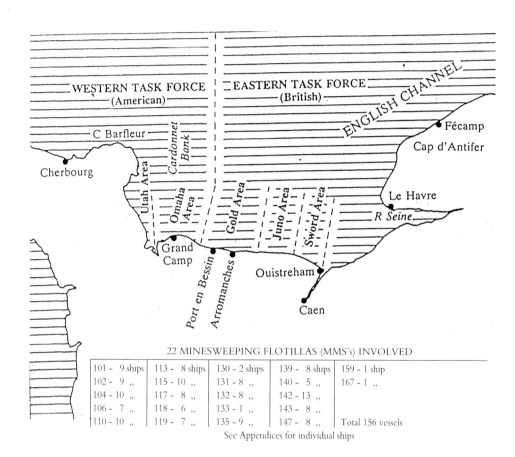

22 MINESWEEPING FLOTILLAS (MMS's) INVOLVED

101 - 9 ships	113 - 8 ships	130 - 2 ships	139 - 8 ships	159 - 1 ship
102 - 9 ,,	115 - 10 ,,	131 - 8 ,,	140 - 5 ,,	167 - 1 ,,
104 - 10 ,,	117 - 8 ,,	132 - 8 ,,	142 - 13 ,,	
106 - 7 ,,	118 - 6 ,,	133 - 1 ,,	143 - 8 ,,	
110 - 10 ,,	119 - 7 ,,	135 - 9 ,,	147 - 8 ,,	Total 156 vessels

See Appendices for individual ships

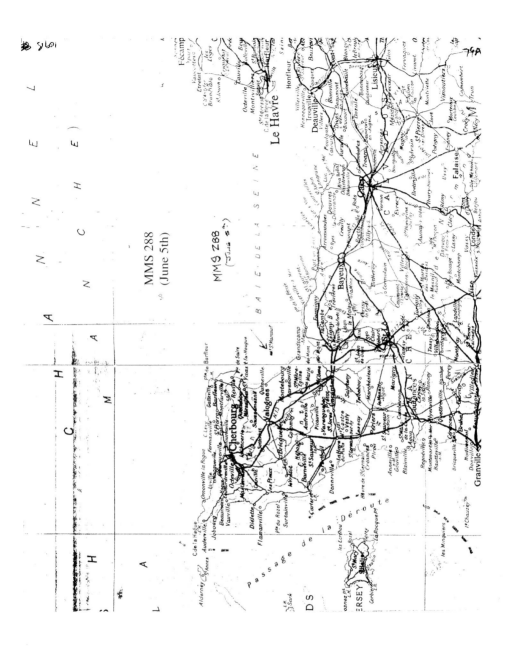

MMS 288
(June 5th)

MMS 288
(June 5th)

Island Waters Free of Mines Soon

Gallant Crews of "Sweepers" Ending Dangerous Mission

EARLY O.K. FOR MAILBOATS

Within a short time Guernsey will have to bid au revoir to the men of the minesweepers who, during the past few months, have been engaged in the tedious and dangerous task of making the waters around our coasts safe for shipping.

Especially at the time the Island was liberated, explosions at sea bore testimony to the efficient way in which these brave fellows have carried out their work. Their vessels have been a source of interest and attraction since the first day they entered the harbour.

Now, in a few days, with the job completed, these members of the " Suicide Squad," as the minesweepers are often called, are to return to their base at Plymouth. Since they first made the acquaintance of islanders, fast friendships have been forged, and although pressure of work compels them to leave, it is hoped they will return in the not-too-distant future to renew the bonds so firmly cemented during the past few months.

AFLOAT WITH THE SUICIDE SQUAD

The ".Pawnbroker's Sign " Goes Up

BY A " PRESS " REPORTER
Aboard M.M.S. 244.

S. 1320d.
(Established—May, 1930)
(Revised- June, 1944)

D.7885/21420 7/44 8.333 345 (B&S Ltd. 45.243

S.O. 104th M.S.F. (R) MMS 244, 305, 260

from CDR M/S Le Havre

Your 271515. Congratulations to you and your Flotilla
on the successful completion of a difficult piece of
minesweeping

271724/45

Distribution 1.2.3.

Hand   P/L   In Transit   HW   27/2/45

MMS 260 passage via Caledonian Canal

Chapter Seven

Operation Kalender

With the capture of the Port of Antwerp by the Allied Forces on the 2nd. September 1944, arrangements were set in hand to clear a channel from the Southern North Sea to the entrance of the River Schelde, then up river to Antwerp Harbour where the facilities were urgently required to land the necessary stores and equipment to meet the needs of the troops. An additional channel was to be cleared to the Port of Ostend.

Sweeping commenced on the 8th. September with the 15th. Minesweeping Flotilla , which had at that stage been transferred from the Royal Navy to Coastal Forces Nore Command covering the East coast from Sheerness to Grimsby.

The Motor Minesweepers came into the picture where there was a requirement to sweep in shallow waters and mainly the Eastern area of the Schelde approaches. It should be borne in mind that the shore line including the Port of Ostend was still in enemy hands, so posed a threat to any activity taking place in the region.

Added to that the ships had little or no protection, but some kind of cover was offered in the shape of Motor Torpedo Boats making smoke. For all the good it did, one would have achieved better results or at least just as good results by puffing a cigarette on the bridge.

Sweepers were well within the range of German shore batteries, which were inclined to take potshots every now and again, creating a great deal of harrassment as well as fright. It was a hazardous business which had to be done one way or another, and by many different flotillas of minesweeping craft.

Because of the activities of so many ships, there is a great deal of confusion as to where actual ships were at any given time.

It would appear however that there were seven MMS Flotillas initially involved in the Kalendar Operation...the 102nd., 110th., 116th., 118th., 139th.,140th., and 145th., consisting of 56 vessels as follows:

102nd. MMS's 19,40,41,44,45,53,59,71,79,82,113,181,267		13
110th. MMS's 4,9,16,26,32,38,47,48,69,80,81,92,110,115,116,171		16
116th. MMS's 285,286,290		3
118th. MMS's 187,188,191,193 (Belgian)		4
139th. MMS's 54,138,227,231,237,270,271,272,284,292 (Dutch)		10
140th. MMS's 57,60,109,137,149,211,283		7
145th. MMS's 252,253,257		3
	Total	56

Turbine excursion vessel St. Tudno *(2,326 gross ton)*
St. Tudno *MMS Baseship Sheerness*

MMS 191 Operational 1945

MV Ungava *(ex MMS 192) Quebec 1952*

Reference is made in the records available, to other ships from the 117th., the 144th. and 142nd. MSF's when MMS's 190, 192, 242, 43, 77, 112, 182, 186, 189, 73, 226, 234, and 237 arrived on the scene as replacement vessels or as additional backup for the operation and found themselves very much involved in the hostilities. It was none too easy to get away from the action as there was always plenty to keep each crew busy.

It was during this crucial stage of the operation that groups of 'E' Boats began to make a nuisance of themselves, crossing the channel and laying mines off the Norfolk coast. They invariably carried torpedoes, and created havoc at times with the mine clearance which was taking place in preparation for the bombardment of the Island of Walcheren.

As was the practice, it was necessary to clear the channels for a combined force of warships consisting of HMS *Warspite, Erebus*, and *Roberts*, this being the run up to the clearing of the River Schelde, being the one and only supply line to the Port of Antwerp, already in the hands of the Allies.

It was known that Walcheren was the site of the German gun known as 'Big Bertha', capable of firing shells across the North Sea, and striking terror into the East Anglian coast.

This combined attack did not materialise until November 1st., due mainly to the aforementioned problems, but on that date the island fell to the allies ashore, as well as the remainder of the enemy positions in that area, thus making it possible to begin the major task of sweeping the Schelde River, which had become by that time more urgent than ever.

In the December issue of the Listener 1944, Commander Anthony Kimmins made the following comments about the clearance of the River Schelde, and it spells out in very few words just how difficult the task turned out to be:

> There had been no navigational information about this particular stretch of water for over four years. It was known as one of the most hazardous channels in the world . . . a positive menace, and the success of Operation Kalendar depended very much on the expertise of one of the Schelde pilots who had escaped to England in 1940...a man by the name of Mr. Hook.
>
> There were over seventy mines accounted for in the initial sweep of Flushing, carried out under fire from the enemy shore batteries. The blasts between that of the shore batteries and the shells exploding, together with the detonated mines were so many, that they were impossible to count.
>
> With 70 miles of channel to be swept, sown with every conceivable and most diabolic type of mine, together with numerous wrecks and blockships, this made the operation a positive nightmare.
>
> Of all the heroes of the minesweeping game, claims the Commander, those who had to serve below decks in the engine room, who never left their posts unless they were either blown out or had to abandon ship, these were the greatest heroes of them all.
>
> In general the men joked a lot and they laughed a lot, but by the end they were becoming desperately tired, not so much because of the long hours on the bridge, at the winches or in the engine rooms, but because of something they would never admit – the constant strain of wondering whether the next one would go off under them.

There were indeed few who doubted the difficulty of the task, because the enemy had had two months prior to the capture of Antwerp to thoroughly mine the river leading to the docks.

Equally it was not known how far up the river it would be possible to rely on the use of the standard Double L sweep, which depended for its effectiveness on the electrical conductivity of salt water.

The sweeping of fresh water such as the Schelde was in the upper reaches, posed problems, for there were few sweepers fitted out to do this type of work, and crews had to be specially trained. Such crews were in short supply.

It was arranged however that the Western area of the river should be the responsibility of the Harwich Force under Captain M/S Harwich,(Force 'B'), already based at Ostend following its fall to the allies, whilst the inner part of the approach channel and the 50 miles of river should be tackled by Force 'A', from Sheerness under Captain Hopper.

The orders were:

> To sweep and buoy a channel as soon as possible from the Eastern end of the North foreland Schelde channel into the mouth of the Schelde off Flushing, and to sweep and buoy where necessary a channel up the River Schelde to the Port of Antwerp, and finally to sweep the river at Antwerp and to assist in the clearance of the basins and docks.

The fact that the ships had to cope with a tidal river, plus the problem of the salinity, to say nothing of the diabolical devices under the water, gave the crews something of a headache, including those who manned the store, survey and refuelling trawlers.

There were four flotillas of MMS's in Force 'A' accompanied by three flotillas of BYMS's (i.e. those built in the USA for 'lease and lend'.) Eight MMS's were fitted with light anti-aircraft guns as protection against enemy aircraft.

It was 'Out Sweeps' for Force 'B' on the 2nd. November, but operations were abandoned due to shellfire from the vicinity of Knokke on the southern shore of Westerschelde and about twenty miles from Ostend. That battery was captured on the same day and sweeping continued on the 3rd. But the ships again were shelled and suffered damage and a number of casualties.

Because of this hive of activity Force 'A',totalling 45 ships anchored in the Downs, an area off the Kent coast, was delayed in their effort to make a start, but finally made the crossing on the night of 3/4th. November, while Force 'B' was sweeping its way up the Schelde as far as Ternheuzen on the South bank, about ten miles up stream.

Ternheuzen had already been earmarked as a minesweeping base, with arrangements already in hand to sail HMS St.Tudno, the M/S base ship at Queenborough on the River Medway, to that position.

It came as something of a surprise to most of the Queenborough and Sheerness ratings to see *St. Tudno* leave the quay, apart that is, from her annual duty free run outside the three mile boundary. But sail she did, having had a dummy run as early as June 1943, when the preparations for Operation Kalendar had been devised, to see if she was capable of doing the job.

In fact it was precisely because *St.Tudno* passed the test with flying colours that Queenborough and Sheerness were established as minesweeping basis.

Both forces, in spite of considerable enemy shellfire, finally and with the assistance of Commander M/S Belgium, cleared the river and its approaches, with a total of 51 mines to their credit.

This figure does not tally with that reported in the Listener in 1944, but as Commander Kimmins points out, the actual mine detonations were difficult to count. The figure 51 is a Public Records Office figure and therefore more likely to be accurate.

Following one of the most intricate and hazardous sweeping operations of the whole war, the first sweeper got through on the evening of the 4th. November, and a signal from the Secretary to the Admiralty reported that:

> The operations in the River Schelde are likely to give the impression that it was a simple task entailing very little risk, but it was one of the most difficult minesweeping operations of the war; and it was only due to the efficiency of and the unremitting energy and zeal of the minesweepers, working under the inspired leadership of Captain H.G.Hopper R.N., that the clearance was effected in twenty two working days, the only casualty being the Motor Launch 916 and her gallant crew, whose loss I deeply regret.

On 26th. November 1944, the first three coasters were able to tie up at Berth 219, having been able to reach the port of Antwerp safely.

In spite of that report, casualties there were, as the task to clear the remainder of the river continued.

No mention is made of the loss of MMS 257 on the 11th. December 1944, five days after she joined the task force with MMS's 252 and 253 from the U.K. They had been allocated on a permanent basis for service in Terheuzen. For that crew, the word 'permanent' came to mean more than simply for the duration of the war, for some never returned home.

MMS 216 is reported as picking up the casualties, two of which were fatal.

MMS 216 was with the 117th. MSF and apparently her ship's company distinguished itself by rescueing two guards and 16 frightened German prisoners from a sinking DUKW. They were landed and marched to an Army H.Q.

MMS 175 also from the 117th. had a near miss and spent a whole night frantically working the pumps. It may not be generally known that apart from those mechanically operated pumps in the engine room, there was only one manual pump on board. Near misses invariably meant that the seams of the ship opened up below the water line, and once that happened there was little chance of being able to keep afloat without the use of some mechanical help.

In such circumstances the crippled ship would be supported by two sister ships port and starboard. The crew of the 175 must have had quite a busy time, and the story goes that as she was being towed to safety, she was holed by a sunken wreck. Hard work at the pumps prevailed and she was later repaired and brought back into service. Chief Engineer Harris was awarded the D.S.M. and no doubt arranged for an on board celebration.

The enemy meanwhile, were not inactive. The Hook of Holland was still in German possession, from whence came at regular intervals the dreaded 'E' boats.

Added to that and much more of a problem, were the obstructions laid across the river bed and across the moored mines in the channel. This made the sweeping of the mines impossible and while the MMS's could not deal with this, it was left to the Fleet Sweepers of the 18th. MSF to try and drag these obstructions out of the way.

It was a hairy task, not knowing when something was likely to be detonated under the stern, but nevertheless it had to be achieved and one way or another, when completed, it would see the large merchant ships making their way upstream in comparative safety.

Force 'B', forever busy with the approaches to Zeebrugge returned to Harwich on the 28th. and were relieved by the 118th. Minesweeping Flotilla which consisted of those ships manned by Belgian crews. They took on the task of clearing most of the remaining mine infested areas of water around the Belgian coastline. Vessels involved were MMS's 43,77,112,188,191, and 193. MMS 77 was replaced by MMS's 75 and 79 at a later date.

Force 'A' remained operational in the River Schelde until the 23rd. December when they finally returned to Sheerness, sinking a midget submarine on the way. The total mine count for Force 'A' was 217 ground mines and 41 moored.

It would be extremely unfair even to suggest that the MMS flotillas alone made Operation Kalendar a success. That could never be and never was the case.

Many other sweepers played their important role in the task, and that ought not ever to be forgotten. Indeed there were those whom we might call, for the want of another name, "land based sweepers". In official terms the were known as the PPU's or Portable Pulsing Units.

This was in fact a system devised to sweep areas where ships could never go, and each unit consisted of generators mounted on trailers from which the sweep was activated at 2,350 amps, and usually within those waters of low salinity.

Most of this activity took place between 6th. and 13th. January 1945, and was not without its dangerous moments for the crews involved. No one really had any idea where the mines were likely to explode. Many occasions would see a detonation quite close to the shore or alongside the quay of the harbour. It was a risky business and casualties were reported from time to time. In addition to this, when the Acoustic Kango Hammer already mentioned was found to be mostly ineffective, a new idea was introduced to deal with this type of mine, used both at sea and ashore.

It was a simple idea, where ships were fitted out with a quarter inch steel plate about six feet square, through which was poked a 12 foot steel tube.

We called those who operated these devices "Grenadiers", for it was down this tube that hand grenades duly primed by the duty watch the night before, were stuffed at intervals, between round wooden blocks. They were then shoved out of the seaward end by using a wooden pole.

Those of us employed in the engine room and any in the after mess who happened to be trying to get a bit of shut-eye, were made only too well aware of the explosions, lasting for the duration of the sweeping time. There was always the feeling that if the grenade went off prematurely, which some did, it would blow a hole in the side of the ship. It didn't happen in the author's experience, but there were narrow squeaks when some of the grenades went off inside the tube. Seamen were often injured as they dropped the grenade while trying to get it into the tube with the safety pin out – quite easily done especially while handling them with frozen fingers on a cold winter's day.

But as has already been mentioned, any idea was better than none, even though it might not be too effective. Better than having to accept the possibility of constant loss of life, ships and cargo by doing nothing at all.

As time went by problems became almost unsurmountable, particularly with the advent of the Oyster or Pressure mine already mentioned, for which we had no known countermeasure.

Cartoon by P. Fell - MMS 74

Chapter Eight

MSF 101 and 115; Two Among Others

While many flotillas were in action during the period 1941-1946 and indeed beyond those dates (for sweeping continued until 1952 when it was felt that all shipping lanes and minefields had been sufficiently cleared so as to afford safe passage to all kinds of shipping), particular comments need only be made of two, so that the reader might get some idea of the work these craft were called upon to do in one capacity or another.

The 101st. MSF was one of the oldest flotillas, having been formed in 1941. It consisted in those early days of the war of MMS'S 14, 15, 16 and 17, then was augmented from Cardiff by MMS's 25, 26, 27 and 28 as and when they were commissioned.

Many of the earlier years were taken up with routine sweeping day and night, trying as far as was able with limited experience to establish some kind of pattern for those who were to follow. It was mostly trial and error – an experimental exercise, never being too sure whether or not it was likely to work. It was a time of apprehension, of wondering how long the crisis was going to last, and in particular, not knowing what new device was waiting on the next trip out to sea.

It has already been noted that there were very few ships that remained in the same flotilla for the duration of the war and the 101st. was no exception.

MMS 15 left to join MSF 131 and MMS's 16 and 26 added their expertise to the 110th. This was mainly due to the more experienced skippers having to become leaders of the new flotillas as they were formed following their commissioning.

As time went by MMS's 182,186,189, and 219 joined the 101st.

During Operation Overlord, this flotilla was employed on Mulberry escort duties, that is sweeping the lanes clear for the great concrete monsters which when sunk off shore were to be the haven of many ships during the hectic days that followed. MMS 189 rescued seven survivors from a tug whose name is unknown, but which had been torpedoed by an 'E' boat.

MMS 27 managed to pick up a submerged wire around her propellor which could have ripped her hull wide open, but the Commanding Officer, Lieutenant Scott, knowing that there were no divers available to clear the obstruction, safely beached the vessel. The offending wire was cut away, and while awaiting the next tide, he had the crew scrape the ship's bottom.

Lt. Scott must have been well versed in tidal activities, for had the tide been

MMS 189 (101st. MSF 1944)
Sister ships: MMS's 14, 17, 25, 27, 28, 182, 186, 219.

MMS 6 (115th. MSF 1944)
Sister ships: MMS's 7, 22, 30, 55, 79, 91, 139, 165, 205.

on its way out, he would have been left high and dry and at the mercy of enemy gunfire from the shore batteries which were not too far distant. It was a common hazard, which left a ship vulnerable to air attack or indeed from the shore batteries, which reminded the sweepers that the enemy were never too far away.

MMS 19 with the 117th. MSF suffered in a similar manner. She was unfortunate enough to start losing speed during a sweeping operation off the beach-head.

Investigation revealed a couple of ship's rope fenders wrapped around the propellor shaft. In spite of a number of dramatic underwater dives by members of the engine room staff (they were the only members of the ship's company who knew how to use a hacksaw – so the coxswain said!) all of which were unsuccessful due mainly to the men's inability to hold their breath for any length of time, the ship was finally towed back to the Mulberry Harbour where a diver was found to do the necessary work.

On some occasions Motor Launches were sent along with the sweepers to 'make smoke', which afforded little protection especially in anything other than a flat calm. Great gaps in the 'screen' laid the sweepers open to gunfire from ashore, and very often the smoke came at the wrong time or not at all.

Ships invariably returned to their anchorage peppered with shrapnel holes. With only a couple of Oerlikons and a pair of Lewis guns port and starboard, the sweepers of this class became sitting ducks with little chance of meaningful retaliation.

Daily routine sweeps from the Mulberry anchorage continued, beginning with first light and stopping only when darkness fell. The work varied from day to day depending upon where the need was greatest. Night time was taken up with 'minespotting duties', meaning that the ship would lay at anchor somewhere near the coastal front line, reporting any mines deposited overnight by enemy aircraft, so the crews did not have a great deal of rest.

The adverse weather conditions, not only at the start of the operation, but during the months that followed, gave the ship's company many a rough passage and interrupted any of those occasions when they were likely to have time off, which was not very often. Lying at anchor in high winds, gave little opportunity for rest. Unlike the 'big' ships, the sweepers were tossed around like matchwood.

The sea bed around the landing beaches did not provide good holding ground for ships' anchors, so craft of all shapes and sizes were seen to change position, often out of control when the crew were trying to get some sleep. It was only good seamanship and prompt action of ships' companies that saved many vessels from sustaining severe damage.

By July 1944 it was possible to introduce a system which allowed one ship to stand down for one day in four. This came about mainly due to the arrival of other sweepers on the scene, thus easing the strain on personnel and equipment.

HMS *Adventure*, Pennant Number M23, an ex-minelaying cruiser converted in 1944, acted as repair ship for all the minesweeping craft, which included straightening out the 'A' frame to which was attached the acoustic hammer, on MMS 186.

She had been in a collision with the depot ship which was one of a number of incidents which caused minor hiccups from time to time. Submerged objects were a menace in low water and many sweepers were damaged as a result. Repairs were often carried out on the beach.

Water was always a problem with the MMS's. There was never enough of it, not even to shave. Dhobying was done with salt water soap, which produced as much lather as the froth on a pint of NAAFI beer. Growing beards was the order of the day, that is until the ship returned to the U.K. where the proud sailor, sporting a beautiful set of whiskers, was politely told that because he had not submitted a written request, the offending growth would, before he went ashore, have to be removed.

With razor blades in short supply, and not being too expert with the cut-throat razor (Admiralty pattern) it was quite an exercise to become clean-shaven at such short notice. Many considered it quite unfair with a war on and all that, but regulations were regulations even in the Patrol Service.

Even when nothing untoward happened, the work was long and arduous with very few opportunities for relief. The cramped quarters and the dehydrated food did not help. Powdered egg and red lead (tinned tomatoes) was the usual breakfast if you were lucky enough not to lose it over the side whilst attempting to transport the plate from the galley aft, to the forward mess. Often breakfast was carried away in the wind, and there was no second helping, unless 'cookie' was an 'oppo', when one might get a spare tin of sardines.

Corned (dog)beef and dehydrated spuds, plus the inevitable rice pudding (Chinese wedding cake) offered in many disguises was the usual dinner, adequately salted from the sea spray from which one could never escape, even on the lee side of the ship.

The chance to go ashore was zero, certainly in the early days of Overlord. One or two personnel managed to set foot in Arromanches, but only because they happened to be lucky enough to man the small boat taking the skipper ashore for a briefing.

In many of the ships the engine room staff (usually four) worked five hours on and five off, although this was entirely up to the discretion of the Chief Engineman.

The five hours off were invariably interrupted by enemy action and stokers had to take up positions on the bridge as ammunition carriers or magazine loaders or even in some cases manning the Oerlikon 20 mm machine gun, for which task they had been duly trained at the Naval School of Gunnery at Whale Island. They were always glad to get away from places like that, where everything was very pusser and done at the double.

Sleep was almost an unknown quantity where signalmen and wireless operators were concerned. Ships with more than one 'Bunts' or 'Sparks' were lucky indeed. Cooks spent most of their time in the galley preparing meals or hot cocoa or 'kye' as it was called, and recharging the stock pot with anything edible.

To try and sleep up forward while sweeping operations were in progress was an impossibility with the sound of the acoustic hammer thumping in one's ears immediately below the messdeck.

The after mess was just as bad with the propeller shaft turning and rumbling at 350 revolutions a minute.

Officers were no better off, for they were required to stay on the bridge while the ship was under way. In any case their cabin was situated right above the engine room where there was enough noise and vibration to wake the dead.

The 115th. MSF was as active as any other and consisted at the outset of ten ships MMS's 6,7,22,29,30,55,89,90,139,165.

MMS 30 was replaced by MMS 49, MMS 91 replaced MMS 55 which was sunk in July 1944 off Normandy, MMS 90 went off to spend the rest of her life with the Russian Navy. MMS 205 replaced MMS 89 which went off to the Mediterranean to join the 114th. MSF and was sunk by a mine off Bizerta on the 12th. May 1943.

When the flotilla weighed anchor on June 5th. there were ten vessels, and their first duty was to screen the cruiser HMS *Roberts* on her way to the bombardment area, setting out like her sister ships upon unchartered mine-strewn waters.

Each sweeper carried a balloon (already referred to) plus another attached to an Oropesa float at the end of a wire cable. These presented their own problems, especially in the high winds during those first few days of the assault.

Dawn revealed that many ships had lost their charges, the reason why being obvious to anyone who had anything at all to do with the control of such 'animals' in rough weather, especially those flying at heights beyond 100 feet. They were virtually uncontrollable and could play havoc with a ship's rigging as they pranced about at the end of their cable. They were fine in the right sort of conditions, which did not unfortunately prevail at the beginning of the assault. If the truth be known most of those reported 'lost', were in fact cut away to prevent damage to the ship and the crews.

In addition to the loss of MMS 55 in July, the 115th. had many near misses from German shore batteries, drawing the enemy fire as they approached 'no man's land' as it were. Only MMS 29 sustained any real damage however, but this did not prevent her from continuing her sweeping operations.

Following that first assignment the flotilla arrived at Juno beach-head at 1720 hours on the 6th. June. The next three days were spent in routine sweeping operations, then a return passage to Portsmouth for fuel and stores, then back into the fray, to meet very much the same problems as the 101st. and others.

On the 16th, June MMS 7 had two near misses which caused a great deal of damage. One seaman was killed and the ship almost put out of action, just managing to limp home to the U.K. after a very dicey journey across the channel. Secondhand Watson and Stoker Murray were both awarded the Distinguished

Service Medal.

The bad storm of the 19th.-21st. June brought its own disasters. MMS 29 lost an anchor and had to cut away the second to avoid a collision with a merchant ship which was drifting out of control. MMS 55 (she was still afloat then) parted with her anchor, while MMS 139 suffered damage to her steering.

Any thoughts of sweeping were out of the question, and in many ways, the motor minesweeper, being one of the smallest craft in the whole operation, suffered most of all. They were not designed for heavy weather, but considering all the ships that took part in the 'D' Day landing operations, it is surprising how few casualties there were. At this point it might be as well to list all of those craft which were either lost or damaged during their active service life:

First those in HOME WATERS.

102 MSF

MMS 8 Sunk by a mine	June 26th. 1944
MMS 40 Severely damaged	
MMS 44 Mine damage	November 1941
MMS 45 Shell fire damage	13th.June 1944
MMS 61 Mine damage	
MMS 74 Mine Damage	October 1944
MMS 115 Mine damage	October 1944
MMS 181 Mine damage	July 1944

104 MSF

MMS 279 Acoustic Mine damage	June 1944

105 MSF

MMS 3 Mine damage	1943

109 MSF

MMS 136 Mine damage	May 1942

110 MSF

MMS 9 Mine damage	27th.October 1941
MMS 92 Mine damage	November 1944
MMS 171 Near miss damage	

115 MSF

MMS 7 Bomb damage	June 1944
MMS 49 Mine damage	September 1944
MMS 55 Mined and sunk	July 1944

131 MSF

MMS 59 Mine damage	June 1942
MMS 82 Mine damage	

133 MSF

MMS 16 Mine damage	June 1941

134 MSF
    MMS 174 Hit by bombs   July 1942

135 MSF
    MMS 286 Shore gunfire damage   October 1943

136 MSF
    MMS 175 Mine damage   July 1942

138 MSF
    MMS 229 Sunk   June 1944

139 MSF
    MMS 227 Sunk   May 1944

143 MSF
    MMS 248 Sunk River Schelde   January 1945
    MMS 257 Sunk River Schelde   December 1944

147 MSF
    MMS 288 Damaged by shore gunfire

205 MSF
    MMS 297 Gunfire and mine damage   17th. June 1944
    MMS 278 Sunk in Lawrence River St.Malo 14th.September 1944

146 MSF
    MMS 144 Damaged in aircraft attack

163 MSF
    MMS 241 Mine damage July 1944
    MMS 39 was the first MMS casualty of the war mined August 1941.

The list from overseas is that much shorter but nevertheless, and we need to be constantly reminded, there were many of these particular craft in service in foreign waters, mainly in the Mediterranean, doing a first class job, and without whom the task of winning the war would not have been accomplished.

103 MSF
    MMS 68 sunk off the shores of Greece   4th. February 1945

111 MSF
    MMS 117 mined and sunk in Italy   1st. September 1944
    MMS 168 sunk in Genoa Harbour   25th. June 1945
    MMS 170 sunk of Gorgona Island, Italy.   12th. December 1944

114 MSF
    MMS 89 sunk off Bizerta   May 1943

117 MSF

    MMS 70 sunk at Taranto   September 1943

120MSF

MMS 101 sunk off Salonika   29th. September 1944
MMS's 51 and 52 were scuttled in Java   1942
MMS's 93, 94, 95, 96, 123, 124, 125, 126, 127, and 128 were lost when
Singapore was captured. They were being built there.
MMS 147 was lost in Rangoon
MMS's 152, 153, 161, 162, 163, and 164 were lost in Burma
MMS 166 was lost in Penang.

Other known casualties lost following the war were:
MMS 58 caught fire and sank in the English Channel in April 17th. 1954
MMS 226 sank at Hollandia New Guinea in November 1951
MMS 223 sank in a storm south east of Bermuda on February 25th. 1951

Chapter Nine

The Big Mickey

It is only right that in compiling a history of the Motor Minesweeper, mention of the larger class of vessel is made i.e the 1000 Class or the 126 footer. Following the design and building programme being initiated in 1939-40, suggestions were made that a larger vessel of the same type as the Mickey Mouse would be desirable, for a number of reasons. One being that a larger vessel would be capable of sweeping in much less sheltered waters, and providing that the shallow draught as specified for the smaller ships of eight feet was not insisted upon, much deeper waters could be covered. Another was that larger craft would be able to make ocean passages without the worry of having insufficient fuel or fresh water.

A design was subsequently prepared and submitted for approval by the Director of Naval Construction and passed for onward transmission to the builders. The dimensions were 140' overall, by 27' 11" x 8½' draught, with a displacement of 360 tons against the smaller vessel's 256 tons. The engine capacity was the same at 500 horse power with a speed of 10 knots.

The endurance however was doubled i.e. from 2000 miles to 4000 miles. The extra space provided for four extra crew making a total ships company of 25. They were known as the 'Big Mickeys' or the 1000 Class to distinguish them from their smaller sister ships. Pennant numbers ranged from 1001 to 1090.

Other differences were mainly in improved mechanical and electrical facilities, with the Double 'L' reel being power driven rather than hand wound. Manual steering was replaced with hydraulics and the ship's structure strengthened to make them very able sea-boats.

The 87 vessels which finally came into service did exactly the same job as the 105 footer, although Oropesa sweeps became standard fittings at a later date. Those who were privileged to serve aboard one of these larger ships gained some advantage from the extra 20 feet of messing space, a little more comfort for the duration of the war, but still not comfortable enough to disqualify the crews from the 'hard laying' money which never changed from the princely sum of one shilling a day. In fact the crews, after a quick visit, with a trip around the Solent in a flat calm and aboard a destroyer by Lady Astor, nearly lost that privilege. She claimed that the crews quarters seemed to be quite adequate. Fortunately however the Navy won the day.

This type of craft was built in the main by the same yards who had gained experience with the 105 footers, and on completion constituted nine flotillas, the 201st. to the 209th. They did not start coming into service until December 1942, and by May of 1944 there were 49, of a total number of 90 vessels planned.

Twenty-four of these were completed by overseas Canadian companies, Vaughan, Wagstaff, and Clare. Three were cancelled MMS's 1071,1072 and 1073. The remainder served with those flotillas already mentioned with the exception of MMS's 1083 and 1084 operating with the smaller craft in Flotillas 102 and 117 respectively.

MMS's 1079 and 1080 were utilised mainly as dan layers at Dover and the Humber while MMS's 1085 and 1086 served with the Norwegian Navy. Only recently has the Norwegian Naval Museum been seeking drawings of these vessels in order to build models. It would appear that drawings are not available. All the 'Big Mickey' flotillas were in action around the coast of Britain but mainly on the eastern shores.

In addition to the 90 ships already mentioned, there were 16 named vessels ordered, six completed in 1945, and four in 1946. Six were cancelled. Of this group ordered in 1943, and known as the 'Lake' Class, all were shipped off to serve with the USSR Navy.

These vessels all bearing the name of a tree and not a lake e.g. Fir Lake..Ash Lake..Alder Lake etc.,began their lives in Canadian Yards. Midland Boats, Ontario; Vancouver Shipyard; Port Carling Co. Ontario; Taylor of Toronto; Mac Craft, Sarnia; and a number of other comparatively unknown but very competent builders.

There is only one recorded loss of this type of vessel.

MMS 1019 was mined off Cherbourg on the 2nd July 1944. MMS 1004 was sold in Singapore in 1961, 1023 and 1005 went to join her sisters in the USSR, 1016 was wrecked in Jutland in 1946 while serving with the Danish Navy following the end of hostilities.

Some vessels, like MMS 1003 served for a time as degaussing vessels.(Gauss is an electrical term connected with magnetism and takes its name from the German mathematician Johann Karl Friedrich Gauss). Many of the ships ended up as hulks like those illustrated, and it would seem that there are none left in existence today.

It might be mentioned here that there were a further ten 105 foot class ships built in Canada which were named rather than numbered and were manned by Royal Canadian Naval personnel. These craft were operational along the Pacific Coast, two of which were completed in 1942, and eight in 1944. Most were sold off by 1947, but there was apparently one survivor the *Daerwood* until 1973 when she was lost at sea.

It might be helpful to say something here about Pennant Numbers which are to say the least confusing, even among those who knew the minesweepers well.

With the 105 foot class the ships were numbered 1 to 313. Some had no prefix letters, while others have FYPT which stands, not as some would have it, for fishing, yachts, patrol and tugs, but is an abbreviation for Fishery Pennant. Others had the FY without the PT, but in addition to the minesweepers, anti-submarine, dan laying, degaussing, minewiping and mine recovery vessels, wore the same pennant.

It is said that all Canadian Naval sweepers wore the Pennant 'J', but so did some of the others built in the UK, as photographs clearly show. Some of the 105 foot class had the figure '5' in front of their number as in MMS 566. These alterations are understandable in order to identify one ship from another, but photographs also reveal ships with the additional figure '6'. It could have been a painter's error.

If the smaller boats numbers were difficult, the larger and particularly the British Yard sweepers were worse, with some using the Flag 3 (as the photograph), and it is understood that this confusion existed throughout the whole of the war, basically one must suppose because of the many different kinds of ships being utilised.

The BYMS's had exactly the same numbers as the small MMS's and it was not until the beginning of 1944 that 2000 was added to their number, thereby bringing to an end what must have been something of a problem in the area of communications. It might also be of interest to note that all lease-lend ships were prefixed by the letter 'B' as seen on some of the fleet sweepers such as the Algerine Class built in Canada.

MMS 1017

125

MMS 1042

MMS 1083 (Hulk Medway)

UK BUILDERS 126 FOOT MMS

Camper and Nicholson Gosport	1001..1002..1003..1004..(4)
Curtis Par/Looe	1032..1033..1034..1035..1036..1040..1075..1076 1077..1078..1079..1080..1087..1088 (14)
Doig Grimsby	1022..1026..1081..1082 (4)
East Anglian Constr. Oulton Broad	1005..1007..1008..1027..1046..1074..1085..1086 1089 (9)
Forbes Peterhead	1013..1045 (2)
Forbes Sandhaven	1017..1024..1049 (3)
Hancocks Pembroke	1039 (1)
Harris Appledore	1014..1031 (2)
Herd & Mackenzie Buckie	1015..1016..1047 (3)
Humphrey & Smith Grimsby	1023..1025..1042..1043 (4)
Noble Frazerburgh	1021..1048 (2)
Philips Dartmouth	1030..1090 (2)
W.Reekie Anstruther	1018..1041 (2)
Richards Lowestoft	1006..1037..1038 (3)
Upham Brixham	1019..1020..1029 (3)
Wivenhoe S/Y	1009..1010..1011..1012..1028..1044..1083.. 1084 (8)

Total 66

OVERSEAS BUILDERS 126 FOOT MMS

Clare S/B Co.Canada	1050..1051..1052..1053..1054..1055..1056..1057 1058..1059..1060..1061 (12)
Vaughan Canada	1068..1069..1070..1071..1072,,1073 (6)
Wagstaff & Hatfield Canada	1062..1063..1064..1065..1066..1067 (6)

Total 24

BUILDING PROGRAMME 1943 126 foot MMS United Kingdom

	Jan	Feb	Mar	Apr	May	Jne	Jly	Aug	Sep	Oct	Nov	Dec	
Camper/Nicholson						1001		1003					2
Curtis						1035	1032				1036 1033		4
Doig		1022				1026					1081		3
East Ang	1005					1007		1008				1027	4
Forbes		1017			1013	1024				1045	1049		5
Hancocks													
Harris						1014					1031		2
Herd & Mac						1015			1016				2
Humphrey	1023				1025				1042 1043				4
Noble				1021					1048				2
Philips										1030			1
Reekie							1018						1
Richards			1006	1037						1038			3
Upham								1019					1
Wivenhoe		1009				1010		1011		1012			4
													38
Totals	3	2	1	2	2	5	4	4	5	4	5	1	
Prog/Totals	3	5	6	8	10	15	19	23	28	32	37	38	

BUILDING PROGRAMME 1944 126 foot MMS United Kingdom

	Jan	Feb	Mar	Apr	May	Jne	Jly	Aug	Sep	Oct	Nov	Dec
Camper & N	1002 1004											2
Curtis		1075		1040		1034	1076				1077 1033	5
Doig	1082											1
East Ang			1046		1074		1085			1086		4
Hancocks									1039			1
Herd & Mac	1047											1
Reekie		1041										1
Upham		1020										1
Wivenhoe	1028							1044		1083		3
												19
Totals	5	3	1	1	1	1	2	1	1	2	1	
Prog/Totals	43	46	47	48	49	50	52	53	54	56	57	57

BUILDING PROGRAMME 1943 126 foot MMS United Kingdom

	Jan	Feb	Mar	Apr	May	Jne	Jly	Aug	Sep	Oct	Nov	Dec	
Curtis			1078		1087								
			1079										
			1080										
			1088										5
East Ang			1089										1
Philips	1090												1
Upham			1029										1
Wivenhoe			1084										1
Total	1		7		1								9
Prog/Total	58		65		66								66

BUILDING PROGRAMME 1944 126 foot MMS Overseas

	Jan	Feb	Mar	Apr	May	Jne	Jly	Aug	Sep	Oct	Nov	Dec	
Clare							1050	1051	1052	1053		1054	
												1055	6
Wagstaff						1062	1063		1064			1065	4
Vaughan								1068		1069	1070		3
Totals						1	2	2	2	2	1	3	
Prog/Totals						1	3	5	7	9	10	13	13

1945

	Jan	Feb	Mar	Apr	May	Jne	Jly	Aug	Sep	Oct	Nov	Dec	
Clare	1056	1058	1059		1060	1061							
	1057												6-
Wagstaff		1067	1066										2
Total	2	2	2		1	1							8
Prog/Totals	15	17	19		20	21							

1071/72/73 Cancelled in 1944

Summary:

United Kingdom built		66
Canada built		21
Cancelled		3
	Total	—
		90

130

MMS 126 foot Flotillas Vessel Comparison Tables

201st Yar/Har	202nd Lwt/NWE	203rd Harwich	204th Dvr/N.Sh	
1001	1013	1022	1024	
1005	1015	1031	1030	
1012	1017	1042	1032	
1014	1018	1044	1033	
1023	1021	1046	1035	
1025	1034	1081	1036	
1026	1041	1082	1039	
1027	1075		1040	
1043	1076			
1049				
10	9	7	8	Total 34

205th Pt/Grt/Lt	206th Lvpl/Yar	207th Grby	208th N.Sh/Dvr	
1003	1002	1050	1028	
1006	1004	1051	1029	
1007	1016	1052	1045	
1008	1019	1053	1057	
1009	1020	1062	1058	
1010	1047	1063	1066	
1011	1048	1064	1078	
1037	1077	1068	1087	
	1089			
	1090			
8	10	8	8	Total 34

209th. (Ply)	
1054	
1055	
1065	
1069	
1070	
5	Total 5

Grand Total 73

Seventeen vessels are not listed under specific flotillas but served as under:
1038 Leith; 1056 Plymouth; 1059/60/61/67 North Shields;
1071/72/73 Cancelled; 1074 Sold to Holland; 1079 Danlayer Dover
1080 Danlayer Humber; 1083 with 102nd and 1084 with 117th.
1085/86/88 were sold to Norway.

LEGEND:

Dvr	-	Dover
Grt	-	Granton
Grby	-	Grimsby
Har	-	Harwich
Lwt	-	Lowestoft
Lvpl	-	Liverpool

N.Sh	-	North Shields
NWE	-	North West Europe
Pt	-	Portsmouth
Ply	-	Plymouth
Yar	-	Yarmouth

POSTSCRIPT ON 126 foot MMS

Sixteen ships of a similar type were ordered and called the LAKE CLASS.
Of these eight were cancelled and the remainder not completed until the August of 1945. All were earmarked to serve with the Russian Navy.

Ten additional 105 foot MMS's were built to serve mainly on the Pacific Coast. They were as under:

				Sold
LLWELLYN	}			
	}	Chantier Maritime		1942
LLOYD GEORGE	}			1951
KALAMALKA	}		]	1947
	}	AC Benson Vancouver	]	
LA VALLEE	}		]	1945
	}			
ST. JOSEPH	}		]	1947
	}	Newcastle S/Y Nanaimo	]	1944
COQUITLAM	}		]	1946
			]	
CRANBROOK	}		]	1947
	}	Star S/Y	]	
REVELSTOKE	}		]	1957
			]	
ROSSLAND	}		]	1946
	}	Vancouver S/Y	]	
DAERWOOD	}		]	1947

MMS 126 foot Flotilla Checklist
Pt No/Flot

	43	44	45	46	47	48	49	50	51	52	53	54	55	56	57	58	59

100 1201>>>>>>>>>>>>>
2   206>>>>>>SH>>DV>>>>>>>>>>>DG
3   205>>>>>>>>>>>>>>>>C>>>>>>>>>>DG>>RY
4   206>>>>>>>>>C>>>>>>>>>>DG>>>>>>SP>>>>>>>>>>>>>>>>Sold 61
5   201>>>Russia T121
6   205>>>>>>>>>>>>>> Sold
7   205>>>>>>>>>>>Sheerness 46 sold 47 Dicky
8   205>>>>>>>>>>>>>>>>Sold
9   205>>>>>>>>>>>>>>>>Sold
10   205>>>>>>>>>>Sold
11   205 Chatham 46 DG 50 Sold 68
12   201 Sold and rebought for DG Prestige Sold BU 58
13   202 Sold Uddu
14   H201 203 Tholen BU
15   202 Sold
16   206 Vernon D Wrecked Jutland 46
17   202 201 206Sheerness RNVR Curzon>>>>>>>>>> Sold BU 58
18   202 Sold
19   206 >>Sunk 2.7.44 Cherbourg
20   206 >>>>>>>118 B>>>>>>——————————————Sold 55
21   202 >>>>>>Sold 46
22   H203 >>>>>>>>>>>>>>>>>>>>>>>>>>>Walcheren Deleted 53
23   201Russia>>>till 1963
24   204 F(D343) Sold 48
25   H201 203 Wierengen BU 49
26   H201 Ijsselmonde Indonesia 52
27   xxx 201 Sold Solnes
28   xxx NS 208 Sold 46
29   xxxxxx 208 Dover and Salcombe
30   204 202 Sheerness 46 RNVR Hull 47, Humber 48-54 Sold 59
31   203 201 Sold 46
32   204 >>>>>>>>>F(D342) 46 Sold 51
33   204 >>>>>>>>>F(D345) 46 Sold 48
34   xxxxxxx 202 Sheerness 46 RNVR Belfast 47 Kilmoray 48-54 Sold 55
35   204 >>>>>>>>>F46 Ptsmth 48 Broadway 53 Sold 54
36   204 >>>>>>>>>F(D346) 46 Sold 51
37   205 >>>>>>>>>>>>>>>Sold 47 Trappes foundered 49
38   LTH >>>>>>D 45-50 Chatham 51, 51st.MSF Rosyth 54, hulked 59
39   xxx 204 >>>>>>F(D341) 46 Sold 48
40   xxx 204 >>>>>>F(D344) 46 Sold 48
41   xxx 202 >>>>>>Sold 46
42   203 201>>D 45——————————>C>>>>>P>>>>>C>>>>>>>>>Sold 57 BU
43   201 S D 203>>>>>>>>>>>>>>>>>>>>>>>>>>>BU 52
44   xxx 203 D 45——————————>C>>>>>>>P>>>C>>>Sold 54
45   NS >>>>208>>>>>>>>>>>>Sold 48
46   Hxxx >>> 203>>>>>>>>>>>>>>>>>>>>>>>>>>>>BU 52 Overflakkee
47   xxx 206>>>>>>>Sold 46
48   206 >>>>>>>>>>SH RNVR Clyde '47, Graham '48-50 C>>'52 Sold 57

133

	43	44	45	46	47	48	49	50	51	52	53	54	55	56	57	58	59

1049 201 >>>>Vernon 44 Sold 46
  50 xxx 207>>>>>>>sold 46 Eliesor
  51 xxx 207>>>>>>>sold 46 Timann
  52 xxx 207>>>>>>>sold 46 Arcus
  53 xxx 207>>>>>>>sold 46 Thor-bjorn
  54 xxxxxxx 209 F>sold 46 Dolphin
  55 xxxxxxx 209 F>sold 46 Havbrant
  56 xxxxxxx Ply>>>sold 46 Jane Lolk
  57 xxxxxxx 208>>>sold 46
  58 xxxxxxx 208>>>sold 46 Jorgen Claus
  59 xxxxxxx Nth.Sh sold 46
  60 xxxxxxx Nth Sh 60th. Rosyth 47. RNVR St.Mungo 53-54, Sold 58
  61 xxxxxxx Nth Sh 60th.>>>>>301st 50, RNVR Mersey 54 Sold 57 BU
  62 xxx 207>>>>>>>sold 46
  63 xxx 207>>>>>>>sold 46
  64 xxx 207>>>>>>>sold 46 Krohnoy
  65 xxxxxxx F(D343)sold 46
  66 xxxxxxx 208>>>>sold 46 Lady Patricia Photo hulk Medway
  67 xxxxxxx Nth Sh sold 46
  68 xxx 207>>>>>>Sold 46
  69 xxx 209>>>>F(D341)sold 46
  70 xxx 209>>>>F(D345)sold 46
  71 Cancelled 44
  72 Cancelled 44
  73 Cancelled 44
  74 Sold to Holland 44 Duiveland
  75 xxx 202>>>Sheerness 46 RNVR Mersey 48-54 sold 56
  76 xxx 202>>>>>>>>>>>>>Sold 47 Fenmore
  77 xxx 206>>>>Chatham 46 RNVR Montrose 48-55 Sold 56 BU
  78 xxxxxxx 208 Dover and Salcombe
  79 xxxxxxx Danlayer Dover 46 sold 46
  80 xxxxxxx Danlayer Humber 45 Dover 46 Sold 46 Benn
  81 203 201 >>>>Sold 46
  82 xxx 203 H 44 Schokland>>>>>>>>>>>BU 49
  83 xxx 102>208 Sold 46 Salcombe
  84 xxxxxxx 117 Sold 46 Admiral Hawkins
  85 xxx Norway Orkla
  86 xxx Norway Vefsna 49 Franklin Rooseelt
  87 xxxxxxx 208 Plymth 46 Sold Salcombe46
  88 xxxxxxxxxxSold 46 Sveip
  89 xxxxxxx 206 Sheerness 47 RNVR Forth 48 Killiecrankie 51-54 Sold 57
  90 xxxxxxx 206 Sheerness 47 RNVR Coquet Tyne 48
               renamed RNVR Bernicia 48
               renamed RNVR Northumbria 54 Sold 58

LEGEND:

BU	–	Broken Up	F	–	France	Ry	–	Rosyth
C	–	Chatham	H	–	Holland	SH	–	Sheerness
D	–	Denmark	NS	–	North Shields	SP	–	Singapore
DG	–	Degaussing	P	–	Portsmouth			
DV	–	Devenport	Ply	–	Plymouth			

Chapter Ten

The BYMS

Wooden minesweepers were not merely the prerogative of the British government. America had a hand in producing under the Lend Lease Act, those craft known as the British Yard Minesweeper, none of which were built in the U.K. although they were serviced from time to time in various ports around the British Isles.

The vessels were brought over from their various yards,(see Appendix A) by British crews, some of whom claimed to have been on something of a holiday, until that is, the ship was ready to sail, telling tales of arriving in the States only to find their ship half built.

That meant a waiting time of some months during which they were fêted by our American allies. What follows is but a brief summary of these ships' activities during and beyond their time of Service life, some lasting and active to the present day, but in a different role.

There were twenty four flotillas (see appendix B), operational in many areas around the world. Compared with the Mickey Mice, they were luxury vessels, with many fittings not found in the British craft. The outfit of stores and comforts was on much more generous lines than was usual in the Royal Navy.

One ship's company was seen to sport a full grown pig, housed in a suitable 'sty' on the port side of the ship, and fed on whatever was left over from the galley meals; being 'fattened up' so they claimed, for the Christmas roast!

Refrigerators and cold water drinking fountains, with hot and cold running water, made life on board at least tolerable, unlike most of the small Mickeys, whose crews had to put up with salt water showers, and with the only hot water available coming from the galley in a bucket, having taken hours to heat up on the galley stove, (coal/coke for the use of or if one was lucky, diesel fired.)

The BYMS had a complement of 30 officers and ratings, and certainly enjoyed a better standard of vitualling than most of their counterparts.

The Yard Minesweepers were prefixed by the letter B, which was interpreted by some to mean British or Brooklyn. Why Brooklyn no one seems to know, as it is clear from to the records that no ships of this type were built in Brooklyn. Both suggestions would appear to be misnomers.

It is more likely that the letter 'B' was added because as previously stated in this book, these were vessels, like many others, which came to Britain on Lease-Lend, and were of course required to be returned to the USA on completion of their duties. Some made it and many did not.

As in the MMS's there was considerable confusion with pennant numbers, so much so in fact, that they were prefixed by 2000, so that BYMS 1 became 2001 and so on. Photographs can be seen with the prefix '3'.

No one appears to know why, but it is the author's guess that a B can easily become a 3 if the upright is removed. Ours not to reason why but to record the facts as they are found!

There were 284 (Pennant Numbers range from 1-284) originally planned to be built, but only 150 managed any sea-going time. Many numbers are therefore missing e.g. 2081 to 2136..2138 to 2140..2143 to 2147..2151..2158 to 2160..2163 to 2166..2169 and 2170..2176 to 2180..2183 and 2184..2192 and 2193..2195 to 2201..2207 and 2208..2215 and 2216..2218 to 2220..2222..2224..2226 to 2228..2231..2235..2237 to 2239..2241 to 2243..2245..2247 to 2251..2259 and 2260..2262 and 2263..2265 to 2276.. 2281 and 2283.

In general BYMS and MMS's did not mix, although they complemented one another in the work they were called upon to do.

By June 1944 there were 90 craft operational with 14 flotillas, and in due time they became operational in practically every sphere of the war, and many with distinguished service.

In all there were 14 ships lost. Details of the crews are not to hand although some of the officers and ratings who served on board are still alive and well and can be found listed with the other crew members under their respective ships.

BYMS 2182 (Refit 1945 Herd & McKenzie, Buckie, Scotland)

BYMS awaiting disposal

BYMS 2028(28)   BYMS 2141(141)
Note: Prefix   3PT

OVERSEAS BUILDERS

Builder	Ship Numbers	Count
American Car and Foundry Wilminton	2001..2002..2003..2004..2031..2032..2034..2035..2036	9
Assoc. of Shipbuilders Seattle	2009..2010..2011..2012..2014	5
Astoria Marine Const.	2137..2141..2142	3
Ballard Marine Seattle	2025..2026..2027..2028	4
Barbour Boatworks New Bern	2029..2030..2037..2038..2039..2040..2041..2042	8
Bellingham Marine Rly	2017..2018..2019..2020	4
Berger, Wisconsin	2155..2156..2157..2161..2162	5
Campbell, San Diego	2152..2153..2154	3
Dachel Carter Michigan	2015..2016..2167..2168	4
Gibbs/Jackson/Florida	2043..2044..2045..2046..2047..2048..2049..2050..2051 2052..2053..2054	12
H.C. Grebe Chicago	2171..2172..2173..2174..2175..2181..2182..2185..2279 2280	10
Greenpoint Basin, Long Island	2186..2187..2188..2189..2190..2191..2194	7
C. Hiltebrant DD New York	2202..2203..2204..2205..2206	5
Robert Jacob New York	2209..2210..2211..2212..2213..2214	6
J. Martinac, Tacoma	2217..2221..2277..2278	4
Hojean & Erikson Tacoma	2223..2225	2
Sample, Booth Bay, Maine	2229..2230..2232..2233..2234	5
San Diego Maritime Const.	2221..2222..2223..2224..2282..2284	6
South Coast Co. Newport California	2261..2264	2
Stadium Yacht Co., Cleveland	2236..2240	2
Tacoma Boat Bldg Co.	2244..2246	2
Weaver S/Y Orange Texas	2252..2253..2254..2255..2256..2257..2258	7
Wesstergard Tacoma	2055..2056..2057..2058..2059..2060..2061..2062..2063 2064	10
Western Boat Building, Tacoma	2148..2149..2150	3
Wheeler Ship Building Whitestone New York	2005..2006..2007..2008..2065..2066..2067..2068..2069 2070..2071..2072..2073..2074..2075..2076..2077..2078 2079..2080	20

This brings the total ships completed to 150.

It should be noted that the BYMS were not renumbered till the beginning of 1944, so it is found that many ex-service personnel would have known their ship by her original number.

As has already been said, 2000 was added to avoid confusion with those other ships which were unfortunate enough not to have a name.

BYMS SPECIFICATION DATA

Construction	Wood
Length	135.5 feet O.A.
Beam	24.5 feet
Draught	7.5/8.5 feet
Machinery	General Motors Twin Shaft diesel 1200 bhp
Speed	14 knots
Displacement	335 tons
Endurance	2.500 miles at 10 knots
Armament	One 3 inch AA forward. Two 20mm Oerlikon
Complement	30

Captain and crew of BYMS 2012

COMPARISON TABLES
Inter Flotilla Check List

MSF 150 Portsmouth/Yarmouth/Copenhagen/Dover

42	43	44	45	46	47	48
2001	2001	2001	2001	2001		
2002	2002	2002	2002	2002		
2004	2004	2004	2004	2004		
2016	2016	2016	2016	2016		
2015	2015	2015	2029(2)			
2030	2030	2030	2214(2)			
2003	2003	2062(3)	2221(2)			
	2059	2059(1)	2034(2)			
7	7	6	5	4		29

MSF 151 Eastern Fleet/Mediterranean

42	43	44	45	46	47	48
	2011	2011	2011	2011		
	2012	2012	2012	2012		
	2020	2020	2020	2020		
	2023	2023	2023	2023		
	2005(1)	2005	2013(2)	2013		
	2006(1)	2006	2014(2)	2014		
	2007(1)	2007	2024(2)	2024		
	2008(1)	2008	2028(2)	2028		

MSF 152 West Africa/Eastern Fleet/East Indies/Malaya

42	43	44	45	46	47	48
	2013(1)	2013	2005(2)	2005		
	2044	2044	2044			
	2028(1)	2028	2006(2)	2006		
	2024(1)	2024	2007(2)	2007		
	2043(1)		2008(2)	2008		
	2045(1)		2148(2)	2148		
	2046(1)		2217(2)	2217		
			2223(2)	2223		

MSF 153 Mediterrranean

42	43	44	45	46	47	48
	2026	2026	2026	2026		
	2037(2)	2037	2037	2037		
	2171	2171	2171	2171		
	2172	2172	2172	2172		
	2009(1)	2009	2009			
	2027(1)	2027	2027			
	2022	2022	2022			
	2077	2077				
	2019					

Comparison Tables (contd.)

MSF 154 West Africa

42	43	44	45	46	47	48
	2010	2010	2010	2010		
	2025	2025	2025	2025		
	2017(1)	2149	2149	2149		
	2021(1)	2244(2)				
		2261(2)	2261			

MSF 156 Mediterranean

42	43	44	45	46	47	48
	2031	2031	2031	2031		
	2187	2187	2187	2187		
	2209	2209	2209	2209		
	2049(1)	2056(2)	2056	2009(2)		
	2068(1)	2068	2068	2075(2)		
	2072	2174(2)	2174	2174		
	2073(1)	2175(2)	2175	2175		
	2156(1)	2053(2)		2212(3)		
	2190(1)			2027(2)		
	2191(2)					

MSF 157 Great Yarmouth

42	43	44	45	46	47	48
	2034(1)	2141(2)	2141	2141		
	2038(1)	2038				
	2076(1)	2076				
	2213(1)	2213				
	2214(1)	2214				
	2230(1)	2230				
	2039(1)	2221(1)				
	2078(1)					

MSF 159 GRimsby/Normandy Invasion Force

42	43	44	45	46	47	48
	2032	2032	2032	2032		
	2052	2052	2052	2052		
	2070	2070	2070	2070		
	2071	2071	2071	2071		
	2157	2157	2157	2157		
	2173	2173	2173	2173		
	2211	2211	2211	2211		
			2253(2)	2253		

Cmparison Tables (contd.)

MSF 160 Levant (Palestine Coast) Mainly Greek manned

42	43	44	45	46	47	48
	2065	2065	2065	2065		
	2066	2066	2066	2066		
	2067	2067	2067	2067		
	2185	2185	2185	2185		
	2186	2186	2186	2186		
	2229	2229	2229	2229		
	2037(1)	2191(2)				
	2047(1)					
	2048(1)					
	2212(1)					

MSF 161 Eastern Fleet

42	43	44	45	46	47	48
	2148(1)	2148				
	2217(1)	2217				
	2223(1)	2223				
	2137(1)					

MSF 162 Levant (Palestine Coast)

42	43	44	45	46	47	48
	2240	2240	2240	2240		
	2033	2033	2033	2033		
	2075(1)	2075	2075	2056(3)		
	2174(1)	2190(2)	2190	2190		
	2175(1)	2212(2)	2212	2068(2)		
	2074	2074				
	2056(1)	2073(2)				
	2053(1)					

MSF 163 Lowestoft/Great Yarmouth/North West Europe

42	43	44	45	46	47	48
	2040	2040	2040	2040		
	2057	2057	2057	2057		
	2079	2079	2079	2079		
	2167	2167	2167	2167	2167	
	2194(2)	2194	2194	2194		
	2036(1)	2039	2039	2039		
	2080(1)	2078(2)	2078	2078		
	2161(1)	2003(2)	2003	2003		
				2044(3)		
				2142(3)		
				2142(3)		
				2189(2)		

Comparison Tables (contd.)

MSF 164 West Africa

42	43	44	45	46	47	48
		2150(1)	2150			
		2043(2)				
		2137(2)				
		2141(1)				
		2142(1)				
		2225(1)				
		2246(1)				
		2264(1)				
		2284(1)				

MSF 165 Harwich

42	43	44	45	46	47	48
	2035	2035	2035	2035		
	2041	2041	2041	2041		
	2058	2058	2058	2058		
	2202	2202	2202	2202		
	2233	2233	2233	2233		
	2252	2252	2252	2252		
	2205(1)	2205	2076(2)	2076		
	2206(1)	2206	2261(3)	2051(3)		

MSF 166 Eastern Fleet

42	43	44	45	46	47	48
	2060	2060	2060	2060		
	2168	2168	2168	2168		
	2181	2181	2181	2181		
	2203	2203	2203	2203		
	2204	2204	2204	2204		
	2232	2232	2232	2232		
	2236	2236	2236	2236		
	2062(1)	2162	2162	2162		
	2194(1)					
	2244(1)					
	2261(1)					

MSF 167 Normandy Invasion Force/North West Europe/Portsmouth/Humber

42	43	44	45	46	47	48
	2156(2)	2156	2156	2156		
	2155(2)	2155	2155	2155		
	2182(1)	2182	2182	2048(3)		
	2210	2210	2210	2210		
	2061(1)	2061	2038(2)	2038		
	2047(2)	2256(2)	2256	2188(2)		
	2051(1)		2046(3)	2046		
	2069(1)		2230(2)	2230		
			2254(2)	2254		

Comparison Tables (contd.)

MSF 168 Normandy Invasion Force/East Indies 1945

42	43	44	45	46	47	48
		2279(1)	2279			
		2280(1)	2280			
		2062(2)				
		2063(1)				
		2234(1)				
		2253(1)				
		2254(1)				

MSF 169 Dover

42	43	44	45	46	47	48
	2152	2152	2152	2152		
	2153(1)	2047(3)	2047	2047		
	2255	2255	2213(2)	2213		
		2277	2277	2277		
		2278	2278	2278		
		2049(3)	2049	2049		
		2050(3)	2050	2050		
		2064(1)	2055(2)	2055		
		2284(1)	2069(3)	2069		
		2154	2154			

MSF 170 Earmarked for Eastern Fleet 1943/Served Swansea/Grimsby/N.W.E.

42	43	44	45	46	47	48
	2044(1)	2048(2)	2048			
	2045(1)	2051(2)	2051			
	2046(1)	2042(2)	2042			
		2188(1)	2188			
		2189(1)	2189			
		2049(2)				
		2056(2)				
		2069(2)				
		2256(1)				
		2282(2)				

MSF 180 Swansea/South West Pacific

42	43	44	45	46	47	48
		2017(2)	2017	2017		
		2018(2)	2018	2018		
		2045(3)	2045	2045		
		2064(2)	2064	2064		
		2153(2)	2153	2153		
		2246(2)	2246	2246		
		2225(2)	2225	2284(3)		
		2080(2)				
		2021(2)				
		2036(2)				

Comparison Tables (contd.)

MSF 181 East Indies/Singapore

42	43	44	45	46	47	48
		2161(2)	2043(2)	2043		
			2244(3)	2244		
			2059(2)			
			2015(2)			
			2061(2)			
			2063(2)			
			2205(2)			
			2206(2)			

MSF 182 Plymouth/South West Pacific/Singapore

42	43	44	45	46	47	48
			2021(3)	2021		
			2036(3)	2036		
			2064(3)	2064		
			2161(3)	2161		
			2258(3)	2258		
			2264(2)	2264		
			2059(3)	2206(3)		
			2234(2)	2225(3)		
			2282(2)			
			2043(3)			

MSF 183 Dover

42	43	44	45	46	47	48
				2021(4)		
				2063(3)		
				2150(2)		
				2234(3)		
				2256(3)		
				2257(3)		
				2280(3)		

Note: Many Pennant Numbers are followed by a bracketed figure (1) etc. These denote movements of vessels, some of which were attached to as many as four different flotillas during the period of their operational life, e.g. BYMS 2021 started off with MSF 154 in 1943, then MSF 180 in '44, 182 in '45 and finally with 183 in '46.

2029 Chatham/Lowestoft
2054 Port Edgar/Vernon
2257 Trinidad 1944/Harwich 1945
2258 Trinidad 1944/Lowestoft 1945
2279 Peterhead 1945
2280 Peterhead 1945

There is a mention in some of the records of Minesweeping Flotilla 155, but there is no indication of any of the 150 vessels being attached to that Flotilla. The 155th is said to have operated out of Yarmouth in 1943 and Dover in 1946.

BYMS FLOTILLAS AT HOME

	1942	1943	1944	1945	1946	1947

150 xxxx PO--------------------------YA----------CO---------DO

155 xxxxxxxxxxxxxxxxYA --------------------------------------DO

157 xxxxxxxxxxxxxxxxYA---

159 xxxxxxxxxxxxxxxxxGR----------NIF-----------------------DO

163 xxxxxxxxxxxxxxxxxLO------------GR----------NWE--------LO

165 xxxxxxxxxxxxxxxxxxHA---

167 xxxxxxxxxxxxxxxxxxAR-----------NIF----------HA-----------NWE-----------

168 xxxxxxxxxxxxxxxxxxxxxxxxxxxxxxxNIF/PO-----EI-----------------

169 xxxxxxxxxxxxxxxxxxxxxxxxxxxxxxxxxxDO----------------------------

170 xxxxxxxxxxxxxxxxxxEF------------SW----------GR/SWE----------

180 xxxxxxxxxxxxxxxxxxxxxxxxxxxxxxxSW------------------------EI/SI-----------

182 xxxxxxxxxxxxxxxxxxxxxxxxxxxxxxxxxxxxxxxxxxxxxxxPO------------SWP/SI

183 xxxxxxxxxxxxxxxxxxxxxxxxxxxxxxxxxxxxxxxxxxxxxxxxxxxxxxxxxxxxxDO

LEGEND:

NIF	Normandy Invasion Force		SWE	South West Europe
SWP	South West Pacific		NWE	North West Europe
AR	Ardrossan		HA	Harwich
EI	East Indies		SI	Singapore
DO	Dover		SW	Swansea
PL	Plymouth		PO	Portsmouth
LO	Lowestoft		EF	Eastern Fleet
CO	Copenhagen		YA	Yarmouth
GR	Grimsby			

BYMS FLOTILLAS ABROAD

	1942	1943	1944	1945	1946	1947

```
151  xxxxxxxxxxxxxxxxxxxEF-------------------------MD-------------
152  xxxxxxxxxxxxxxxxxxWA/EF---------------------MD------------
153  xxxxxxxxxxxxxxxxxxxMD-----------------------------------------
154  xxxxxxxxxxxxxxxxxxxWA----------------------------
156  xxxxxxxxxxxxxxxxxxxMD-----------------------------------------
160  xxxxxxxxxxxxxxxxxxxLV-----------------------------------------
161  xxxxxxxxxxxxxxxxxxxxxxxxxxxxxxxxxEF----------------
162  xxxxxxxxxxxxxxxxxxxLV-----------------------------------------
164  xxxxxxxxxxxxxxxxxxxxxxxxxxxxxxxxxxxxWA--------------------------
166  xxxxxxxxxxxxxxxxxxxEF-----------------------------------------
170  xxxxxxxxxxxxxxxxxxxEF-----------------------------------------
```

LEGEND:

MD	Mediterranean	EF	Eastern Fleet
WA	West Africa	LV	Levant

BYMS FLOTILLAS OPERATIONAL ABROAD

MSF 151	MSF 152	MSF 153	MSF 154	MSF 156	MSF 160	
2005	2005(2)	2009	2010	2009(2)	2037	
2006	2006(2)	2019	2017	2027(2)	2047	
2007	2007(2)	2022	2018	2031	2048	
2008	2008(2)	2026	2021	2042	2065	
2011	2013	2027	2025	2049	2066	
2012	2014	2037(2)	2149(1)	2053(2)	2067	
2013(2)	2024	2077	2244(2)	2056(2)	2074(2)	
2014(2)	2028	2169(2)	2261(2)	2068(1)	2185	
2020	2043	2171		2072	2186	
2023	2044(2)	2172		2073(1)	2191(2)	
2024(2)	2045(2)			2073(3)	2212(1)	
2028(2)	2046(2)			2075(2)	2229	
2141(3)	2148(2)			2149(2)		
	2217(2)					
	2059(2)					
8	5	9	6	6	10	44

MSF 161	MSF 162	MSF 164	MSF 166	MSF 170		
2148(1)	2033	2043(2)	2060	2044		
2137(1)	2053(2)	2137(2)	2062	2045		
2217(1)	2056	2141(1)	2162	2046		
2223(1)	2068(2)	2142(1)	2168	2048(2)		
	2073(2)	2150(1)	2181	2049(2)		
	2074(1)	2225(1)	2194(1)	2051(2)		
	2075(1)	2246(1)	2203	2137(3)		
	2175(1)	2264(1)	2204	2142(2)		
	2190(2)	2282(1)	2232	2188(1)		
	2212(2)		2236	2189(1)		
	2240		2244(1)	2256(1)		
			2261(1)	2282(2)		
4	6	7	12	6	35	
					44	
					79	

BYMS FLOTILLAS OPERATIONAL AT HOME

MSF 150	MSF 157	MSF 159	MSF 163	MSF 165	MSF 167
2001	2034(1)	2032	2003(2)	2035	2038(2)
2002	2038	2052	2036	2041	2046(3)
2003	2039	2055	2039(2)	2051(3)	2047(2)
2004	2076(1)	2070	2040	2058	2048(3)
2015	2078(1)	2071	2044(3)	2076(2)	2050
2016	2141(2)	2157	2057	2202	2051
2029	2213(1)	2173	2078(2)	2205(1)	2061
2030	2214(1)	2211	2079	2206(1)	2069(1)
2059(1)	2221(1)	2253(2)	2080(1)	2233	2055(2)
2062(3)	2230(1)		2142(3)	2252	2156(2)
2214(2)			2161(1)	2261(2)	2182(1)
2221(2)			2167		2188(2)
2279(2)			2188(2)		2210
2034(2)			2194(2)		2230(2)
			2282(3)		2254
					2256(2)
9	9	8	7	8	7

MSF 168	MSF 169	MSF 180	MSF 181	MSF 182	MSF 183
2062(2)	2047(3)	2017	2015(2)	2021(3)	2021(4)
2063	2049(2)	2018(2)	2043(4)	2036(3)	2063(3)
2234(2)	2055(2)	2021(2)	2059(2)	2043(3)	2150(3)
2253(1)	2064	2036(2)	2061(2)	2059(3)	2182(2)
2254	2069(3)	2045(3)	2063(2)	2061(3)	
2279(1)	2152	2064(2)	2161(2)	2161(3)	
2280(1)	2154	2069(2)	2205(2)	2206(3)	
	2213(2)	2080(2)	2206(2)	2225(3)	
	2255(3)	2153(2)	2244(3)	2234(2)	
	2277	2225(2)		2258	
	2278	2246(2)		2264(2)	
	2284(1)	2284(3)		2284(2)	
5	6	1	–	1	–

Total ships at home 61 plus BYMS 2054 based at Port Edgar Total 62

NOTE: As ships were transferred so often from one flotilla to another, the moves are given in brackets. Those with no brackets stayed with the same flotilla throughout their service life.

An example would be BYMS 2063 permanently with MSF 168 while BYMS 2021 started with MSF 154 in West Africa then came home to join MSF 180 at Swansea in 1944 for a brief spell, then the 182 MSF at Plymouth in 1945 and finally ended up in the 183rd, at Dover in 1946.

The flotillas abroad suffered more or less the same fate.

BYMS FLOTILLA SERVICE AND FINAL DISPOSAL

Pt. No.	1942	1943	1944	1945	1946	1947	1948	1949
2001	PE	150			H	S		
2002	150				P	S		
2003	150		163		L	S		
2004	150				P	S		
2005	xxxxxxxx	151		152	M	A		
2006	xxxxxxxx	152		152	M	A		
2007	xxxxxxxx	151		152		A		
2008	xxxxxxxx	151		152	M	A		
2009	xxxxxxxx	153		156M	I	Anemone till 66		
2010	xxxxxxxx	154				S		
2011	xxxxxxxx	151			M	S	Joe Young/Belg	
2012	xxxxxxxx	151			M	I	Biancospino/66	
2013 ★	xxxxxx	152		151	M	E	Gaza Lost 50	
2014	xxxxxxxx	152		151		I	Geranio till 66	
2015	150			181	SB	S		
2016	150				P		S	
2017 ★	xxxxxx	154	180		K		C Lost 48	
2018	xxxxxxxx	154	180			A		
2019 ★	xxxxxx	153	Mined near Cotone Italy 19.9.43 CTL					
2020	xxxxxxxx	151			M	S		
2021	xxxxxxxx	154	180	182	183P	S		
2022 ★	xxxxxx	153	Mined Frejus Gulf, S. France 10.8.44					
2023	xxxxxxxx	151				I	Mughetto till 66	
2024	xxxxxxxx	152		151	M	I	Narciso till 66	
2025	xxxxxxxx	154			RU	S		
2026	xxxxxxxx	153			M	S	Calypso	
2027	xxxxxxxx	153			156M	I	Oleandro till 66	
2028	xxxxxxxx	152		151	M	E	Arish Sold 67	
2029	CH	LT		150	P		S	
2030 ★	150		Mined Le Havre 081044					
2031	xxxxxxxx	156			M	S		
2032	xxxxxxxx	159		D		FL	Tampammenpaa 58	
2033	xxxxxxxx	162			G		Kalymnos	
2034	xxxxxxxx	157		150		P/S		

BYMS FLOTILLA SERVICE AND FINAL DISPOSAL (contd)

Pt. No.	1942	1943	1944	1945	1946	1947	1948	1949
2035	xxxxxxxx	165			SH	E	Malek Faud S 67	
2036	xxxxxxxx	163	180	182	SB			
2037	(RCN)xx	160 153			M	I	Orchidea del 66	
2038	xxxxxxxx	157		167	HL		Marrsdiep S 62	
2039	xxxxxxxx	157	163		F		S	
2040	xxxxxxxx	163			P	RU/S		
2041	xxxxxxxx	165			SH	E/AL Darfour/Sidi Fradj		
2042	xxxxxxxxxxxxxxx		150	PO/RU		S		
2043	xxxxxxxx	152	164	181 182	RU		S	
2004	xxxxxxxx	170 152			163D	F	FL	Purunpaa
2045	xxxxxxxx	170 152	180		K/RU	S		
2046	xxxxxxxx	170 152	167		HL	Westerschelde del 48		
2047	(RCN)xx	160 167	169			F	FL	Katanpaa
2048	(RCN)xx	160	170			167	RU/HL Zuidersdiep 62	
2049	(RCN)xx	156	170 169		SH	F	FL	Vahterpaa
2050	(RCN)xx	156	170 167		HL/183	Hollandsh Diep del 58		
2051	xxxxxxxx	167	170		165P	S		
2052	xxxxxxxx	159			SH	S		
2053	★xxxxxxx	162	156	Mined off Porto Corsini, Italy 28.4.45				
2054	xxxxxxxx	PE						S/G Aura 62
2055	xxxxxxxx	159		169	SH	F	S	
2056	xxxxxxxx	162	156		162 G Karteria			
2057	xxxxxxxx	163			P	RU/S		
2058	xxxxxxxx	165			P	G Ariadni 61		
2059	★xxxxxxx	150		181 182	SP Lost on passage 24.8.46			
2060	★xxxxxxx	166			RU/reported scuttled 5.3.48			
2061	xxxxxxxx	167		181 182	RU	SB		

Pt. No. 1942	1943	1944	1945	1946	1947	1948	1949
2062 xxxxxxxx	166	168 150	D	RU	S		
2063 xxxxxxxxxxxxxx		168	181	183/SH	F	S	
2064 xxxxxxxxxxxxxx		169 180		K/RU	S		
2065 xxxxxxxx	160	Greek Paxi				del.69	
2066 xxxxxxxx	160	G Paralos		Greek Navy			
2067 xxxxxxxx	160	G Salaminia		Greek Navy		till	66
2068 xxxxxxxx	156			162/ G Lefkas		till	66
2069 (RCN)xx	167	180	169	SH	E Naharia S 67		
2070 xxxxxxxx	159			SH	F	S	
2071 xxxxxxxx	159			P	S		
2072 *xxxxxxx	156 Lost Beirut November 1943						
2073 xxxxxxxx	156	162		156M	I Begonia Customs		
2074 *xxxxxxx	162 160 G Kassos Mined off Piraeus 151044						
2075 xxxxxxxx	162			156M	E Kaisaria S 67		
2076 xxxxxxxx	157		165	SH	G Prokyon del 68		
2077 *xxxxxxx	153 Mined Gulf of Corinth 241044						
2078 xxxxxxxx	157	163		SH		G Vegas 57	
2079 xxxxxxxx	163			F		S	
2080 xxxxxxxx	163	180		K	S		
2137 (USA)xxx	160	164		HW S	Calisto		
2141 (USA)xxx	164	157		151M	I Dalia Customs 66		
2142		164		163SH	I Azalia del 66		
2148 xxxxxxxx	161		152	FM	A		
2149 (USA)xxxxxxxxx		154	WV	156M	E Rafah		
2150 (USA)xxxxxxxxx		164	YM	183SH	I Gardenia		66
2152 xxxxxxxx	169			P	S G Kleio 67		
2153 *xxxxxxx	169	180		KRU	CTL		
2154 xxxxxxxx	169		HWRU		S		
2155 (RCN)xx	156 167			HL	Vlliestroom	S 62	
2156 (RCN)xx	156 167		HL Texelstroom del 58				
2157 xxxxxxxx	159			P	S		

BYMS FLOTILLA SERVICE AND FINAL DISPOSAL (contd)

Pt. No.	1942	1943	1944	1945	1946	1947	1948	1949
2161	xxxxxxxx	163	181	182	FM	S in USA		
2162	xxxxxxxxxxxxxx		166		FM	S in USA		
2167	xxxxxxxx	163			D	F	S	
2168	xxxxxxxx	166			U	SB		
2171	ʌʌʌʌʌʌʌʌ	153			G Kefalinia	del 66		
2172	xxxxxxxx	153			G Kerkkyra			
2173	xxxxxxxx	159			D	F	S	
2174	xxxxxxxx	162	156		M	S Sliema/Sidquisem/		
2175	*xxxxxxxx	162	156			E Tor wrecked 0463		
2181	xxxxxxxx	166			SP RU	SB		
2182	xxxxxxxx	167		BK	183 SH		S	
2185	xxxxxxxx	G Afroessa			Greek Navy			
2186	(RCN)xx	160 G Leros			Greek Navy			
2187	xxxxxxxx	156			M	S Lord Strickland		
2188	(RCN)xxxxxxxx		170		167	HL Volkerak del 58		
2189	(RCN)xxxxxxxx		170		163D	S		
2190	xxxxxxxx	156	162G		Simi	del 66		
2191	*xxxxxxxx	156	160G		Kos Mined 150444			
2194	(USA)xx	166 163			SH	I Tulipano del 66		
2202	xxxxxxxx	165			SH		S	
2203	xxxxxxxx166				FM	S in USA		
2204	xxxxxxxx	166			RU	SB		
2205	xxxxxxxx	165		181	SPU	SB		
2206	xxxxxxxx	165		181	182M	I Magnolia del 66		
2209	xxxxxxxx	156			G Zakynthos			
2210	(RCN)xxx	167			HL Borndiep		S 62	
2211	xxxxxxxx	159			SH	PL		
2212	(RCN)xx	160	162		156M	E Kordofan	S 67	
2213	xxxxxxxx	157		169	P	RU	S	
2214	xxxxxxxx	157		150	SH	S Clubship Rainham		
2217	xxxxxxxx	161		152	RU		S	
2221	xxxxxxxxxxxxxx		157	150	SH	S G Pigassos	del 68	
2223	xxxxxxxx	161		152	MY/RU	S		

BYMS FLOTILLA SERVICE AND FINAL DISPOSAL (contd)

Pt. No.	1942	1943	1944	1945	1946	1947	1948	1949
2225	xxxxxxxxxxxxxx		164		182MY/RU/	A		
2229	xxxxxxxx	160 G Patmos					del 66	
2230	xxxxxxxx	157		167	RU/HL Oosterschelde S62			
2232	*xxxxxxx	166			RU Scuttled			
2233	xxxxxxxx	165			SH		S	
2234	xxxxxxxxxxxxx		168	182	183P		RU/S	
2236	xxxxxxxx	166			SP/RU/A			
2240	xxxxxxxx	162			G Ithaki		del 66	
2244	xxxxxxxx	166	154	181	SP/MY/	S		
2246	xxxxxxxxxxxxx		164 180		K RU	S		
2252	xxxxxxxx	165			P	RU	S/G Thalia	
2253	xxxxxxxxxxxxx		168	159	SH	F	S	
2254	xxxxxxxxxxxxx		168	167	RU/HL Deurloo			S 62
2255	*xxxxxxx	169	Mined off Boulogne 051044					
2256	xxxxxxxxxxxxx		170 167	IN	183/SH			
2257	xxxxxxxxxxxxx		TR	HA	183	S/PL		
2257	xxxxxxxxxxxxx		TR	L182	MY/RU	A		
2261	(USA)xxx	166	154	165	P	S/G Andromeda	del 67	
2264	xxxxxxxxxxxxx		164	182	MY/RU	S		
2277	xxxxxxxxxxxxx		169		SH	I Fiordaliso	del 66	
2278	xxxxxxxxxxxxx		169		SH	I Primula	del 66	
2279	xxxxxxxxxxxxx		168	PH	150/SH	F	S	
2280	xxxxxxxxxxxxx		168	PH	183/S	I Verrbena	del 66	
2282	xxxxxxxxxxxxx		164 170		163/D	PL		
2284	xxxxxxxxxxxxx		169	182	180/K/RU	S		

2000 was added to the Pennant Numbers between December '43 & April '44

LEGEND:

A	American Army	AL	Algeria	B	Buckie
C	China	CTL	Complete total loss	CH	Chatham
D	Devonport	del	Deleted	E	Egypt
F	Falmouth	G	Greece	H	Hartlepool
HL	Holland	I	Italy	IN	Inverness
K	Hong Kong	L	Lowestoft	M	Malta
P	Pembroke	PE	Port Edgar	PO	Poland
PT	Peterhead	RU	Return USA	SH	Sheerness
SP	Singapore	S	Sold	SB	Subic Bay
TR	Trinidad				

Vessels marked ★ were lost or sunk due to enemy action.
Subic Bay is in the Philippines.

155

FINAL DISPOSAL

The undermentioned vessels were sold out of service and used in civilian roles. Some were given names and these are listed on page 157.

2001, 2002, 2003, 2004, 2010, 2011, 2016, 2020, 2021, 2025, 2026, 2029, 2031, 2034, 2039, 2040, 2042, 2045, 2051, 2052, 2054, 2055, 2057, 2062, 2063, 2064, 2070, 2071, 2079, 2080, 2137, 2154, 2157, 2161, 2162, 2167, 2173, 2182, 2189, 2202, 2203, 2213, 2214, 2217, 2221, 2223, 2233, 2234, 2246, 2252, 2253, 2256, 2279, 2284.

54

US Army:
2202, 2206, 2207, 2208, 2018, 2148, 2225, 2236, 2258

9

Malta:
2174, 2187

2

Italy:
2009, 2012, 2014, 2023, 2024, 2027, 2037, 2073, 2141, 2142, 2150, 2194, 2206, 2277, 2278, 2280.

16

Egypt:
2028, 2035, 2041, 2069, 2075, 2076, 2149, 2175, 2212

9

Finland:
2032, 2044, 2047, 2049

4

Greece:
2033, 2056, 2058, 2066, 2067, 2068, 2078, 2152, 2171, 2172, 2185, 2186, 2190, 2191, 2209, 2229, 2240, 2261

19

Holland:
2038, 2046, 2048, 2050, 2155, 2156, 2188, 2210, 2230, 2254

10

Poland:
2211, 2257, 2282

3

Malaya:
2244, 2264

2

Subic:
2015, 2036, 2043, 2061, 2168, 2181, 2204, 2205

8

Lost:
2013, 2017, 2019, 2022, 2030, 2053, 2059, 2060, 2072, 2074, 2077, 2153, 2232, 2255

14

Total   150

SHIPNAME OF BYMS

2009	Anemone	I	2011	Joe Young	M
2012	Biancospino	I	2013	Gaza	E
2014	Geranio	I	2024	Narciso	I
2026	Calypso	M	2027	Oleandro	I
2028	Arish	E	2032	Tampammenpaa	F
2033	Kalymnos	G	2035	Malek Faud	E
2037	Orchidea	I	2038	Marsdiep	H
2041	Darfour	E	2044	Purunpaa	F
2046	Westerschelde	H	2047	Katanpaa	F
2048	Zuidersdiep	H	2049	Vahterpaa	F
2050	Hollandsh Diep	H	2054	Aura	G
2056	Karteria	G	2058	Ariadni	G
2065	Paxi	G	2066	Paralos	G
2067	Salaminia	G	2068	Lefkas	G
2069	Naharia	E	2073	Begonia	I
2074	Kassos	G	2075	Kaisaria	E
2076	Prokyon	G	2078	Vegas	G
2137	Calisto	UK	2141	Dalia	I
2142	Azalea	I	2149	Rafah	E
2150	Gardenia	I	2152	Kleio	G
2155	Vliestroom	H	2156	Texelstroom	H
2171	Kefalinia	G	2172	Kerkyra	G
2174	Sliemaa/Sidqusem/Caramy	M	2175	Tor	E
2185	Afroessa	G	2186	Leros	G
2187	Lord Strickland/		2188	Volkerak	H
	Amiral de Joinville	M	2190	Simi	G
2191	Kos	G	2194	Tulipano	I
2206	Magnolia	I	2209	Zakynthos	G
2210	Borndiep	H	2212	Kordofan	E
2221	Pigassos	G	2229	Patmos	G
2230	Oosterschelde	H	2240	Ithaki	G
2252	Thalia	G	2254	Duerloo	H
2261	Andromeda	G	2277	Fiordaliso	I
2278	Primula	I	2280	Verrbena	I
					67

Italy:
Anemone, Biancospino, Geranio, Narciso, Oleandro, Orchidea, Begonia, Tulipano,
Primula, Verbena, Gardenia, Dalia, Magnolia, Fiordaliso, Azalea 15

Greece:
Aura, Paralos, Vegas, Leros, Patmos, Thalia, Kassos, Salaminia, Karteria, Ariadni, Lefkas,
Kleio, Kefalinia, Simi, Andromeda, Ithaki, Pigassos, Zakynthos, Kos, Afroessa,
Kerkyra, Prokyon, Paxi 23

Egypt:
Rafah, Kaisaria, Naharia, Kordofan, Tor, Arish, Gaza, Darfour, Malek Faud 10

Holland:
Texelstroom, Volkerak, Borndiep, Deurloo, Oosterschelde, Vliestroom, Westerscheld,
Zuidersdiep, Marsdiep, Hollandsh Diep 10

Malta:
Lord Strickland/Amiral de Joinville, Joe Young, Calypso, Sliema/Sidqusem/Caramy 4

Finland:
Vahterpaa, Katanpaa, Parunpaa, Yanpammenpaa 4

UK:
Calisto 1

Total 67

Chapter Eleven

The Final Countdown

It was not everybody's good fortune (or was it misfortune?) to have been engaged in what some might like to call the heroics of war...meaning in the battle line. There were men from all walks of life, as history (and indeed letters from those who survived) has shown, who served in many capacities in what can only be described as very remote areas of the United Kingdom and abroad, who were involved in nothing more or less than the routine sweeping of those lanes which were vital for the survival of the country and indeed the winning of the war.

There were those ships and crews from Leith and Granton on the River Forth of the 137th. Minesweeping Flotilla.. MMS's 36. 83. 260. 279. 280. 305 and 307.

MMS's 305 and 260 had a couple of years with the 104th. MSF, assisting with the 'D' Day landings as indeed had MMS 307 for a year in 1944, but for the most part that flotilla swept a total of 2,500 miles of water in the Forth area alone.

MSF 107 consisted in 1942 of seven vessels, MMS's 72,110,115,149,150,176 and 181, and spent its time keeping the lanes clear in the Northern Ireland and River Clyde areas, offering a incident free run for the liberty ships arriving from the USA with much needed stores and equipment. The flotilla lost six ships to other flotillas almost immediately it was formed, leaving MMS 72 to 'hold the fort' for a year in 1943. The 116th. MSF served in the Northern hemisphere of Scotland at Scapa Flow in 1944, consisting of three solitary craft MMS's 285, 286 and 290 in a very isolated situation.

Scapa was no holiday centre even in the peak of summer. The work was routine...out sweep...in sweep, day in day out, a monotonous dreary rigid routine offering very little in the way of satisfaction, let alone glory!

Mines were seldom detonated if at all in those latter days, but the work had to go on in spite of being fed up with one anothers' faces, habits and cramped quarters. There was little to attract anyone ashore, but perhaps on the whole they were the lucky ones, who went home when it was all over.

When the war finally came to its close, first with Germany in 1945, then with Japan the year following, the majority of the Royal Naval Patrol Service personnel anxiously awaited, like most others in uniform, for their demobilisation number to come up.

It was then a case of winding their weary way home, some travelling by boat from various ports in the Mediterranean where their ships had been 'paid off',and the crews surplus to requirememnts, to places like Marseilles, there to board a rattling old train for a two-day journey across France to Toulouse, and thence by

Hulks Whitewall Creek, Kent

MMS 298 Hulk, Portsmouth

boat to a utility 'demob' suit and home.

Many had spent the majority of the war years seeking to eliminate these horrors of the deep the magnetic, acoustic and oyster mines, and serving on many of the small craft which, apart from the Dunkirk episode, did not make the headlines.

Their craft were, in the main, handed over to the allies, who were requested to sweep their own waters, still infested with mines of all categories, lying outside the swept and cleared channels which the flotillas, because of the lack of both time and ships, had not tackled.

There were of course hundreds of ships at the end of the war. Minesweepers galore – far too many for the job – but all of which came too late. They were needed at the start and we were found wanting, certainly in the area of minesweeping, as this book clearly shows. We were not prepared, and as a result nearly did not make it.

Many ships went to France on loan;

MMS's 9(D252), 21(D361), 47(D251), 118(D262) and 116(D261) were already manned by French naval personnel.

They were joined by MMS's 49(D377), 67(D375), 91, 204, 213(D378), 220(D373), and 221(D371).

Belgian naval crews commanded MMS's 75, 79, 112, 182(M940), 187(M941), 188(M(942), 189(M943), 191(M944), 193,(M945) and 266(M946), while Denmark retained MMS's 36, 83, 84, 263 and 207.

Others such as MMS's 1(Chimarra), 5(Mikonos), 46(Tepelini), 53(Korytsa), 58(Argyrokastion), 143(Thios), 144(Tinos), 310(Andres) and 313 (Syros) went to Greece.

Holland too had her share of sweepers in this class, MMS's 54(Marken 2),[MMS 227(Marken 1) was sunk], 138(Putten), 173(Texel), 226(Vlieland), 231(Ameland), and 234(Terschelling),[this was the second ship named Terschelling, the first being MMS 174 which was returned to the Royal Navy in 1942], 237(Beveland), and 292(Rozenberg).

Italy borrowed fourteen vessels namely MMS's 10, 32(DR202), 34(DR203), 35(DR204), 48(DR205), 50(DR206), 99, 100, 102, 104, 105, 135(DR212), 167(DR213), 172(DR214), and 185(DR215), [DR stands for Dragamine, the Italian word for minesweeper}.

India had ten vessels MMS's 130, 132, 145, 148, 131, 151, 154, 97, 98, and 129 and Malta three 34, 35 and 172.

Most of these ships eventually returned to the U.K. following extensive sweeping operations in the areas to which they had been assigned.

For the record there were a few other named MMS's, for instance 88(Bartin) which went with MMS's 63, 65, 140 and 150 to Turkey.

Also MMS'S 141 and 142 were named Burin and Cottel. MMS'S 238,239,240 and 241 were named Fichot, Jude, Quirpon, and St. Barbe. Whether they were known by these names during their active service, each serving with different flotillas, is difficult to determine, but it it likely that having been given the names

MMS 1728(228)   MMS 1586(86)

Seamoor ex MMS 86

in Canada where they were built, they probably reverted to their Pennant numbers in order to avoid any confusion. All these ships served out of Grimsby and with the Normandy Invasion Force.

Most of the craft mentioned in this book were disposed of in 1946, sold out of service as no longer of value, to the breakers yards like Pounds of Portsmouth who was in the ideal and most convenient place to acquire such ships if required.

The breakers were concerned in the main with making a quick turn over, either by a straight sale which was more beneficial, or through the laborious task of removing anything that would sell on the memorabilia market. Indeed everything made of metal, most of which was copper and brass, was stripped out.

Some however, though not many, escaped the humility of the breaker's yard. The longest survivors in service were those with the Russian navy, MMS's 90, 202, and 212, operational till 1961.

The Air Ministry had four for use with their Air Sea Rescue Squadrons, MMS's 86(Seamoor), 245(Airmoor III), 247(Airmoor I), and 256(Airmoor II), who were probably the best people to take these vessels in hand, being as they were, expensive to run and maintain.

But it was inevitable that most of these unique craft should disappear from the scene. In all there were forty-three losses in one way or another, some as has already been mentioned, lost before they even touched the water, in places like Singapore, Burma, and Hong Kong, where members of the Commonwealth were doing there bit to help the war effort. There were thirteen cancellations.

In 1951, five years after the war had finished there was a total of 60 MMS's in service with the Royal Navy, 26 active, two with the Royal Naval Volunteer Reserve, two in training and 30 in reserve, most of them being laid up at Chatham on the River Medway.

The line up was as follows:

32, 34, 35, 36, 48, 56, 50, 57, 69, 79, 83, 84, 86, 99, 100, 102, 103, 104, 105, 106, 109, 110, 135, 167, 172, 181, 185, 224, 228, 233, 236, 261, 263, 271, 272, 275, 283, 285, 286, 288, 289, 290, 294, 296, 297, 301 and 307.

Italy by this time had returned all the vessels they had on loan, while Greece still retained eight.

Four craft were allocated to Israel, but the Pennant numbers are not known.

Russia had three already mentioned and Turkey also three. Out of the ten which had gone to India, only three remained MMS's 130, 132 and 154.

Pakistan was the proud possessor of two MMS's 129 and 131. Belgium retained seven, Burma two, MMS's 197 and 201, while Bermuda used MMS's 222 (Amber) and 223 (Jade) for ferry services in that part of the world. MMS 10 was renumbered TRV20 and used as a torpedo recovery vessel and 217 utilised as a mine location ship.

This strength was maintained even when the Ton Class Minesweeper was introduced into service in 1952, through until 1956 when it was reduced to 25 craft, which included all those(asterisked) which had returned from overseas:

MMS's 5★, 36, 46★, 50, 53★, 56, 57, 79, 84, 86, 109, 132★, 144★, 154★, 181, 228, 233, 261, 272, 283, 286, 289, 297, 301 and 307.

All these ships were allocated new Pennant Numbers in so far as they were prefixed by 15,16, and 17. Pennants 1–99 were prefixed by 15 making 23 into 1523, the next 100 up to 199 by 16 making 123 into 1623. 307 became 1807.

Why these were changed it is not known. It may have been simply to bring them into line with the Ton Class Sweepers all of which had four figures in the numbers, as indeed had the Motor Launches.

By 1957 the Admiralty had disposed of MMS's 5, 53, 57, 109, 144, 228, 261, 272, 283, 301, and 307, leaving the sum total of fourteen ships in service.

Another seven went in 1958 and the last four MMS's 56, 79, 132, and 154 making their final bow in 1959.

Those in the Netherlands were all struck off in 1958, as were those in Turkey. The Russian trio were deleted in 1962, being the longest serving MMS's with any Navy.

So the history of the 'Mickey Mouse' is brief, but in many ways heroic.

Not all however have disappeared, as research into their background has revealed. If one cares to take a trip to California they might just get a glimpse of a luxury vessel that looks strangely like a 'Big Mickey' or a BYMS as some would claim. Up till a few years ago she belonged to the actor John Wayne, who, just before his death, sold her to a Californian lawyer.

She is called the 'Wild Goose.'and is still afloat although somewhat different from the original.

John Wayne's Wild Goose ex BYMS

Elizabeth Smit ex MMS 54 Holland 1982

MMS 54 was sold to the Netherlands Navy and renamed Marken, ending her active service with the Dutch Sea Scouts. This vessel was given a new lease of life, following her purchase by a shipbuilder by the name of Smit from Muiden in Holland. The 54 is now a three masted barquentine used on regular charter cruises on the Ijsselmeer. Her name 'Elizabeth Smit'.

MMS 46 was sold out of service to the shipbreakers Pounds of Portsmouth, and from there, contrary to the information received that she had been stripped out and 'burned up', was sold to Messrs. Caledonian MacBrayne of Greenock in Scotland in 1957.

She was converted into a ferry boat, renamed the 'Loch Arkaig, and served that company until 1982, faithfully transporting people from the mainland at Mallaig to the Islands of Rum and Egg and beyond.

She was holed during an extra low tide, by a projection on the jetty, and sold off to the breakers as a total loss. That would seem to have been the end of the journey for the old '46', but no!

She was sold to someone in Dubai and set sail for that destination from Milford Haven in September of 1982, calling on the way at Gibralter where she must have taken some respite on her journey from Greece back to the U.K. in 1951 which was also in the month of September.

Loch Arkaig never reached her destination for on the 13th. of the same month she foundered off Almeria in Southern Spain in a very deep and dangerous zone.

One member of the crew was lost. It is not known what the weather was like, but the incident is listed under number 8507016 in Lloyd's Register. And there the 'Fighting 46' as the crew named her, ended her valiant days.

And valiant they were, assisting to clear the channels for the heavy 'battle waggons' and indeed the harbours and canals for much needed supplies. And not too far from the place where she is now at rest.

MMS 1791(291), sold to a Mr. Pierce of Canvey Island, lies, or should it be said, that the remains of another valiant ship lies, on the banks of the River Medway, where if the truth is known many of these vessels ended their day, as the photograph of Whitewall Creek shows (page 159).

She kept the lanes clear on the western shores of Britain and joined forces with others in the Normandy Invasion. She has been used as a houseboat, now almost a wreck, but still with her mast clearly visible from Rochester Bridge facing upstream on the starboard side.

Not far away downstream at Stoke Creek lies the only remaining vessel of her kind and the only one which bears any kind of resemblance to the original design.

MMS 191 was discovered and that is the only word to describe it, during the research stages of this book in 1978.

Following extensive inquiries as to the possible whereabouts of any of these unique vessels, MMS 191 was found, unrecognised by the many people who saw her from day to day, lying on the mud in Otterham Quay. There was nothing found aboard the vessel to say what ship she in fact was. Somewhat disguised by a false funnel, plus the fact that the mast had been removed, she was identified by the writer by the unmistakeable shape of her bow and stern.

She is now in the process of being restored for posterity, being unique in so far as she is the only remaining vessel of her class. She lies safely at Stoke Creek. There has been a long holding operation by the MMS Trust, but it is just that and no more.

What the Trust has done has been amateurish in the extreme, but the main objective is to try and keep her afloat until, hopefully, the right nail is struck and someone comes along with the necessary cash to make a first class job of the restoration.

Stoke Creek is not the best of places to be, but because of the generosity of the owner of the site, she can be kept there free of charge. She is subject to winds and tides and all kind of weather conditions which make working conditions very difficult indeed.

As far as is known, MMS 191 served all her war years out of Harwich with the 118th. Minesweeping Flotilla, being involved finally in Operation Kalendar, already mentioned in a previous chapter.

She was ordered in September 1941, completed in May 1942, and commissioned by a Belgian crew under the command of Lieutenant Commander H.A.G. Ceulemans, who until mid-1990 was alive and well and residing at Frinton-on-Sea in Essex, not too far from where his old ship peacefully lies, and where she may end her days.

Built by the MacDuff Engineering and Shipbuilding Co. of MacDuff in Scotland, and who are still building ships to this day, she is basically sound and afloat, although needing regular weekly visits to keep the bilges dry.

How is it known that the ship is in fact MMS 191?

A number was discovered painted on her port bow under many layers of old paint. This was painstakingly scraped off with a penknife and the number M944 was revealed which proved to be according to official records, the Pennant number given to MMS 191 on her transfer to the Belgian Navy following hostilities.

So here, with this ship, we have the last of the line. It is hoped that she will prove to be a worthwhile project for restoration, for as the last of a unique breed of vessel, whose story is partly told in these pages, it is important that she is kept, as indeed other vessels are being restored, to show future generations what their forefathers did to help keep the freedom and the peace in this and other lands, and often under very difficult conditions.

People today do not believe that 20 men lived, ate and slept in such conditions, but it is a fact, for I served in two other ships just like her . . .

MMS 191 under restoration 1991

Loch Arkaig ex MMS 46

MMS 944 ex 191 Belgium

167

Chapter Twelve

Conclusion

While this book is written primarily as a record of the development, design, and deployment of the 105 foot Motor Minesweeper, it is equally aimed at what might be termed as the inefficiency of the War Office or would it be better to say the government of the day, in being unable to provide the resources required to meet the problems which undersea warfare presented and in particular in the area of mine clearance.

A great deal was done, but it was all too late, and inadequate. During the year of grace earned by Mr. Chamberlain's attempts to keep the wolf at bay, there was little done to provide even the basic necessities for a wartime minesweeping programme. It seems that there were many who did little or nothing to meet the urgent requirements of day to day channel clearance.

Most of the craft designed for the job became effective only long after the war commenced. A brief inspection of any Naval book on the subject of the availability of ships tells the same tale.

True, things gathered momentum after a while, but at the beginning we had virtually nothing to cope with the mine menace, and when it did come it was all a bit of a 'hit and miss' affair, even right up to the end of the war.

When the magnetic mine (our own invention) was discovered, it brought about an air of confusion, and as the enemy perfected and developed it with his delayed action mechanisms and clocks, then introducing the acoustic and pressure mines, we ought to have been able to envisage what he was likely to do next, but that did not seem to be the case.

A reader somewhere will probably get up on his hind legs and claim that this is not so, but to date, the records say differently.

Much of the information passed to magazines such as War Illustrated contained a lot of 'eye wash', supposedly for propaganda purposes which was necessary at the time, but the truth reveals the shortfalls in our preparation and equipment.

It was not the Navy's fault. They did the best they could with the equipment provided, but it was difficult in the extreme to cope with crews who sometimes did not know one end of a ship from the other.

The effectiveness of mine warfare can be seen when whole flotillas of ships cannot move, and are paralysed until the danger is removed.

It is said that all one needed to do, even today, is to drop an unidentified object into a shipping channel and *everything* stops for tea! Nothing must move till the object, which could be an old 40-gallon drum, is identified and removed.

Grand Harbour in Malta in 1942 was a prime example. The story of the Baltic Evacuation in 1945, is another, as the Germans sought to transport 62,000 refugees from East Prussia and Danzig through those waters to safety.

The Royal Air Force flew 750 sorties over the area and dropped 3,211 mines, sending to the bottom of the ocean 112 ships amounting to 304,712 tons.

When the Falklands crisis reared its ugly head, it was fortunate for the British assault force that the Argentinians did not have any of the waterways heavily mined.

There would have been no need for the Exocet missile! It may be of course that those of us who stand on the outside are not aware of the defence arrangements made by Argentina, but the accounts given of the engagement reveal little or no problems with sea mines.

A few pressure mines around the shore line would have stopped any invasion fleet in its tracks. That may be a bald statement from one who is not 'au fait' with the secrets of the Ministry of Defence, who may very well have had the necessary equipment to deal with such dastardly underwater weapons, but if it was anything like that used in clearing the Suez Canal, operating in virtually peacetime conditions, and free to search the waters without too much hindrance, and which proved to be a slow and laborious task, a different tale may have been told.

The news that four sea-going metal hulled trawlers were on their way to deal with the minesweeping task in the Falklands, suggested that either someone had once again seriously underestimated the task involved, or information had been received that sea mines were not going to present a problem.

The fact that it didn't, proves nothing. Cards of varying sorts are often held up contestants' sleeves, and we might have been caught out once again with our trousers around our ankles.

There is a great deal of talk in defence circles about the de-escalation of nuclear weapons, and the fact that something positive is at last being done about the situation is to be applauded.

Conventional ways of defence means a strong navy and the ability to deal with those who would from time to time, seek to create havoc with peaceful nations, sometimes with weapons we know nothing about. The Iraqi conflict is just one such incident, and it is no use stating that mines presented no problem.

Damage amounting to millions of pounds was caused not with any kind of sophisticated weapon like the pressure or magnetic mine, but with the old barnacle covered moored affair, which is still a menace if it happens to get in the way.

The combined efforts of NATO were needed to keep the channels clear and even then, and quite contrary to any news in Britain that there were no casualties, it was reported that the American assault ship *Tripoli* was severely damaged by a mine, with a 16 x 20 foot hole below the waterline.

An influence mine put the cruiser *Princeton* out of commission, damaging one of the propellors and opening a large crack in the hull. Three sailors were injured. The minesweepers again did an excellent job, but the opposition was slight, and they were able to get on with the task without fear of interruption.

Those of us who are not experts or have no up-to-date knowledge of mine warfare, perhaps ought not to be too critical, or indeed too inquisitive, but it is hoped that if a conventional war did take place, we would not be quite so long in producing the goods as we were last time.

SALUTE TO THE WAVY NAVY

SOMETIMES I SHUDDER WHEN I THINK

OF ALL THE PAPER AND THE INK,

I SACRIFICED TO DON THIS JACKET,

AND GET MYSELF INTO THIS RACKET.

YES, I AGREE IS SEEMS ABSURD

THAT JOBS LIKE THESE WE HAVE INCURRED;

BUT WHEN ONE SEES THE MANY FAULTS

OF STRAIGHT-STRIPED MEN, AND THOSE OLD SALTS,

I'M GLAD TO THINK THAT IN THE NAVY

I WEAR MY BRAID, NOT STRAIGHT, BUT WAVY.

Group photo of Newhaven Skippers reading from left to right.
Top row: J.H.M. McKay, S/Lt G.B. Woods, S/Lt R.B. Anderton, S/Lt H. Arbuckle,
Lt J. Comfort, Lt G. Miles, Lt J. Randall, S/Lt Whitling, Lt McEchnie, S/Lt S. Blyth, S/Lt Smith.

Bottom row: Lt H.E. Williams, Lt R. Neville, Lt Rogers, Lt/Cdr Leyland, (Unidentified)
Lt/Cdr Hansen, Lt Mackie, Lt Beaver, Lt J. Whyte.
Not in photo but belonging to the Newhaven flotillas:
Lt R. Copper, Lt J. Bowie, Lt/Cdr H. Galsworthy, Lt/Cdr J. Harrison DSC.

Chapter Thirteen

Postscript

Recent research has revealed additional information regarding some of the Motor Minesweepers following hostilities.

In late 1951 there were six MMS's brought out of reserve to be refitted at Gravesend, for service in the Korean war and to be based at Singapore.

The squadron as it was called, consisted of

MMS's 1556 (ex 56), 1536 (ex 36),1579 (ex 79) and half-leader,
1786 (ex 286), 1584 (ex 84) and 1797 (ex 297).

Following the refit which was a hurried effort, the dispatch of the squadron being no more than a gesture of support at the time, the ships set sail on the 28th. January 1952.

The story is taken up with notes from Mrs. Nelson Curryer's late husband's letters. He was the C.O. of MMS 1579, and half-leader.

The first problem was that 1579's engine (an eight cylinder Crossley 2 stroke) would not start (the author knows something of that problem and hopes that they did not have to revert to putting a bucket of lighted diesel under the air intake).

They managed to get away an hour later, heading for Harwich and testing the guns en route. Minor engine troubles persisted, plus a problem with jammed steering which resulted in the need for a tow from a Harwich tug.

After repairs and trials, on February 27th. another attempt was made to get away and after encountering fog and haze finally arrived at Portland on the 29th.

The squadron eventually set off on the 4th. March in a force 6 wind and rough seas, escorted by the frigate HMS *Widemouth Bay*, having rendezvoused at Polperro, in Cornwall on the southern English coast.

It was not too long before the 1579's steering gave up again and took an hour to fix. Then there was trouble with the electrics, caused by sea water coming over the ship's side, when oil lamps had to be used.

Power was restored with an emergency 'lash-up'. The weather became so bad that the squadron had to run for shelter on the Spanish Coast at a place called Ria del Barquero.

Following a let up in the weather and repairs being carried out by the staff of the frigate, the squadron headed south, but not for long. On the next day the ship had trouble with the stern gland, and was taken in tow for two hours while repairs were effected, arriving in Gibraltar on the 11th. March.

The programme was to set sail from Gibraltar on the 17th. to Malta, following repairs, where they hoped to arrive by the 23rd, then it was on to Port Said, with an ETA of April 1st.

That was the plan, but owing to a slight hitch meaning that 'lubricating oil was spouting up the funnel', plus stern gland trouble once again, plus a force 8-9 gale, the squadron headed for Bizerta after two days at sea.

There, the French Naval dockyard offered first class facilities for their troubles. Leaving Bizerta on the 20th. the ships after 24 hours steaming time safely anchored in Malta.

After a great deal of discussion about the defects in 1579, spares now being required, it was decided that the five other ships should sail and leave 1579 to follow after the monsoon season.

But they were not without their troubles. Four of them arrived in Aden on the 27th. April. MMS 1536 was reported as having caught fire and others with stern gland problems.

1579 was dogged with further troubles, but finally made the passage to the Far East spending her last days in China.

The whole sorry mess for such it was, is summed up by Lt. Nelson Curryer, when he says in his notes.

"These ships were built 11 years ago to sweep quietly in and out of ports, on which ports they were based and to which they returned at the end of each day's sweeping. They are now older than they were ever expected to be, and they are being used as fleet units, sent on ocean trips and expected to carry out prolonged sweeps away from their base.....that is what is wrong with them."

Nevertheless in spite of what the lieutenant says, the ships proved to be very worthy of the tasks they were called upon to do. One would guess that one of the major difficulties lay in the hastiness of the refit at Gravesend.

MMS 1579 ex 79 on passage to Korea 1951

This book reveals that most of the vessels did many sweeping hours, some travelling across the Atlantic and others making the journey out into the Mediterranean without too many hiccups. It could be that 1579 was something of a rogue vessel.

The owners of the Celtic Lord mentioned in this book, claimed that she was the finest seagoing ship they ever had, and she operated among the North Sea oil rigs until the mid eighties, so they can't all have been bad! One of the questions that might be asked in this connections is,

"Why was it necessary to send the UK ships out to Korea when there were already eight MMS's in Malta with the 108th. MSF?"

Surely it would have been the wise thing to send six from Malta, with the 108th. being supplemented from the UK after the ships had been tested thoroughly?

Not knowing what the circumstances were at that time, perhaps it is better not to judge, for indeed it is all water under the bridge.

Celtic Lord ex Seamoor ex MMS 86.
Scrapped Inverkeithing 1982.

Addendum I

Additional information has come to hand regarding some of the Motor Minesweepers mentioned in this book.

MMS 6 was broken up in 1982 after being utilised as a dry cargo vessel by the owners Andreassen of Stamsund in Norway.

MMS 92 was broken up in 1980 following a spell in fishing in Norway.

MMS 135, sold to Magro Brothers in Malta in 1955 was renamed *Trevisan* in 1970 then the *Queen of Peace*. On route to Benghazi in North Libya from Reggio Calabria on the southernmost tip of Italy, she foundered and was lost in the Gulf of Sirte.

MMS 172 was sold to Joseph Gasan of Malta in 1956 then to some unknown buyer in Greece in 1957.

MMS 247 was broken up in 1983 in Turkey.

MMS 261 is owned by W.A. Mason from Preston in the UK. No trace of the owner.

MMS 277 is at present owned by FORDYAR LANDGSTYRI and is used as a ferry in the Faroe Islands, but see note below.

MMS 279 still sails under the name of *Frydenlund* out of Kirkeveien in Norway. The owner cannot be traced.

MMS 285 (Usus) is owned by Ali Anatjeh of Khorranshaht, Iran.

MMS 1051 named *Mina C* is owned by Brian A. Johnston, in Canada and is still operational.

MMS 1086 once named *Franklin Rooseveldt* and now goes under the name of *Rezak*, can be found in Split, Yugoslavia.

BYMS 2038 now *Siriri* is still operating in Brazil and owned by a Professor Nelson Ribeira. No trace of the owner. Mail returned.

BYMS 2026 named *Calypso* is owned by Captain Cousteau of underwater photography fame, who made the purchase from J. Gasan of Malta. Mail sent to the owner has been returned.

BYMS 2031 was renamed MV *Nanridi* by A. Theuma of Malta in 1947 and chartered to J. Gasan of Malta for ferry work. In 1950 she sailed to Messina and was sold to an M. Galea of Gibraltar, and renamed *Monte Carmelo*. She later sailed to Tangier and was captured off Palermo by the Italian authorities while attempting to smuggle tobacco into Italy. The vessel was confiscated.

BYMS 2044 is called *Paramera* and is the property of a company in Finland.

Pireaus in Greece is the base of BYMS 2252, owned by a company called Nashar Saudi Lines.

BYMS 2187 according to one source was sold to Anglia Shipping Company of Malta in 1947, renamed *Lord Strickland*★ and chartered by J. Gasan, providing

★Then *Amiral de Jointree* (see page 157).

temporary ferry facilities between Mgarr and Marfa. In 1948 she was doing the Malta/Syracuse run and was finally sold off to a company in Puerto Limon in 1952.

She was subsequently renamed *Admiral Strickland* then *Centaur*, and has her home in Houston Texas, where the present owner resides, according to Lloyd's Register.

Confirmation regarding the current state of *Wild Goose*, owned by John Wayne until his death, is being investigated, but it is known that the vessel, an ex-BYMS and now a luxury craft, is still in use on the coast of California.

Addendum II

Letters sent out in connection with the above craft have all come back, annotated "Return to sender", "not known", or "gone away", which would seem to bring the final curtain down on any vessels which might have survived. One bit of information came regarding MMS 277, which was bought by the Faroes Government, named *Tennan* and used as a passenger carrying ferry on domestic routes. She was subsequently used as a guard and life-saving ship around the islands and sold to a margerine factory in Thorshaven. She was finally disposed of in a package deal with another ferry by the name of *Trondur*, but the MMS was in such a bad shape that she was sunk. So ends the lesson. That was in 1968, so she did not do so badly as some.

To date the writer has explored every field known for information regarding these particular vessels. This book is the result, and it is hoped that it will prove helpful to those who served and indeed to any Naval historians who have found a gap in their information regarding the minesweeping activities of World War II. Indeed there are few in the British Navy of today who have ever heard of these craft. That is not their fault entirely, because the Royal Naval Patrol Service was never regarded as being an authentic part of the Royal Navy even though the White Ensign was proudly displayed on every ship.

APPENDIX A

CREWS BY SHIPS

Note: The names listed against the following vessels, have been gathered over a period of 12 years via many forms of correspondence, and not through any official channels. MOD is most reluctant to divulge such information.
It is regretted therefore that the lists are limited, and that many names have no reference either to the person's rank or to the trade in which he served.

MMS 1★ Dundas A.; Lt. B. Cross (CO).
MMS 2 Pearce H.; Watt J. (Cox); Price H.
MMS 3 Lt/Cdr. G. Winrow (CO); Young (Eng).
MMS 4 Barnett H. (Eng); Barber T. (Cox); Lt. D. Baddeley (C); Lt. B. Cross (No 1);
Lt. P. Brady; Lt. C. Holmes (CO).
MMS 5 Lt. Steel H. (CO); Lt. A. Sharpe; Sparkes R. (Stk); Lt. R. Christian; Lt. H. Soley;
Lt. A. Turner.
MMS 6★ Lt. T. Muir DSC (CO); Lt. G. Jones (CO); Bowman (Sig); McLoughlan; Midlane (C/Eng);
Groomsbridge (Sea/Gnr); Harris (Stwd); Chester (L/Sea); Griggs; Page (Tel); Reid (Sea);
Lt. P. Daniel; Lt. E. Lacey; Lt. E. Bell; Lt. K. Swayne.
MMS 7 Watson T. DSM; Murray DSM; Lt. G. Hardy (CO); Lt. R. Privett; Lt. A. Sharpe;
Lt. A. Turner; Lt. Steel H.
MMS 8★ Atkinson; Messenger J. (Stk); Jones H.J. (L/Ck); Butler J. (W/M); Parsons H.C.;
Vincent; Lt. J. Barratt (CO).
MMS 9 Laity DSM; Richardson H.J. (W/M0); Canham A.; Parsons H.C.
MMS 10★ Earl (Cox); Jones E.G. (Tel); Holden F.; Lt. D. Wolff (CO); Mancini M. (Eng);
Lt. P. Quine (CO); Lt. P. Palette (No 1).
MMS 11
MMS 12★
MMS 13★ Fisher E.; Turner L. (W/M); Lt. G. Patience (C/O).
MMS 14★ Lt. J. Randell (CO); Dunn J.
MMS 15
MMS 16★ Trundley P. (Sig); Jones W.E. (Eng); Iness K. (Cox); Glennie (C/Eng); Rousseau DSM (L/Sea);
Hunt (Stk); Harris (Sea/Gnr); Lt. Faulkner (No 1); Geddes W. (Cox); Monroe A. (C/Eng);
Fallo (L/Sea); Lacey (Sea); Higgenbottom (Sea); Ambller N. (Sig); Parsons H.
MMS 17 Osbourne G.; Mason A.; Vaughan L.
MMS 18 Easton T.N.
MMS 19 Lt. R. Snell (CO); Lt. Churchman (No 1); Lt. G. Fox (No 1); Lt. Lewis DSC:
Lt. D. bass (No 1); Melvin M.J. (Stk); Varley G. (C/Eng);   O'Shea (L/Sea);
Horseburgh J. (L/S); Scarlett G. DSM (L/Sea); McLeoud D. (Stwd); Taaylor J. (Sea);
Turner (Sea); Hartley (Sea); Pulford (Cook); Hunter (Tel); Reeves (Sig); Lack G.;
Petersen; Rousee; McLeod J. (Sea); Herriet R. (Sea); Noble J.
MMS 20 Fisher E.; Cotter.
MMS 21 Harrison DSM; Mercer G.
MMS 22 Sparkes R. (Eng); Lt. J. Easton (CO); Lt. W. Fautleyy; Lt. J. Simpson DSC & Bar.
MMS 23 Samford; Watson DSO (CO).
MMS 24★ Lt. Morrison (CO); Lt. Bell; Bishop (L/Sea); Splange K. (Sea); Jenkins (Stwd);
Hughes P.; Bond W. (Sea); Lt. Hawthorn; Mercer G.; Lt. Darton (CO); Farquar B. (Sea).
MMS 25 Lt/Cdr Warren (CO); Roach H.
MMS 26
MMS 27★ Jones, Roberts (Cox); Harvey (Sea); Lt. Worthington (CO); Crewdson J. (Tel).
MMS 28★ Lt. Stretton (CO); Lt. S. Smith (CO); Phillips J.; Hawkins (Cox).
MMS 29 Colyer DSM (L/Sea); McBain DSM (Eng); Lt. D. Stephenson (CO); Lt. F. Blowers;
Lt. J. Miller; Lt. J. Mitchell; Lt. J. Ridd.
MMS 30 Sandford; Lewis; Sparkes R. (A/C/Eng); Lt. W. Ellery (CO); Lt. F. Copestake);
Lt. Cdr T. Stobbs DSC; Lt. G. Swan; Lt. P. Ward.
MMS 31 Davidson G. (Eng); Lt. J. Plowright (CO); Sutherland W.; West D. (W/M); Dexter D.
MMS 32★ Sandford; Lt/Cdr F. Fails (CO).
MMS 33 Corp K. (Sig).

177

MMS	34★	Lt. B. Blackburn (CO); Lt. B. Abbott; S/Lt P. Quayle.
MMS	35	Cowen H.; Lt. Cookson (CO); Lt. Laidlaw (No 1).
MMS	36★	
MMS	37	Lt. M. Munro (CO).
MMS	38	Andrew C. (CO); Lt. J. Leney; Cadwalader (Cox); McKay (L/Sea); Brittain (Sea); Oram (Sea); Cooper (Stwd); Alexander (Stk); Winder (Sea); Clark.
MMS	39	Haddock H. (Sea).
MMS	40★	Maffey D. (Cook); King D; Davis DSM (L/Sea); Bugden DSM (L/Sea); Thorpe W.; Lt. N. Lewis (CO); Meyers H.
MMS	41	Mustard R.
MMS	42	Sandford; Ellis; Lt. Jones N. (CO).
MMS	43	
MMS	44	Lt. G. Fox (CO); Lt. H. Greenwood; R. Pamment (Tel); Peach (C/Eng); Kitchen (Stk); Bull (Stk); Watkins (Stk); Craig (W/M): Grace (Sea); Bedddows (Cook); Andrew (L/Sea); Ringshaw (Sea); Nightingale (Sea); Hodge (Sea); Mackinnon (Sea); Dobson (Sea); Bygrave (Stwd).
MMS	45	Dunn W.L.; Lt. Menzies; Lt. Beresford Smith (CO); Lt. E. Cash.
MMS	46★	Michael Melvin (L/Stk); Duncan (Eng); Thomas Russell (Sea); William main (Sea); Joseph Nice (Stk); Donald Rabjohn (Sig); Sydney Page (Sea); Lt. Smith (CO); John Bland (W/M); G. Cassar (L/Stwd); William Dale (Cox); Fred Godwin (Stwd); Henry Hall (Eng); Sydney Harris (L/Sea); Albert Huntley (Tel); rupert Issott (L/Stk); J. Jarvis (Tel); John Lownie (Eng); T. Lee (Sea); Angus MacLeod (Sea); George McGowan (Sea); Stanley White (Cook); No 1 from New Zealand; Lt. Every-Clayton; Lt. J. Raven.
MMS	47	Cuppage T. (CO).
MMS	48★	Holland I.
MMS	49	Sparkes R. (Eng); Lt. E. Fenn; Lt. J. Grundy; Lt. E. Nesbitt; Lt. L. Newham; Lt. L. Percival; Lt. J. Trundell; Lt. I. Webb.
MMS	50	Church F. (Cox); Lt. P. Reid (CO); Lt. N. Partington (No 1); S/Lt. W. Eardley (No 1); Duthie G. (C/Eng); Gledhill G. (C/Eng); Hyke F. (C/Eng); Willoughby W. (Stk); Dickson (Sig); Carr J. (W/M); Rawlinson G. Stwd); Redman J. (L/Sea); Cornwall J. (L/Sea); Carroll J. (Sea); Storey W. (Sea); Lightburn E. (Sea); Jackman R. (Sea); Perratt R.
MMS	51	
MMS	52	
MMS	53	Edwards F. (C/Eng).
MMS	54	
MMS	55	Thornbury M. (Stk).
MMS	56	Anderson (L/Sea); Travers J.; Gooding E.
MMS	57★	Webb E. (Sig); W.E. Allsopp (Eng); Lester R.; Kelly R.J. (Sea); Bradley (L/Sea); Wrey J. (Cox); Lt. J. Dussock (No 1); Insole J.; Wilson D. (Cook).
MMS	58★	Stone DSM (Eng); Earl A. (L/Sea).
MMS	59	Smith A.D. (W/M): Batty H.; Lt. F. Coggins (CO); Jock Porteous Hawk; Joe Heaton; Manchester F.; Pendlebury B.; McDowell R.; Pearson B.; Farrow.
MMS	60★	Humphries R. (W/M); Lewis DSM (Eng); Lt. Neville R. (CO).
MMS	61★	Lt. J. Randell (No 1); Lt. Hanson (CO); Parsons H.
MMS	62	Clementson A. DSM (C/Eng); Fearn H. (C/Eng); Wilson H. (Cox).
MMS	63★	Lt. D. Brigham (CO).
MMS	64★	Lt. Mackie (CO); S/Lt Whitling.
MMS	65	Brown K. (L/Tel); Lt. Alexander (CO); S/Lt. Powell (No 1); Lt. N. Edge; Sloan W. (C/Eng); Skinner (Cox); Nelson J. (Stwd); Brown G. (W/M); Patience A. (Sea); Johnson N. (Sea/Gnr); Bird (Cook); Gilmore (Sea); Adams (Sig); Gourley (Sea); Fallowner (Sea).
MMS	66★	Lt. Jones (CO); Pease B.; Small DSM; Harrison F.; Lt. J. Easton; Lt. E. Bellamy.
MMS	67	Cringle DSM (Stk); Lt. R. Copper; Lt. G. Miles.
MMS	68	Marshall G.; Hankey J.
MMS	69★	
MMS	70	

MMS 71	Lt. G. Gare (CO).	
MMS 72	Barron A.	
MMS 73★		
MMS 74	Lt/Cdr H. Drake (CO); Nixey H. (W/M); Brodie W. (Cox); Cameron J. (Stwd); Clarke C. (Sig); O'Brian T. (Stk); Davison R. (Stk); Williams S. (Eng); Johnson A. (Sea); Tarburn R. (Sea); Ashley G. (L/Sea); Wilkes J. (Sea); Ball J. (Eng); Jeffrey W. (Sea); Cunningham D. (Sea); England J. (Tel); Sharples J. (Cook); Lt. A. Niblick (CO).	
MMS 75	O'Donnell DSM (A/C/Eng); Lt. R. Bennett (CO).	
MMS 76		
MMS 77★	Smith.	
MMS 78	Richie DSM (Eng); Roach H.	
MMS 79★	Holdsworth DSM (Eng); Broad G. (Tel); Lt/Cdr. Collier J. (CO); Gawne H. (Cox); R. Creswell; Weaver N. (Sig).	
MMS 80		
MMS 81★	Lt. J. Bowie (CO); Weldon D.	
MMS 82		
MMS 83		
MMS 84	Lt. W. Kyle (CO).	
MMS 85	Yerrell F.G.	
MMS 86★	Lt. A. Chancellor (CO); Bray DSM (Stk); Sutherland.	
MMS 87	Allan A.	
MMS 88		
MMS 89	Lt. R. Rogers (CO).	
MMS 90	Lt. Dunwoodie DSM (A/CO); Lt. C. Warren (CO).	
MMS 91	Lt. R. Christian (CO); Ward (Sig); Lt. E. Packham.	
MMS 92★	Lt. S. Linder (CO).	
MMS 93	No crew; lost Singapore incomplete.	
MMS 94	No crew; lost Singapore incomplete.	
MMS 95	No crew; lost Singapore incomplete.	
MMS 96	No crew; lost Singapore incomplete.	
MMS 97	Indian Navy.	
MMS 98	Indian Navy.	
MMS 99		
MMS 100	Easton R.	
MMS 101	Rourke E.	
MMS 102★	Loundes J.; Lt. Thoburn (CO); Lt. Browell (No 1); Sutton L.; S/Lt. Simpson; Organ (L/Sea); Kidd (Tel); Bald L. (C/Eng); Solly (Cook); Harper A. (Stk); Demain-Stone A. (Cox); Kirkham J. (Eng); Brand P. (Stwd); Kimberley B. (Tel); Lewis T. (W/M); Watson A. (Sig); Lt. B. Pounds (CO); Strong F. (Sea/Gnr); Lt. McCallum (CO); S/Lt. Keating; Hinkin (L/Sea).	
MMS 103		
MMS 104		
MMS 105		
MMs 106★	Lt. C. Andrew (CO); Whelan (L/Sea); Williams (Eng); Barker (L/Sea); Gillies (Sea); Grayson (L/W/M); Clark (C/Eng); Bicknell (Cook); Bradbury K. (L/Sig); Treghurst (Sea); Smith (C/Eng); S/Lt P. Acott (No 1); Roy R. (Cox); Bowes (Stwd).	
MMS 107★		
MMS 108		
MMS 109★	Webb E. (Sig).	
MMS 110★	Jones N.; Ellis; Thorpe W.H.; Lt/Cdr N. Jones (SO); Boiston F.	
MMS 111	Lt. S. Rogers (CO); S/Lt Arbuckle.	
MMS 112★	May A.E.	
MMS 113★	Lt. D. Hackett (CO); Marlow D.; Taylor R.G. (Tel); Webb, G.; King D.	
MMS 114	Lt. D. Bass (CO).	
MMS 115	Lt. W. McLaughlin (CO).	
MMS 117	Lt/Cdr G. Johnson.	
MMS 118	Brennan B.	

179

MMS 119	Woods A.W.
MMS 120	
MMS 121	
MMS 122	
MMS 123	Lost on stocks. No crew.
MMS 124	Lost on stocks. No crew.
MMS 125	Lost on stocks. No crew.
MMS 126	Lost on stocks. No crew.
MMS 127	Lost on stocks. No crew.
MMS 128	Lost on stocks. No crew.
MMS 129	Indian Navy.
MMS 130	Indian Navy.
MMS 131	Indian Navy.
MMS 132	Indian Navy.
MMS 133	Lt. D. Jacobs (CO); Horn DSM (Eng).
MMS 134	Edginton H.
MMS 135★	Quennell P.
MMS 136	
MMS 137★	Lt. S. Linder (CO).
MMS 138★	
MMS 139	Royle H. (Sig); Pearce (Cox); Jones; Lt. B. Lewis (CO); Lt. B. Fidler.
MMS 140★?	
MMS 141	
MMS 142	
MMS 143	
MMS 144	
MMS 145	
MMS 146	No crew. Cancelled.
MMS 147	No crew. Lost on stocks.
MMS 148	
MMS 149	Humphries (L/Sea).
MMS 150	Lt. H. Greenwood (CO).
MMS 151	
MMS 152	No crew. Cancelled.
MMS 153	Lost on stocks.
MMS 154	
MMS 155	
MMS 156	Lost on stocks.
MMS 157	No crew. Cancelled.
MMS 158	No crew. Cancelled.
MMS 159	No crew. Cancelled.
MMS 160	No crew. Cancelled.
MMS 161	Lost on stocks.
MMS 162	Lost on stocks.
MMS 163	Lost on stocks.
MMS 164	Lost on stocks.
MMS 165	Lt. E. Hudson (CO); Lt. G. Lloyd.
MMS 166	Lost on stocks.
MMS 167	Robinson F.; Lt/Cdr/ Jensen.
MMS 168★	Lt. A. Tucker RNR DSC (CO); Lt. A. Watt (CO); C. Hughes (C/Eng); I. Andrew (Eng); E. Carter (L/Stk); Ewbank(L/Stk); Meenz (Tel); McGroarty J. (Sig); Harper (Cook); Parish (W/M); Jackson R. (L/Sea); Alexander E. (Sea); Clements H. (Sea); Ballantyne W. (Sea); Bennett P. (Sea); Smith R.
MMS 169	
MMS 170	Lt. R. Savage (CO);
MMS 171	
MMS 172	

MMS 173★	Lt. S. Linder (CO); Simpson J. (W/M).
MMS 174	Blackie V.; Lt/Cdr. J. Newstead (CO); Lt. Talbot; Coombs G. (Sig); Barnes J. (Sea); Myers A. (Sea); Palmer P. (Sea); Simmonds W. (Stwd); Marshall H. (Tel); Leigh P. (W/M); Treble F.
MMS 175	Harris DSM (C/Eng).
MMS 176	Midshipman J. McKay (E/O).
MMS 177	
MMS 178	Dexter, D.
MMS 179	
MMS 180	
MMS 181★	Lt. J. Grieve (CO); Lt. J. Alcorn (CO); S/Lt. C. Petersen (No 1); S/Lt. Ashley (No 1); Atkinson R. (Tel); Guthrie J. (Eng); Barrett N. (Stk); Corry J. (Sea); Kockleberg (Stk); Chatfield W. (Sea); Holt E. (W/M); O'Brien N.; Underwood G. (Sea).
MMS 182	
MMS 183	Smith H.; Gooding E.; Barnes G. (Tel).
MMS 184	
MMS 185★	Sargent G.; Lt. D. Laidlaw; Lt. D. Brigham (CO); PUrches B.
MMS 186	Cook R.
MMS 187★	Williams R.
MMS 188★	
MMS 189★	Turner F.
MMS 190	Simpson J. (W/M); Nind L.E.; Lt. C. Gotto (CO).
MMS 191★	Lt/Cdr H. Ceulemans (CO); DeGruyter R.; Rageart G.; Voss M.; Lt. Vervynck; Gollier; S/Lt. McEntegart.
MMS 192★	Lt. A. Christopherson (CO).
MMS 193★	
MMS 194	No crew. Cancelled.
MMS 195	No crew. Cancelled.
MMS 196	Blandford J. (Tel).
MMS 197	
MMS 198	
MMS 199★	Lt. I. Robertson (No 1); Whittaker R. (Eng); Reeves N. (W/M).
MMS 200★	Haines R. (Tel); Lt. Petheridge RNR (CO); Savage; Sommerville A. (Sig).
MMS 201	Lanfear D. (Tel); Vincent C.
MMS 202	Howard D. (L/Sea); Lt. I. Robertson (No 1); Lt. P. Daniel.
MMS 203	Lt. Ethridge DSM (A/CO).
MMS 204	Lt. F. Copestake (CO); Lucas H.G.; Sparkes R. (Eng); Lt. K. Smith.
MMS 205	Lt. G. Dargavel (CO); Lt. J. Hartnell; Lt. C. Hippisley; Lt. D. Stephenson.
MMS 206	Breach G.A.; McLeod J. (L/Sea); Lt. Cruikkshank (CO); Edwards J. (Sea); King J. (Sea); Bawden A. (Sea); Porter (Tel).
MMS 207	
MMS 208	
MMS 209	Barrow A. (Stk); Dilworth F. (Stk); Milton F. (Stk).
MMS 210	
MMS 211★	Taylor G.; Lt/Cdr F. Pewter (CO).
MMS 212	Cartmell J.R. (C/Eng); Dreer F. (Stk).
MMS 213	Lt. T. Every-Clayton (CO); Little T. (Sig); Pease; Lt. R. Privett.
MMS 214	Thorpe W.H.; Barnett S. (C/Eng); D. Hume.
MMS 215	
MMS 216	Blackie V.
MMS 217	Halloway R. (W/M); Sir J. McKay (CO); Lewis V. (tel).
MMS 218	
MMS 219★	Logan A. (Seea/G); McClure (C/Eng); Stuart W. (Eng); Dickson (Sig); Lester R.
MMS 220	Lt. F. Bass (No 1); Lt. Blowers (CO); Cookson (Sig); Tomlinson (Tel); Lt. P. Daniel; Ward R. (Sig).

MMS 221	Lucas H. (Sig); Lt. D. Roe (CO); Lt. J. Rodriguez (CO); Lt. J. Stirling (CO); Lt. P. Wishaw (No 1); S/Lt F. Atkinson; Meikle G. (Cox); Gattie J. (C/Eng); Strachan C. (Eng); Armstrong G. (C/Eng); Sullivan (Eng); Turfrey J.; Jacobsen J. (Cook); Jelfs C. (Cook); Parry R. (Cook); Gerry C. (Cook); Parkin H. (Cook); Ratcliffe C. (Stwd); Allen R. (W/M); Allsop (W/M); Bate (Sea); Coffin (Sea); Pryor J. (Sea); Riley P. (Sea); Carmichael D. (Sea); Nichols J. (Sea); Skivington A. (Sea); Mayne J. (Sea); Grimes A. (Tel); Hardaker J. (Tel); Eglinton C. (L/Sea); Graham J. (L/Sea); Bottom K. (Stk); Harris Y. (Stk); Horan J. (Stk); Shaw R. (Stk); Prudden; Sparkes R.; Lt. G. Hardy; Banks A. (Cox); Jones H. (Sea/Gnr).
MMS 222	
MMS 223	
MMS 224★	Gerrie W.; Henning D.
MMS 225	
MMS 226	
MMS 227	
MMS 228★	
MMS 229	
MMS 230	Bate R. (Sig); Lt. Seivewright (CO); Lt. J. Titlow; Lt. A. Dunbar.
MMS 231	
MMS 232	Lt/Cdr Goldsworthy (CO); Wren E.
MMS 233	
MMS 234	
MMS 235	
MMS 236	
MMS 237	
MMS 238	
MMS 239	Pearce G. (Cox); Lt. C. White (No 1).
MMS 240	
MMS 241	Ridehalgh J. (Stk).
MMS 242	
MMS 243	
MMS 244★	Lt. H. Greenwood (CO); McPherson W. (C/Eng).
MMS 245	Scovell DSM (Eng).
MMS 246	
MMS 247	
MMS 248	Kemp W.F.; McDonald (CO); Blease G.
MMS 249	
MMS 250	Chambers J. W.
MMS 251★	Ridehalgh J. (Stk); Lt. J. Moore (No 1); Lt. Thomas (CO).
MMS 252	Cross K.
MMS 253	
MMS 254	
MMS 255	
MMS 256	
MMS 257	Lt. D. Medlicott.
MMS 258	
MMS 259	
MMS 260★	Lt. C. Andrew (CO); Turnbull R.; Lt. J. Addison; S/Lt. E. Gale; Wilson J. (Eng); Goodson E. (Stk); Armes A. (L/W/M); Yates A. (L/Cook); Brown E. (Stwd); Gordon A. (L/Sig); White F. (L/Stk); Crichton J. (L/Sea); Harris A. (Sea); Watkins E. (Sea); Brown J. (Sea); Leech A. (Sea); Baker F. (Sea); Upton E. (Sea); Lt/Cdr J. Jones (RCN).
MMS 261	Thomson A.; Lt. Ludlow (CO).
MMS 262	
MMS 263★	
MMS 264	
MMS 265	
MMS 266	Davis A.; May A. (L/Sea).

MMS 267	Yarwood G.
MMS 268	
MMS 269	Dunn J.
MMS 270	
MMS 271	
MMS 272★	Lt/Cdr Harrison (CO); O'Neil P. (Sig).
MMS 274	King D. (L/Sea); Johnston G.
MMS 275	Watson H.
MMS 276	
MMS 277	Quennell P.
MMS 278	Lt. E. Batt (CO).
MMS 279	Lt. Watson DSM (CO); Reed DSM (L/Sea); Eves DSM (Stk); Lt. W. Salenius DSC.
MMS 280	Clark C.; Lt. R. Corney (CO).
MMS 281★	Smith T. (Tel); East G. (W/M); Salter W. (Stwd); Dunn R.; Lt. W. Main (No 1); Brown S. DSM (Sea); Maullin T. (Sea); Boiston F.
MMS 282★	Claxton M.
MMS 283★	Tither C.
MMS 284	Appleton DSM (Stwd).
MMS 285	
MMS 286★	Norton C.H. (Tel).
MMS 287	Cook K. (Eng); Elliot G. (Stwd).
MMS 288	Phillips J.
MMS 289★	Lt/Cdr M. Grant.
MMS 290★	
MMS 291★	Phillips J.; Duffet; Horne C.
MMS 292	
MMS 293★	
MMS 295	Creswell R.
MMS 296★	Handford F.; Prudden A.; Heasman A.; Walton J.
MMS 297★	Edwards C.; Whitlock T. (Cox); Lt/Cdr Forbes (CO).
MMS 298★	Lt Anderton (No 1); Lt. R. Neville (CO).
MMS 299	
MMS 300	Williams R.
MMS 301	Camfield S.; Lt. Clutterbuck (CO); Wagstaff.
MMS 302	
MMS 303	
MMS 304	Gibb H.
MMS 305	Lt. G. Blair (CO); Hollis.
MMS 306	
MMS 307★	Lt. A. Christofferson (CO).
MMS 308	Lt. W. Hall (CO); Lt. C. Deaton (No 1); Cropley L. (Cox); Hemmings C. (L/Sea); Pentney L. (Sea); Saxon N. (Sea); Roach J. (Sea); McDonald H. (Sig); Balls W. (Sea); Finlayson J. (C/Eng); Grimshaw H. (Eng); Lt. Hayward DSM (CO); Crawley D. (Stwd); Coles F. (Tel); Greenfield J. (Stk); College H. (Stk).
MMS 309	
MMS 310	Adams C. (Cox).
MMS 311	
MMS 312★	
MMS 313	

Asterisk means photograph

MMS 1000 CLASS CREWS AS KNOWN

1004	B. Brown.
1006	R. Reeve; W. Ellery (CO); R. Whittaker (Eng); C. Vincent DSM (L/Sea); J. Lumbus (CO); K. Roberts (Tel).
1009	J. Cunningham; G. Smith.
1011	W. Brazier (CO).
1017	A. Mason; R. Evans.
1019	K. Bush.
1020	R. Gollier; W. Jenkins (Tel).
1033	W. Watts.
1036	K. Corps.
1039	J. Wilson.
1041	W. Gibson.
1045	J. Crewdson.
1049	E. Turner.
1061	J. Dove.
1062	G. Dove.
1067.	E. Howlett.
1075	J. Cunningham.
1076	H. Moore.
1083	R. Evans.
1084	E. Dunkley.

BYMS CREWS AS KNOWN

2002	J. Rigby (Eng).
2003	R. Stewart; M. Bennett.
2004	J. Wilson.
2007	D. Ransley; D. King; Jolley S.
2009	L. Copping.
2012	D. Wolff (CO).
2013	O. McKenna.
2014	F. Edwards.
2017	R. Feek.
2018	R. Reeve.
2020	S. Coleman.
2021	H. Beeby; G. Stevens; R. Huckle.
2022	G. Richards; F. Edwards.
2023	W. Cook; J. Jolly.
2026	F. Turner; R. Walington; E. Bowdler; R. Cave; J. Peel; P. Norton; J. Pearson; I. Warren; S. Pinchen; H. Thornton; A. Wyllie; S/Lt. Butters; M. Pratt; C. Wright; F. Evans; R. Hayward; J. Worell; J. Buchan; N. Williams; W. Dunn; A. Whitehouse; R. Hawkins; W. Fairbrace; W. Wilkinson; J. Miller; R. Adams; R. Mallen; M. Ryan; Lt. Reves.
2028	J. Wilson.
2029	A. Fridge; D. Gilmour; D. Maycock; F. Watson.
2032	C. Pitcher.
2033	J. Jolly; G. Mustard.
2035	E. Meyers.
2036	G. Webb.
2038	W. Wiltshire.
2040	R. Kay; D. Little.
2042	R. Sparkes.
2045	T. Syrett.
2046	F. Turner.
2052	J. Stepping; S. Cox.
2053	T. Loosley; J. Plater; J. Dove.
2057	D. Little; R. Evans.
2061	R. Williams.
2062	J. Stepping.
2063	G. Webb; A. Bell.
2068	G. Stevens.
2069	R. Vincent.
2070	R. Wiltshire.
2071	G. Webb.
2074	J. Wilcock.
2075	L. Watkinson.
2076	A. Barron.
2077	S. Jolley.
2082	C. Pitcher.
2137	R. Feek.
2148	T. Buntin.
2150	L. Sewell.
2153	D. Ovett; D. Powell.
2155.	W. Ambrose.

2156	G. Stevens.
2161	H. Gibb.
2162	A. Cowie.
2167	P. Titterall.
2168	H. Jones.
2172	J. Plater; J. Steppings.
2173	D. Tester; B. Purches.
2175	J. Jolly; A. Mason.
2181	B. Beakhouse; W. Woodhouse.
2182	R. Wiltshire; C. Pitcher.
2188	P. Griffiths.
2189	J. Ackroyd.
2194	R. Williams.
2204	T. Harrison.
2205	D. Lawson; G. Smith; J. Hodge; R. Draper.
2207	E. Ward; S. Jolley.
2209	H. Risedale.
2211	P. Griffiths.
2213	F. Gratix.
2217	D. Bailey; D. Benstead.
2225	H. Gibb.
2232	D. Burgess.
2240	J. Jolly.
2246	G. Harrison; S. Forbes (CO).
2256	R. Forsythe.
2258	F. Holland; H. Wellburn.
2264	D. Taylor; P. Griffiths; C. Horne.
2278	J. Ward (Cook).
2280	C. Ellerton; D. Dexter.
2282	M. Bennett.

APPENDIX B

THE MINESWEEPER ANTHEM

Tune: John Brown's Body.

> Norton sits up in the Operations Room
> Norton sits up in the Operations Room,
> Norton sits up in the Operations Room,
> And he don't do right by us.
>
> CHORUS;
>
>> Every day we get our orders,
>> Every day we get our orders,
>> Every day we get our orders,
>> But we don't get the one's we want.

Tune: In and out the window.

> Oh you will sweep the Barrow,
> You will sweep the Barrow,
> You will sweep the Barrow,
> As you have done before.

Tune: Camp down races.

> Oh, we have got the Dumpton sweep,
> Bugger! Bugger!
> We have got the Dumpton sweep,
> Bugger, bugger, blast!
> Goin' to sweep all night!
> Goin' to sweep all day,
> I'll leave my sweep on an old can buoy,
> And bitch up my S.A.

Tune: Rose o' Tralee;

> The pale dawn was rising above Sheppey Island,
> My Number One's face was repulsive to me,
> As I let go my stern rope and shouted 'Port twenty,'
> And rang 'Half ahead' and went off to the sea.

Tune: I passed by your window;

> I steamed by St. Tudno in my little craft,
> My crew with their caps on, both for'ad and aft,
> I blew on my whistle a long piercing peeeeep,
> But Hopper was down in the wardroom asleep.

> Oh!

187

Tune: Whistle as you work.

> Whistle as you pass
> Whistle as you pass
> For all the good it does, you could
> Just stick it up ....!

Tune: Mountains of Mourne;

> O Garrison Point is a wonderful sight,
> Where they flash at you "What ship?"
> From morning till night.
> So I wake up my Bunting and spell out my name,
> Then I stream out my sweep and then lower my frame.

Tune: Comin' thru' the Rye;

> Gin a sweeper meet a sweeper,
> Comin' through the boom,
> Gin a sweeper go to starboard
> Will his tail go straight.

Tune: Shipmates of mine;

> Tell me tell me, where are you steering
>   Coxswain o' mine,
> I think you are chasing the compass,
>   Coxswain o' mine.
> Over your helm.
> 'Steady at that', I'm constantly calling,
> Steer, till we get back to port
> and you go in the rattle,
> Coxswain o' mine.
>
>   But

Tune: Bonnie;

> My bond it is down on St. Tudno,
> My bond lies on Deck Number 3
> My bond it is down on St. Tudno,
> O send half my bond back to me.
> Meachem...Meachem
> O send half my bond back to me to me,
> Meachem...Meachem
> O send half my bond back to me.

188

Tune: While shepherds watched;

> While Sheppard shifted 221
> And Smith the two three nought,
> The silly ass went full astern,
> And rammed the bloody lot.

Tune: Old Bull and Bush

> Come, come, come and drink beer with me
> Down at the old Bell and Lion tararara,
> Come, come, stick up your ear with me
> Down at the old Bell and Lion
> You will hear the latest buzz
> All the most secret dope,
> Hear about my hundreth mine;
> Come, come, come and shoot a line with me
> Down at the old Bell and Lion.

Tune: Keel Row

> We've cracked our diaphragm, our diaphragm, our diaphragm,
> We've cracked our diaphragm, we've failed the bloody range,
> There's plenty in the dockyard, the dockyard the dockyard,
> There's plenty in the dockyard, but not on Queenborough Pier.

Tune: Nellie Dean

> There's a leak right through my deck B-C-Q,
> And it drips right down my neck B-C-Q,
> My defect list is a farce
> Not an item will you pass
> You can_____B-C-Q.

Tune: Nuts in May

> Here we go gathering wrecks and buoys,
> Wrecks and buoys, wrecks and buoys,
> Here we go gathering wrecks and buoys,
> In the Barrow deep in the morning.

Tune: Here comes the Bogey Man

> Oh, Bang, Bang, Bang,
> There goes a bloody mine,
> Now hurry up and fill in the form
> And sign the dotted line.
> How far is it, we want a bearing too,
> And how long had we pulsed, and was it red or was it blue.

Tune: Something about a Soldier

> Oh there's something about a diesel,
> Something about a diesel,
> Something about a diesel that is rum, rum, rum,
> It may be a blooming Paxman,
> It may be a ruddy Lister,
> But it seems to be always going on the bum, bum, bum.

for

Tune: Pop goes the Weasel

> Oil it up for half an hour,
> With oil as thick as treacle,
> Every time you start to sweep,
> Pop goes the diesel.

Oh its

Tune: Any old iron

> Any old ir'n, any old ir'n,
> Any, any, any old ir'n,
> Coggins says its oke,
> Firin' every stroke,
> Says that the trouble is..the stoker is a soak.
> All the while
> Says it with a smile
> But its just a blooming try-on,
> But I'd swop you half a dozen for a Ford V8
> Old ir'n, old ir'n.

Tune: Daisy Bell

> Port ship, port ship, look to your steering do,
> I'm half crazy trying to follow you,
> I've tried hard but I'm not able
> To keep within a cable,
> And all the while
> Your half a mile
> From the channel that's marked for you.

Tune: Lets put out the lights

> No more mines are left to sweep,
> In the convoy let us keep,
> What's to do about it
> Let's put out the lights and go to sleep.

Tune: O dear what can the matter be.

O dear, where has our beacon gone,
Dear, dear, where has our beacon gone,
O dear where has our beacon gone,
Why am I stuck on the spit.
I went on the 'putty' by Queenboro' beacon,
Avoiding a barge that had got a slight leak on,
I didn't know twas on top of the beacon,
And here I am right in the ....

Tune: Barnacle Bill

Where am I going to berth tonight
Said 79 the sailor,
Where am I going to berth tonight,
Said 79 the sailor.
You can berth at number five
Said the aged piermaster
You can berth at number five
Said the aged piermaster.

Tune: Roamin' in the Gloamin'

Roamin' in the gloamin'
By the side of Queenboro' pier,
Shovin' thru' the boom drifters
That have no business here,
When the wind is in the West
And the tugs have gone to rest
O its bloody trying, to come alongside.

Tune: Painting the clouds with Sunshine

When I am in my bunk
The Piermaster...the skunk
He's always routing me out to shift me.

Tune: All over the place

All over the place,
They shift you to here they shift you to there,
They think that your ship,
Can fly in the air.
All over the place.

Tune: Another little drink

And now a little drink, and now a little drink,
And now a little drink won't do us any harm.

191

Tune: Trinity Church

> In order to give him room a-plenty
> I yelled down the voice pipe 'starboard twenty,'
> He like a fool went hard-a-port,
> I was the M.U.G.,
> Down in the river I met my doom,
> Tied up my sweep on the bloody boom,
> Bottles they'll dish me out in plenty,
> That's what they'll do to me.

Tune: What shall we do with the drunken sailor

> What shall we do with old MacArthur
>
> ,,   ,,   ,, ,, ,,   ,,   ,,
> ,,   ,,   ,, ,, ,,   ,,   ,,
> Early in the morning
> Put him in the wardroom till he's blotto
>
> ,,   ,, ,, ,,   ,,   ,, ,,   ,,
> ,,   ,, ,, ,,   ,,   ,, ,,   ,,
> Early in the morning

Tune: Fall in and follow me

> Fall in and follow me
> We'll have some fish for tea
> I will pulse and you can knock behind,
> Up and down the channel
> To see what we can find
> Fall in and follow me
> Jerry will never see,
> That swweping is a past-time for us sweepin' lads
> Fall in and follow me.

Tune: Widdicombe Fair

> Ben Glas! Ben Glas! take station abeam
> Sunlight and Toscin will follow astern
> For I want to go up the Barrow to sweep
> With Malacolite and Libyan
> Elsie Cam, Soranus,
> Peter Carey, Richard Crofts, Bernard Shaw
> Old uncle Delphinus and all
> Old uncle Delphinus and all.

Tune: Loch Lomond

> O you sweep magnetics, and I'll sweep acoustics,
> The moored ones we'll leave till the morning,
> But the 'oysters' I can tell,
> Will blow us all to hell,
> For the damned things go off without warning.

THE SHORE STAFF LAMENT

Tune: the Dwarf's Song

> We muck about and pull,pull,pull,
> All day and half our nights,
> At stuff which dangles off the pier
> And hangs in damn great bights.
> We are the poor old cable gang
> We swear by all the gods
> That there never were such poor unlucky - gentlemen

CHORUS:

> Oh hell, Oh hell
> We work for double L
> We toil like mutts, and pull our guts
> Half out, as well.
> They say we're swell
> At pulling we excell,
> But all the time we say "To hell
> with double L".

> They dig us from the working hands and from the trawlers crew,
> They take us from the canteen staff and off the mess decks too,
> They work us through stand easy time and in our make and mend
> To pull and pull at something which appears to have no end.
> CHORUS

It would appear that each chorus was written separately by a member of each ship's company, and put together to make up the Anthem.

Comment:
The writer of this book was never unfortunate enough to be detailed for a shore staff "wiping crew."

APPENDIX C

How to use the Appendices

To find the movements and operational areas of individual vessels, check her Pennant number against App D which will indicate the Flotilla with which she served.

App F will identify those ships with which your ship was in company.

App G will tell you the area of operation.

It is hoped that the reader will find these cross references helpful while following the text, especially when trying to identify the sister-ships which sailed in the same flotilla.

It will be noted that while some vessels e.g. MMS's 17 and 25 remained with the same flotilla for the whole of their active life, others are seen to move from one flotilla to the other.

Reasons for this are unknown, but it may well have been because of the lack of experience in certain flotillas, and those with longer experience in minesweeping techniques were sent to command or as half leader.

In any case, as the strength of the M/S force grew it was inevitable that some re-arranging would have to be done.

APPENDIX D

VESSEL FLOTILLA CHECK LIST

Pt/No	41	42	43	44	45	46	47	48	49	50	51	52	Legend
1	102	103	G	xxx	xxx	xxx	xxx	xxx	xxx	xxx	xxx	xxx	A Air Ministry
2	108	105	109		116	xxx	xxx	xxx	xxx	xxx	xxx	xxx	B Belgium
3	108	105				xxx	xxx	xxx	xxx	xxx	xxx	xxx	BM Bermuda
4	108	105	110	105			xxx	xxx	xxx	xxx	xxx	xxx	BR Burma
5	114				G								BU Broken up
6	114	115				xxx	xxx	xxx	xxx	xxx	xxx	xxx	C Chatham
7	114	115				xxx	xxx	xxx	xxx	xxx	xxx	xxx	CH China
8	102		S	xxx	xxx	xxx	xxx	xxx	xxx	xxx	xxx	xxx	CL Cancelled
9	110		F			xxx	xxx	xxx	xxx	xxx	xxx	xxx	D Denmark
10	109	105			I	M							DR Dover
11	109			135		xxx	xxx	xxx	xxx	xxx	xxx	xxx	F France
12	109		107			xxx	xxx	xxx	xxx	xxx	xxx	xxx	G Greece
13	108			M		xxx	xxx	xxx	xxx	xxx	xxx	xxx	GB Gibraltar
14	101					xxx	xxx	xxx	xxx	xxx	xxx	xxx	HK Hong Kong
15	101		131			xxx	xxx	xxx	xxx	xxx	xxx	xxx	I Italy
16	101		110			xxx	xxx	xxx	xxx	xxx	xxx	xxx	J Jugoslavia
17	101					xxx	xxx	xxx	xxx	xxx	xxx	xxx	L Lost
18	116			135		xxx	xxx	xxx	xxx	xxx	xxx	xxx	LT Lowestoft
19	102		117		xxx	xxx	xxx	xxx	xxx	xxx	xxx	xxx	M Malta
20	108				M	xxx	xxx	xxx	xxx	xxx	xxx	xxx	N Netherlands
21	109	108	F								C	xxx	P Portsmouth
22	114	115				xxx	xxx	xxx	xxx	xxx	xxx	xxx	PL Plymouth
23	xxx	116	135		xxx	xxx	xxx	xxx	xxx	xxx	xxx	xxx	R Russia
24	112			B	xxx	xxx	xxx	xxx	xxx	xxx	xxx	xxx	RIN India
25	101					xxx	xxx	xxx	xxx	xxx	xxx	xxx	RN Royal Navy
26	101		110			xxx	xxx	xxx	xxx	xxx	xxx	xxx	RY Rosyth
27	101					xxx	xxx	xxx	xxx	xxx	xxx	xxx	S Sunk
28	101					xxx	xxx	xxx	xxx	xxx	xxx	xxx	SC Salcombe
29	114	115				xxx	xxx	xxx	xxx	xxx	xxx	xxx	SH Shanghai
30	114	115	119		xxx	xxx	xxx	xxx	xxx	xxx	xxx	xxx	SN Sheerness
31	104					xxx	xxx	xxx	xxx	xxx	xxx	xxx	T Turkey
32	109		110	105	I						108		WV Wivenhoe
33	108				M	xxx	xxx	xxx	xxx	xxx	xxx	xxx	
34	108	105		M	I						108	M	
35	109		105	M	I								
36	104		137		D						120	CH	
37	104			143	SCxxx	xxx	xxx	xxx	xxx	xxx	xxx	xxx	
38	110	111			Mxxx	xxx	xxx	xxx	xxx	xxx	xxx	xxx	
39	S	xxx	xxx	xxx	xxx	xxx	xxx	xxx	xxx	xxx	xxx	xxx	
40	117		102			xxx	xxx	xxx	xxx	xxx	xxx	xxx	
41	117		102		SNxxx	xxx	xxx	xxx	xxx	xxx	xxx	xxx	
42	112		144	138	xxx	xxx	xxx	xxx	xxx	xxx	xxx	xxx	
43	112		118		SNxxx	xxx	xxx	xxx	xxx	xxx	xxx	xxx	
44	117		102			xxx	xxx	xxx	xxx	xxx	xxx	xxx	
45	117		102		xxxxx L	xxx	xxx	xxx	xxx	xxx	xxx	xxx	
46	114				G							C	
47	110		F		C	C	C	C	C	C		C	

197

VESSEL FLOTILLA CHECK LIST (contd)

Pt/No	41	42	43	44	45	46	47	48	49	50	51	52	Legend
48	110	111				I	M						
49		114	119	115	119	F	xxx	xxx	xxx	xxx	xxx	xxx	
50	108	105				I	M	C	C	C	C	C	
51		SD	xxx	xxx	xxx	xxx	xxx	xxx	xxx	xxx	xxx	xxx	
52		L	xxx	xxx	xxx	xxx	xxx	xxx	xxx	xxx	xxx	xxx	
53	102	103			M	G						C	
54	103	102			139	N	xxx	xxx	xxx	xxx	xxx	xxx	
55	114	115		S		xxx	xxx	xxx	xxx	xxx	xxx	xxx	
56	102	131				C					120	HK	
57		106	140										
58		118	114			G						C	
59	102	131				xxx	xxx	xxx	xxx	xxx	xxx	xxx	
60	106		140	102		xxx	xxx	xxx	xxx	xxx	xxx	xxx	
61	106					xxx	xxx	xxx	xxx	xxx	xxx	xxx	
62		106		145	144	xxx	xxx	xxx	xxx	xxx	xxx	xxx	
63	xxx	144				T	xxx	xxx	xxx	xxx	xxx	xxx	
64	xxx	106				xxx	xxx	xxx	xxx	xxx	xxx	xxx	
65	xxx	116	114			T	xxx	xxx	xxx	xxx	xxx	xxx	
66	xxx	119				xxx	xxx	xxx	xxx	xxx	xxx	xxx	
67	xxx	106			F								
68	xxx	103			S	xxx	xxx	xxx	xxx	xxx	xxx	xxx	
69	xxx	102	103	110		101	104						
70	xxx	103	S	xxx	xxx	xxx	xxx	xxx	xxx	xxx	xxx	xxx	
71	xxx	103		131		xxx	xxx	xxx	xxx	xxx	xxx	xxx	
72	xxx	107	116	107			xxx	xxx	xxx	xxx	xxx	xxx	
73	xxx	N	139	N									
74	104						xxx	xxx	xxx	xxx	xxx	xxx	
75	104						xxx	xxx	xxx	xxx	xxx	xxx	
76	xxx	112		144		xxx	xxx	xxx	xxx	xxx	xxx	xxx	
77	xxx	112		118	L	xxx	xxx	xxx	xxx	xxx	xxx	xxx	
78	112			131		xxx	xxx	xxx	xxx	xxx	xxx	xxx	
79	102	131		144	113	192					120	108	
80	110			113			xxx	xxx	xxx	xxx	xxx	xxx	
81	110			131			xxx	xxx	xxx	xxx	xxx	xxx	
82	102	131		144		xxx	xxx	xxx	xxx	xxx	xxx	xxx	
83	xxx	104		137		D							
84	xxx	104			132	D					120	CH	
85	xxx	103					xxx	xxx	xxx	xxx	xxx	xxx	
86	xxx	104			D							C	
87	xxx	112		144	117	102	xxx	xxx	xxx	xxx	xxx	xxx	
88	xxx	106	114		T								
89	xxx	115	114	S	xxx	xxx	xxx	xxx	xxx	xxx	xxx	xxx	
90	xxx	116	115	R									
91	xxx	119		115	F		xxx	xxx	xxx	xxx	xxx	xxx	
92	xxx	110		117		xxx	xxx	xxx	xxx	xxx	xxx	xxx	
93	xxx	L	xxx	xxx	xxx	xxx	xxx	xxx	xxx	xxx	xxx	xxx	
94	xxx	L	xxx	xxx	xxx	xxx	xxx	xxx	xxx	xxx	xxx	xxx	
95	xxx	L	xxx	xxx	xxx	xxx	xxx	xxx	xxx	xxx	xxx	xxx	

Pt/No	41	42	43	44	45	46	47	48	49	50	51	52	Legend
96	xxx	L	xxxxxxxxxxxxxxxxxxxxxxxxxxxxxxxxxxxxxxxxxxx										
97		RIN				xxxxxxxxxxxxxxxxxxxxxxxxxxxx							
98		RIN				xxxxxxxxxxxxxxxxxxxxxxxxxxxx							
99	xxx	120			I						M	GB	
100	xxx	121	120		I						M	GB	
101	xxx	121	120	S	xxxxxxxxxxxxxxxxxxxxxxxxxxxxxxxxxxxxx								
102	xxx	120		I							M	GB	
103	xxx	120											
104	xxx	120			I						M	GB	
105	xxx	120			I						M	GB	
106	xxx	120										C	
107	xxx	121		122			S						
108	xxx	121		122			S						
109	xxx	116		110		101					301	51	
110	xxx	107	102	110	117	C					104	C	
111	xxxxx		106				xxxxxxxxxxxxxxxxxxxxxxxxxxxxxxxxxxx						
112	xxxxx112	118				xxxxxxxxxxxxxxxxxxxxxxxxxxxxxxx							
113	103	102				xxxxxxxxxxxxxxxxxxxxxxxxxxxxxxx							
114	xxx	103				xxxxxxxxxxxxxxxxxxxxxxxxxxxxxxx							
115	xxx	107	102	110		xxxxxxxxxxxxxxxxxxxxxxxxxxxxxxx							
116	xxx	110		F		xxxxxxxxxxxxxxxxxxxxxxxxxxxxxxx							
117	xxx	111		S	xxxxxxxxxxxxxxxxxxxxxxxxxxxxxxxxxxx								
118	xxx	111	110	F							C	xxx	
119	xxx	114				xxxxxxxxxxxxxxxxxxxxxxxxxxxxxxx							
120	xxx	144				xxxxxxxxxxxxxxxxxxxxxxxxxxxxxxx							
121	xxx	144				xxxxxxxxxxxxxxxxxxxxxxxxxxxxxxx							
122	xxx	144				xxxxxxxxxxxxxxxxxxxxxxxxxxxxxxx							
123	L	xxxxxxxxxxxxxxxxxxxxxxxxxxxxxxxxxxxxxxxxx											
124	L	xxxxxxxxxxxxxxxxxxxxxxxxxxxxxxxxxxxxxxxxx											
125	xxx	L	xxxxxxxxxxxxxxxxxxxxxxxxxxxxxxxxxxxxx										
126	xxx	L	xxxxxxxxxxxxxxxxxxxxxxxxxxxxxxxxxxxxx										
127	xxx	L	xxxxxxxxxxxxxxxxxxxxxxxxxxxxxxxxxxxxx										
128	xxx	L	xxxxxxxxxxxxxxxxxxxxxxxxxxxxxxxxxxxxx										
129		xxxxx	RIN										
130		xxxxx	RIN										
131		xxxxx	RIN										
132		xxxxx	RIN										
133	xxx	109	108	F		xxxxxxxxxxxxxxxxxxxxxxxxxxxxxxx							
134	xxx	105	108	F		xxxxxxxxxxxxxxxxxxxxxxxxxxxxxxx							
135	xxx	105	108		I						108	M	
136	xxx	109			140		xxxxxxxxxxxxxxxxxxxxxxxxxxxx						
137		xxxxx	140	110		xxxxxxxxxxxxxxxxxxxxxxxxxxxxxxx							
138		xxxxx	106	139	N		xxxxxxxxxxxxxxxxxxxxxxxxxxx						
139	xxx	115				xxxxxxxxxxxxxxxxxxxxxxxxxxxxxxx							
140	xxx	114			T								
141		xxxxx	130		LT	xxxxxxxxxxxxxxxxxxxxxxxxxxxx							
142		xxxxx	130		LT	xxxxxxxxxxxxxxxxxxxxxxxxxxxx							

Pt/No	41	42	43	44	45	46	47	48	49	50	51	52	Legend
143	xxxxxxxxxxxxxxxx				143	146	G				M		
144	xxxxxxxxxxxxx146					G					C		
145	xxxxxxxxxxxxxx			RIN									
146	CL		xxxxxxxxxxxxxxxxxxxxxxxxxxxxxxxxxxxxxxxxxxxxxxx										
147	L		xxxxxxxxxxxxxxxxxxxxxxxxxxxxxxxxxxxxxxxxxxxxxxx										
148	xxxxxxxxxxxxxxxxxxxxxxxxxx					RIN		xxxxxxxxxxxxxxxxxxx					
149	xxx	107		140	131		101		xxxxxxxxxxxxxxx				
150	xxx	107	134	145			T						
151	xxxxxxxxxxxxxx			RIN		xxxxxxxxxxxxxxxxxxxxxxxxxxxxxxx							
152	CL		xxxxxxxxxxxxxxxxxxxxxxxxxxxxxxxxxxxxxxxxxxxxxxx										
153	xxx		L	xxxxxxxxxxxxxxxxxxxxxxxxxxxxxxxxxxxxxxxxx									
154	xxxxxxxxxxxxxx			RIN		xxxxxxxxxxxxxxxxxxxxxxxxxxxxxxx							
155	xxxxxxxxxxxxxx			CL		xxxxxxxxxxxxxxxxxxxxxxxxxxxxxxx							
156	xxxxx		L	xxxxxxxxxxxxxxxxxxxxxxxxxxxxxxxxxxxxxxxxx									
157	xxxxxxxxxxxxxx			CL		xxxxxxxxxxxxxxxxxxxxxxxxxxxxxxx							
158	xxxxxxxxxxxxxx			CL		xxxxxxxxxxxxxxxxxxxxxxxxxxxxxxx							
159	xxxxxxxxxxxxxx			CL		xxxxxxxxxxxxxxxxxxxxxxxxxxxxxxx							
160	xxxxxxxxxxxxxx			CL		xxxxxxxxxxxxxxxxxxxxxxxxxxxxxxx							
161	xxx	L	xxxxxxxxxxxxxxxxxxxxxxxxxxxxxxxxxxxxxxxxxxxx										
162	xxx	L	xxxxxxxxxxxxxxxxxxxxxxxxxxxxxxxxxxxxxxxxxxxx										
163	xxx	L	xxxxxxxxxxxxxxxxxxxxxxxxxxxxxxxxxxxxxxxxxxxx										
164	xxx	L	xxxxxxxxxxxxxxxxxxxxxxxxxxxxxxxxxxxxxxxxxxxx										
165	xxx	116	115			xxxxxxxxxxxxxxxxxxxxxxxxxxxxxxx							
166	xxx	L	xxxxxxxxxxxxxxxxxxxxxxxxxxxxxxxxxxxxxxxxxxxx										
167	xxx	111				I					M		
168	xxx	111			S	xxxxxxxxxxxxxxxxxxxxxxxxxxxxxxx							
169	xxx	111				xxxxxxxxxxxxxxxxxxxxxxxxxxxxxxx							
170	xxx	111		S	xxxxxxxxxxxxxxxxxxxxxxxxxxxxxxxxxxxxx								
171	xxx	111	110	131		xxxxxxxxxxxxxxxxxxxxxxxxxxxxxxx							
172	xxx	111				I					108	M	
173	xxxxx		136	140N		xxxxxxxxxxxxxxxxxxxxxxxxxxxxxxx							
174	xxxxx		136N	134	107	104				J			
175	xxx	136		117		xxxxxxxxxxxxxxxxxxxxxxxxxxxxxxx							
176	xxx	107	116	135	SH	xxxxxxxxxxxxxxxxxxxxxxxxxxxxxxx							
177	xxx	113		DR		xxxxxxxxxxxxxxxxxxxxxxxxxxxxxxx							
178	xxxxx	113				xxxxxxxxxxxxxxxxxxxxxxxxxxxxxxx							
179	xxx	113				WV	xxxxxxxxxxxxxxxxxxxxxxxxxxxxx						
180	xxx	L	xxxxxxxxxxxxxxxxxxxxxxxxxxxxxxxxxxxxxxxxxxxxx										
181	xxx	107	102	132		104							
182	xxx	118	133	101		118	B						
183	xxx	113				xxxxxxxxxxxxxxxxxxxxxxxxxxxxxxx							
184	xxx	105	108	F		xxxxxxxxxxxxxxxxxxxxxxxxxxxxxxx							
185	xxx	105				I					108		
186	xxx	118	133	101		xxxxxxxxxxxxxxxxxxxxxxxxxxxxxxx							
187	xxx	118									RN		
188	xxx	118			B								
190	xxx	118	133	117		118	xxxxxxxxxxxxxxxxxxxxxxxxxxxxx						

VESSEL FLOTILLA CHECK LIST (contd)

Pt/No	41	42	43	44	45	46	47	48	49	50	51	52	Legend
191	xxx	118				B							
192	xxx	118	133	117		SC	xxxxxxxxxxxxxxxxxxxxxxxxxx						
193	xxx	118				B							
194	xxxxxxxxxxxxxxxxxx					CL	xxxxxxxxxxxxxxxxxxxxxxxx						
195	xxxxxxxxxxxxxxxxxx					CL	xxxxxxxxxxxxxxxxxxxxxxxx						
196	xxxxx		121	122		SH	xxxxxxxxxxxxxxxxxxxxxxxx						
197	xxxxx		121	122		BU							
198	xxxxx		122			SH	xxxxxxxxxxxxxxxxxxxxxxxx						
199	xxxxx		122				xxxxxxxxxxxxxxxxxxxxxx						
200	xxxxx		122			SH	xxxxxxxxxxxxxxxxxxxxxxxx						
201	xxxxx		122			BU	xxxxxxxxxxxxxxxxxxxxxxxx						
202	xxx	119					xxxxxxxxxxxxxxxxxxxxxx						
203	xxx	R											
204	xxx	119					xxxxxxxxxxxxxxxxxxxxxx						
205	xxx	116			F		xxxxxxxxxxxxxxxxxxxxxx						
206	xxx	131	113		114		xxxxxxxxxxxxxxxxxxxxxx						
207	xxx	134		147		xxxxxxxxxxxxxxxxxxxxxxxxxxxxxx							
208	xxx	CL	xxxxxxxxxxxxxxxxxxxxxxxxxxxxxxxxxx										
209	xxx	131	113	132	104		xxxxxxxxxxxxxxxxxxxxxx						
210	xxx	CL	xxxxxxxxxxxxxxxxxxxxxxxxxxxxxxxxxx										
211	xxx	134		140	132		xxxxxxxxxxxxxxxxxxxxxx						
212	xxx	R											
213	xxx	119			F		xxxxxxxxxxxxxxxxxxxxxx						
214	xxx	134		147			xxxxxxxxxxxxxxxxxxxxxx						
215	xxx	134		147		xxxxxxxxxxxxxxxxxxxxxxxxxxxx							
216	xxxxx	136	117			xxxxxxxxxxxxxxxxxxxxxxxxxxxx							
217	xxx	RN									50		C
218	xxx	131	113				xxxxxxxxxxxxxxxxxxxxxx						
219	xxx	133		101		xxxxxxxxxxxxxxxxxxxxxxxxxxxx							
220	xxx	119			F	P	xxxxxxxxxxxxxxxxxxxxxx						
221	xxx	119			F		xxxxxxxxxxxxxxxxxxxxxx						
222	xxxxxxxxxxxxxxxxxxxx					BM							
223	xxxxxxxxxxxxxxxxxxxx					BM	S	xxxxxxxxxxxxxxxxxxxx					
224	xxx	132	138		117	109					104		C
225	xxx	132	138				xxxxxxxxxxxxxxxxxxxxxx						
226	xxx	N	139										
227	xxx	N	139	S		xxxxxxxxxxxxxxxxxxxxxxxxxxxxxx							
228	xxx	132	138		143	102					104		RNVR
229	xxx	132	138	S		xxxxxxxxxxxxxxxxxxxxxxxxxxxxxx							
230	xxxxxx	135				xxxxxxxxxxxxxxxxxxxxxxxxxxxx							
231	xxx	N	139										
232	xxxxxx	109	135			xxxxxxxxxxxxxxxxxxxxxxxxxxxx							
233	xxx	132		141	132	104		RNVR					
234	xxxxxx	N	139										
235	xxx	CL	xxxxxxxxxxxxxxxxxxxxxxxxxxxxxxxxxxxxxx										
236	xxx	132			116	102						51	
237	xxxxx	N	139										

VESSEL FLOTILLA CHECK LIST (contd)

Pt/No	41	42	43	44	45	46	47	48	49	50	51	52	Legend
238	xxxxxxxxxx			159	163		xxxxxxxxxxxxxxxxxxxxxxxxxx						
239	xxxxxxxxxx			167N	159		xxxxxxxxxxxxxxxxxxxxxxxxxx						
240	xxxxxxxxxx			168			xxxxxxxxxxxxxxxxxxxxxxxxxx						
241	xxxxx		163				xxxxxxxxxxxxxxxxxxxxxxxxxx						
242	xxxxx		142				xxxxxxxxxxxxxxxxxxxxxxxxxx						
243	xxxxx		142					xxxxxxxxxxxxxxxxxxxxxx					
244	xxxxx		142			xxxxxxxxxxxxxxxxxxxxxxxxxxxxxxx							
245	xxxxx		142			A	xxxxxxxxxxxxxxxxxxxxxxxxxxxx						
246	xxxxx		142			xxxxxxxxxxxxxxxxxxxxxxxxxxxxxxx							
247	xxxxx		143			A	xxxxxxxxxxxxxxxxxxxxxxxxxxxx						
248	xxxxx		143			S	xxxxxxxxxxxxxxxxxxxxxxxxxxxx						
249	xxxxxxxxxx			143			xxxxxxxxxxxxxxxxxxxxxxxxxx						
250	xxxxx		142				xxxxxxxxxxxxxxxxxxxxxxxxxx						
251	xxxxx		143				xxxxxxxxxxxxxxxxxxxxxxxxxx						
252	xxxxx		143				xxxxxxxxxxxxxxxxxxxxxxxxxx						
253	xxxxx		143				xxxxxxxxxxxxxxxxxxxxxxxxxx						
254	xxxxx		142	PL			xxxxxxxxxxxxxxxxxxxxxxxxxx						
255	xxxxx		142				xxxxxxxxxxxxxxxxxxxxxxxxxx						
256	xxxxx		143			A	xxxxxxxxxxxxxxxxxxxxxxxxxxxx						
257	xxxxx		143	S	xxxxxxxxxxxxxxxxxxxxxxxxxxxxxxxx								
258	xxxxxxxxxxxxxxxxxxxxxSN					xxxxxxxxxxxxxxxxxxxxxxxxxx							
259	xxxxxxxxxxxxxxxxxxxxxSN					xxxxxxxxxxxxxxxxxxxxxxxxxx							
260	xxxxx		137	104		SC	xxxxxxxxxxxxxxxxxxxxxxxxxx						
261	xxx	132				104		RNVR					
262	xxxxx		CL	xxxxxxxxxxxxxxxxxxxxxxxxxxxxxxxxxxxxxx									
263	xxxxx		137	D							C	P	
264	xxx	CL	xxxxxxxxxxxxxxxxxxxxxxxxxxxxxxxxxxxxxxxxxxxx										
265	xxx	133		117			xxxxxxxxxxxxxxxxxxxxxxxxxx						
266	xxx	133		117		118							
267	xxxxx		117	107	102		xxxxxxxxxxxxxxxxxxxxxxxxxx						
268	xxxxxx		131	113		144	xxxxxxxxxxxxxxxxxxxxxxxxxx						
269	xxxxx		117	107	140	116	xxxxxxxxxxxxxxxxxxxxxxxxxx						
270	xxxxx		135				xxxxxxxxxxxxxxxxxxxxxxxxxx						
271	xxxxx		135		117	102					51	RY	
272	xxxxx		135			101					301	C	
273	xxx	CL	xxxxxxxxxxxxxxxxxxxxxxxxxxxxxxxxxxxxxxxxxxxx										
274	xxxxx		132				xxxxxxxxxxxxxxxxxxxxxxxxxx						
275	xxxxx		134	109	116								
276	xxxxx		141	EI		SH	xxxxxxxxxxxxxxxxxxxxxxxxxx						
277	xxxxxx		132	147	DR	xxxxxxxxxxxxxxxxxxxxxxxxxxxxxx							
278	xxxxx		106	L	xxxxxxxxxxxxxxxxxxxxxxxxxxxxxxxxxxxx								
279	xxxxxxx			137	104		xxxxxxxxxxxxxxxxxxxxxxxxxx						
280	xxxxxxx			137	104		xxxxxxxxxxxxxxxxxxxxxxxxxx						
281	xxxxx		138		116		xxxxxxxxxxxxxxxxxxxxxxxxxx						
282	xxxxx		131	140			xxxxxxxxxxxxxxxxxxxxxxxxxx						
283	xxxxxx		140	132	104	C					104		
284	xxxxx		135				xxxxxxxxxxxxxxxxxxxxxxxxxx						

202

Pt/No	41	42	43	44	45	46	47	48	49	50	51	52	Legend
285	xxxxx		135	116		101					RNVR		
286	xxxxx		135	116		102					51		
287	xxxxx		131	140	116	xxxxxxxxxxxxxxxxxxxxxxxxxxxxx							
288	xxxxx		141	147		102					51	L	
289	xxxxx		141	116		109	C				RNVR		
290	xxxxx		135	116							104		
291	xxxxx		141	147		102					104		
292	xxxxxx		N	139									
293	xxxxx		132	147		102	xxxxxxxxxxxxxxxxxxxxxxxx						
294	xxxxx		131	144	113	104						C	
295	xxxxx		131	144	113	104	xxxxxxxxxxxxxxxxxxxxxxxx						
296	xxxxx		141		132	109					104	C	
297	xxxxx		106	147		101						120	
298	xxxxx		106			xxxxxxxxxxxxxxxxxxxxxxxxxxxxx							
299	xxxxx		CL	xxxxxxxxxxxxxxxxxxxxxxxxxxxxxxxxxxxxxxx									
300	xxxxxxxxxx		EI		SH	xxxxxxxxxxxxxxxxxxxxxxxxxxxx							
301	xxxxx		141	132		104					51		
302	xxxxx		132			xxxxxxxxxxxxxxxxxxxxxxxxxxxxx							
303	xxxxxxxxxx		107	EI	SH	xxxxxxxxxxxxxxxxxxxxxxxxxxxx							
304	xxxxxxxxxx		EI		SH	xxxxxxxxxxxxxxxxxxxxxxxxxxxx							
305	xxxxxxxxxx		137	104	xxxxxxxxxxxxxxxxxxxxxxxxxxxxx								
306	xxxxxxxxxx		CL	xxxxxxxxxxxxxxxxxxxxxxxxxxxxxxxxxxxxx									
307	xxxxxxxxxx		137	D							50		
308	xxxxxxxxxx		141	144	113	xxxxxxxxxxxxxxxxxxxxxxxx							
309	xxxxxxxxxx		107		117	xxxxxxxxxxxxxxxxxxxxxxxx							
310	xxxxxxxxxxxxx			146		G					M	C	
311	xxxxxxxxxxxxx			146		M	xxxxxxxxxxxxxxxxxxxxxx						
312	xxxxxxxxxxxxx			146		M	xxxxxxxxxxxxxxxxxxxxxx						
313	xxxxxxxxxxxxx			146								GM	

VESSELS IN SERVICE BEYOND 1952

Pt/No	53	54	55	56	57	58	59	60	61	62	63
10	M			xxxxxxxxxxxxxxxxxxxxxxxxxxxxxxxxxx							
32	108		M	xxxxxxxxxxxxxxxxxxxxxxxxxxxxxxxxxx							
34	108		M	xxxxxxxxxxxxxxxxxxxxxxxxxxxxxxxxxx							
35	C			xxxxxxxxxxxxxxxxxxxxxxxxxxxxxxxxxx							
36	CH				xxxxxxxxxxxxxxxxxxxxxxxxxxx						
46	C				xxxxxxxxxxxxxxxxxxxxxxxxxxxxx						
48	M		xxxxxxxxxxxxxxxxxxxxxxxxxxxxxxxxxxxx								
50	C				xxxxxxxxxxxxxxxxxxxxxxxxxxxx						
53	GIB		xxxxxxxxxxxxxxxxxxxxxxxxxxxxxxxxxxxx								
56	HK				xxxxxxxxxxxxxxxxxx						
57	GB			xxxxxxxxxxxxxxxxxxxxxxxxxxxxx							
58		xxxxxxxxxxxxxxxxxxxxxxxxxxxxxxxxxxxxxxxxxx									
65		xxxxxxxxxxxxxxxxxxxxxxxxxxxxxxxxxxxxxxxxxx									
69		L	xxxxxxxxxxxxxxxxxxxxxxxxxxxxxxxxxxxxxxxxxx								

Pt/No	41	42	43	44	45	46	47	48	49	50	51	52	Legend
73 N													
79 CH							xxxxxxxxxxxxxxxxxxx						
83 D					xxxxxxxxxxxxxxxxxxxxxxxxxxxx								
84 HK						xxxxxxxxxxxxxxxxxxxxxxxxxx							
86 AM							xxxxxxxxxxxxxxxxxxx						
88 T						xxxxxxxxxxxxxxxxxxxxxxxxxx							
90 R													
99 C			xxxxxxxxxxxxxxxxxxxxxxxxxxxxxxxxxxxxxxxx										
100 P			xxxxxxxxxxxxxxxxxxxxxxxxxxxxxxxxxxxxxxxx										
102 P				xxxxxxxxxxxxxxxxxxxxxxxxxxxxxxxxxxxxxxxx									
103 C				xxxxxxxxxxxxxxxxxxxxxxxxxxxxxxxxxxx									
104 GIB	xxxxxxxxxxxxxxxxxxxxxxxxxxxxxxxxxxxxxxxxxx												
105 GIB	xxxxxxxxxxxxxxxxxxxxxxxxxxxxxxxxxxxxxxxxxx												
106 P				xxxxxxxxxxxxxxxxxxxxxxxxxxxxxxxxxxx									
109 P				xxxxxxxxxxxxxxxxxxxxxxxxxxxxxxxxxxx									
110 C				xxxxxxxxxxxxxxxxxxxxxxxxxxxxxxxxxxx									
130 RIN	xxxxxxxxxxxxxxxxxxxxxxxxxxxxxxxxxxxxx												
135 M				xxxxxxxxxxxxxxxxxxxxxxxxxxxxxxxxxxxxxxxx									
138 N													
140 T													
144 C						xxxxxxxxxxxxxxxxxxxxxxxxxxxx							
150 T													
167 M			xxxxxxxxxxxxxxxxxxxxxxxxxxxxxxxxxxxxxxxx										
172 M			xxxxxxxxxxxxxxxxxxxxxxxxxxxxxxxxxxxxxxxx										
174 J													
181 104						xxxxxxxxxxxxxxxxxxxxxxxx							
182 B			xxxxxxxxxxxxxxxxxxxxxxxxxxxxxxxxxxxxxxxx										
185 P				xxxxxxxxxxxxxxxxxxxxxxxxxxxxxxxxxxx									
187 RN			xxxxxxxxxxxxxxxxxxxxxxxxxxxxxxxxxxxxxxxx										
188 RN			xxxxxxxxxxxxxxxxxxxxxxxxxxxxxxxxxxxxxxxx										
189 B			xxxxxxxxxxxxxxxxxxxxxxxxxxxxxxxxxxxxxxxx										
191 C			xxxxxxxxxxxxxxxxxxxxxxxxxxxxxxxxxxxxxxxx										
193 C						xxxxxxxxxxxxxxxxxxxxxxxx							
197 BU													
203 R													
212 R													
217 RY			xxxxxxxxxxxxxxxxxxxxxxxxxxxxxxxxxxxxxxxxxxxx										
222 BM			xxxxxxxxxxxxxxxxxxxxxxxxxxxxxxxxxxxxxxxx										
224 C	xxxxxxxxxxxxxxxxxxxxxxxxxxxxxxxxxxxxxxxxxxxx												
228 C						xxxxxxxxxxxxxxxxxxxxxxxx							
231 N					xxxxxxxxxxxxxxxxxxxxxxxxxxxx								
233 C						xxxxxxxxxxxxxxxxxxxxxxxx							
234 N					xxxxxxxxxxxxxxxxxxxxxxxxxxxx								
236 SN				xxxxxxxxxxxxxxxxxxxxxxxxxxxxxxxx									
237 N					xxxxxxxxxxxxxxxxxxxxxxxxxxxx								
261 GIB					xxxxxxxxxxxxxxxxxxxxxxxxxxxx								
263 P			xxxxxxxxxxxxxxxxxxxxxxxxxxxxxxxxxxxxxxxx										

VESSEL FLOTILLA CHECK LIST (contd)

Pt/No	41	42	43	44	45	46	47	48	49	50	51	52	Legend
266 P			x	x	x	x	x	x	x	x	x	x	
271 RY						x	x	x	x	x	x		
272 GIB					x	x	x	x	x	x	x		
275 C				x	x	x	x	x	x	x	x	x	
283 C					x	x	x	x	x	x	x		
285 C				x	x	x	x	x	x	x	x		
286 HK					x	x	x	x	x	x	x		
289 C							x	x	x	x	x	x	
290 C				x	x	x	x	x	x	x	x		
291 C				x	x	x	x	x	x	x	x		
292 N					x	x	x	x	x	x	x		
296 C			x	x	x	x	x	x	x	x	x		
297 HK						x	x	x	x	x	x		
301 P					x	x	x	x	x	x	x		
307 C					x	x	x	x	x	x	x		
310 C				x	x	x	x	x	x	x	x		
313 M				x	x	x	x	x	x	x	x		

There were no Motor Minesweepers operational in any part of the world after 1963, the last being the three with the USSR Navy.

APPENDIX E

FLOTILLA CHECK LIST LEGEND

DG	Degaussing	Yar	Yarmouth
RY	Rosyth	Har	Harwich
BU	Broken Up	Lwt	Lowestoft
D	Denmark	H	Holland
F	France	Lth	Leith
Ply	Plymouth	Nth/Sh	North Shields
NWE	North Western Europe	Dvr	Dover
Pt	Portsmouth	Grt	Granton
Lvpl	Liverpool	S	Sold
C	Chatham	Sp	Singapore
Sh	Sheerness	N	Norway

APPENDIX F

COMPARISON TABLES
Inter Flotilla Ship Movements

101 MSF(Sheerness)

Year 41	42	43	44	45	46	47
14	14	14	14	14	14	
15	15	15	182	182	109	
16	16	16	186	186	186	186
17	17	17	17	17	17	
25	25	25	25	25	69	
26	26	26	189	189	272	
27	27	27	27	27	285	
28	28	28	28	28	28	
			219	219	297	

102 MSF(Sheerness)

Year 41	42	43	44	45	46	47
1		110	40	40	40	
8	8	8	8		79	
19	19	19	41	41	41	
53	54	54	44	44	44	
56	69	69	45	45	45	
59	71	71	54		228	
79	82	115	60	60	60	
82	113	113	113	113	236	
		181	267	267	267	
					271	
					286	
					288	288
					291	
					293	

103 MSF(Sheerness/Med)

Year 41	42	43	44	45	46	47
54	1	1	1	14		
113	53	53	53			
	58	68	68	68		
	70	79				
	85	85	85	85	85	
	113	70				
	114	114	114	114	114	

104 MSF(Leith/Nor/Nore)

Year 41	42	43	44	45	46	47
31	31	31	31	31	31	
36	36	36	260	260	261	261
37	37	37	37		233	233
74	74	74	74	74	74	
75	75	75	75		181	181
	83	83	279	279	273	
	84	84	84	283	69	
	86	86	86	86	174	174
			280	280	280	
			305	305	294	
					295	
					301	

COMPARISON TABLES
Inter Flotilla Ship Movements

105 MSF(Liverpool/Med)

Year 41	42	43	44	45	46	47
	2	10	10	10	10	10
	3	3	3	3	3	
	4	185	4	4	4	4
	34	34	34			
	50	50	50	50		
	134	35	35	35		
	135		32	32		
	184					
	185		185	185		

106 MSF(Newhaven

Year 41	42	43	44	45	46	47
60	60	138				
61	61	61	61	61	61	
62	62					
	64	64	64	64		
	67	67	67			
	88	111	111	111		
	57	278	278	278		
		297	288			
		298	298	298	298	

107 MSF(N. Iree./Clyde)

Year 41	42	43	44	45	46	47
	72		72	72	72	
	110		12	12		
	115		303			
	149	149	269			
	150		267			
	176		174	174		
	181	309	309	111		

108 MSF(Liverpool/Med)

Year 41	42	43	44	45	46	47
2	21	21	21	21		
3	184	184	184			
4	133	133	133			
13	13	13	13			
20	20	20	20	20	120	
33	33	33	33	33	33	
34	134	134	134			
50	135	135	135	135		

109 MSF(NI/Liv/Clyde/NWEU)

Year 41	42	43	44	45	46	47
10	10	2	2			
11	11	11				
12	12	12		224		
21	133			290		
32	32			289		
35	35	232	275	275		
	136	136	136	296		

110 MSF(Swan/Med/NWEU)

Year 41	42	43	44	45	46	47
9	9	9	9	69		
38	92	92	16	16	16	
47	47	47	47			
48	116	116	116			
80	80	80	110			
81	81	118	115	115		
	171	171	137	137	137	
	4	109	109			
	32	57	57			
			26	26		

COMPARISON TABLES
Inter Flotilla Ship Movements

111 MSF(Swansea/Med)

Year	41	42	43	44	45	46	47
		38	38	38	38	38	
		48	48	48	48		
		117	117	117			
		118					
		167	167	167			
		168	168	168			
		169	169	169		169	
		170	170	170			
		171					
		172	172	172			

Copper Bottoms

1012MSF(Pl/Hr/Dr/Bf)

Year	41	42	43	44	45	46	47
	24	24	24	24	24	87	
	42	42	42	80		110	
	43	43	43	177		265	
	78	78	78	178		309	
		76	76	179			
		77	77	183			
		87	87	206			
			112	113			
				218			
				268			

113 MSF (Swansea/Dover)

Year	41	42	43	44	45	46	47
		117	117	117	117	117	
		179	179	179	179	179	
		183	183	183	183	183	
			178	178	178	178	
			206	206	79	308	
			209	80	80	80	
			218	218	218	218	
			268	268	294		
					295		
					307		

114 MSF(Prts/Med)

Year	41	42	43	44	45	46	47
	5	5	5	5	5	5	5
	6	49	88	88	88	88	
	7	63	63	63	63		
	22	65	65	65	65		
	29	140	140	140	140	140	
	30		89				
	46	46	46	46	46		
	55	58	58	58	58		

115 MSF(Prts/Nrdy)

Year	41	42	43	44	45	46	47
		6	6	6	6	6	
		7	7	7	7	7	
		22	22	22	22	22	
		29	29	29	29	29	
		30	30	49			
		55	55	55			
		89	205	205	205	205	
		90		91			
		139	139	139	139		
		165	165	165	165		

1106MSF(Cld/Scapa/NWEU)

Year	41	42	43	44	45	46	47
	18	18	18	285	285	2	
		23	23	286	286		
		58	72	290	290		
		65	205		236		
		90	176		269	269	269
		109	109		275		
		165			281		
					287	287	
					289		

COMPARISON TABLES
Inter Flotilla Ship Movements

117 MSF(Sheerness/NWEU)

Year 41	42	43	44	45	46	47
41	41	41	19	19		
44	44	44	92	92		
45	45	45	175	175		
		267	190	190		
		269	192	192		
			216	216		
			265	110		
			266	224		
				228		

118 MSF(Harwich/NIF/EU)

Year 41	42	43	44	45	46	47
40	182	187	187	43	43	43
	186		77	75	75	
	187		187	187	187	187
	188	188	188	188	188	188
	189			79	190	190
	190				112	112
	191	191	191	191	191	182
	192					
	193	193	193	193	266	

119 MSF(Ports/NIF)

Year 41	42	43	44	45	46	47
49	49	49	30	30		
66	66	66	66	66		
202	202	202	202	202	202	
204	204	204	204	49		
212	212	213	213	265		
220	220	220	220	266		
221	221	221	221	271		
	81					

120 MSF(Med)

Year 41	42	43	44	45	46	47
	99	99	99	99		
	102	102	102			
	103	103	103			
	104	104	104	104		
	105	105	105	105		
	106	106	106	106		
		100	100	100		
		101	101			

121 MSF(Med)

Year 41	42	43	44	45	46	47
	100					
	101					
	107	107		107		
	108	108		108		
	196					
	197					

122 MSF(E. Indies)

Year 41	42	43	44	45	46	47
		198	198	198		
		199	199	199		
		200	200	200		
		201	201	201		
			107	107	107	
			108	108	108	
			196	196		
			197	197		

COMPARISON TABLES
Inter Flotilla Ship Movements

130 MSF(Plymouth)   131 MSF(Sheerness)

Year	41	42	43	44	45	46	47	41	42	43	44	45	46	47
			141	141	141	141			56	56	56	56		
			142	142	142	142			59	59	59	59	59	
									79	79	71	71		
									206	268	78			
									209	282	81		81	
									218	287	149	149	149	
										294	171	171		
										295	15	15		

132 MSF(Liverpool/Sheerness)   133 MSF(Sheerness)

Year	41	42	43	44	45	46	47	41	42	43	44	45	46	47
		224	274	181	181				219	219	274			
		225	277	209	84				265	265				
		228	282	211	211				266	266				
		229	287	301	301					182				
		233	233		233					186				
		236	236	236	274	274				189				
		261	261	261	261					190				
			293	283	296					192				
			302	302	302	302								

134 MSF(Belfast)   135 MSF(Scapa/Ports)

Year	41	42	43	44	45	46	47	41	42	43	44	45	46	47
		207	207	174						230	230	230		
		211	211	176						270	270	176		
		214	214							271	271	271		
		215	215							272	272	272		
			275							284	284	284	284	
			150							285	11	11	11	
										286	18	18	18	
										290	23	23		
											232	232		

COMPARISON TABLES
Inter Flotilla Ship Movements

	136 MSF(Sheerness)						137 MSF(Leith)						
Year													
41	42	43	44	45	46	47	41	42	43	44	45	46	47
		173	216						260	36	36		
		174							263	263			
		175							305	83	83		
									307	279	307		
										280			

	138 MSF(Lowestoft/NIF)						139 MSF(Harwich)						
Year													
41	42	43	44	45	46	47	41	42	43	44	45	46	47
		173	216						260	36	36		
		174							263	263			
		175							305	83	83		
									307	279	307		
										280			

	138 MSF(Lowestoft/NIF)						139 MSF(Harwich)						
Year													
41	42	43	44	45	46	47	41	42	43	44	45	46	47
		224	224	42	42				73	73	73		
		225	225	225					138	138	138		
		228	228						226	226	226		
		229	229						227	227	54		
		281	281						231	231	231	231	
			307						234	234	234	292	292
									237	237	237		
									292	292	232		

COMPARISON TABLES
Inter Flotilla Ship Movements

140 MSF(Sheerness/Harwich)

Year 41	42	43	44	45	46	47
		57	109			
		60	149	136		
		137	269	173		
			282	282	282	
			287			

141 MSF(Liverpool)

Year 41	42	43	44	45	46	47
		276	276			
		288				
		289	289			
		291				
		296	296			
		301				
		308				

142 MSF(Plymouth)

Year 41	42	43	44	45	46	47
		242	242	242		
		243	243	243	243	
		244	244	244		
		245	245	245		
		246	246	246		
		250	250	250	250	
		254	254	254	254	
		255	255	255	255	
			202			
			203			
			204			
			205			
			206			

143 MSF(Swansea/NIF)

Year 41	42	43	44	45	46	47
	119	247	247	247	247	
	120	248	248	248		
		251	251	251	251	
		252	252	252	252	
		253	253	253	253	
		256	256	256	256	
		257	257	228		
			249	249		
				37	37	

144 MSF(Grimsby/Dover)

Year 41	42	43	44	45	46	47
		121	119	119	119	
		122	120	120	120	
				121	121	121
				122	122	
				42	62	
				76	76	
				79	206	206
				82	82	
				87	268	
				173		
				294		
				295		
				308		

145 MSF(N/Shields)

Year 41	42	43	44	45	46	47
				62		
				150	150	150

Inter Flotilla Ship Movements

146 MSF(Levant)							147 MSF(NIF)						
41	**42**	**43**	**44**	**45**	**46**	**47**	**41**	**42**	**43**	**44**	**45**	**46**	**47**
			144	144						207	207	244	
				143						214	214		
				310						215	215		
				312	312					277			
				311	311					288	288		
				313	313	313				291	291		
										293	293		
										297	297		

(Year)

159 MSF(NIF/EU)							160 MSF(Grimsby)						
41	**42**	**43**	**44**	**45**	**46**	**47**	**41**	**42**	**43**	**44**	**45**	**46**	**47**
			239	239						241	241	241	
											238	238	

(Year)

165 MSF(Harwich)							167 MSF(NIF)						
41	**42**	**43**	**44**	**45**	**46**	**47**	**41**	**42**	**43**	**44**	**45**	**46**	**47**
			240	240						239			

(Year)

Legend:

Med – Mediterranean	NIF – Normandy Invasion Force
NI – Northern Ireland	NWEU – North West Europe
PL – Plymouth	HR – Harwich
DR – Dover	BF – Belfast
NRDY – Normandy	CLD – Clyde
SHRNS – Sheerness	

COMPARISON TABLES (contd)
VESSEL DISPOSITION FOLLOWING HOSTILITIES 1947–1959

1947

Belg	Dnmk	Fra	Grce	Hlnd	Itly	Ind	Brma	Sgapr	Bmda	Tky	Mlta
189	83	9	46	36	10	129	197	107	222	88	143(2)
191	84	21	53	231	32	130	200	108	223		
193	226	49	58	234	34	132					
266		67	143(1)	237	35	148					
		81	144	263	48	151					
		116	310	307	50	154					
		118(1)	1		99						
		133	5		100						
		184			102						
		204			103						
		213			104						
		220			105						
		221			106						
					135						
					167						
					172						
					185						
4	3	13	8	6	17	6	2	2	2	1	1(64)

Chatham :21, 47, 56, 57, 69, 79, 86, 109, 110, 118(2), 224, 228, 271, 272, 275, 283, 285, 286, 289, 290, 291, 296, 297, 301   Total(23) GT 87

Air Ministry: 245, 247, 256   3   GT. 90

1948

Belgium	Denmark	France	Greece	Holland	Italy	India	Burma	Bermuda	Tky
189	83	49	1	231	10	129	197	222	88
191	84	220	5	234	32	130	200	223	
193	226	221	46	292	35	131	201		
266			53	307	48	151			
			58		50	154			
			144		99				
			310		100				
			313		102				
					103				
					104				
					105				
					106				
					135				
					167				
					172				
					185				
4	3	3	8	4	16	5	3	2	1(46)

Chatham: 36, 47, 56, 57, 69, 79, 86, 109, 110, 224, 228, 263, 272, 275, 283, 285, 286, 288, 289, 290, 291, 294, 296, 297, 301.   Total (25)

MSF 50: 271, MSF 104: 174, 181, 261, MSF 118: 182, 187, 188, 190, MSF 159: 239.

Portsmouth: 49, 236, 237, 293. HMS Vernon 217. RNVR 233.   GT. 86

1949

Belgium	Bombay	Denmark	Greece	Holland	Italy	India	Malta	Tky
191	154	83	1	231	10	129	50(1)	88
193		226	5	234	32	130		
266			46	292	34	151		
			53		35			
			58		48			
			144		50(2)			
			310		99			
			313		100			
					102			
					103			
					104			
					105			
					106			
					135			
					167			
					172			
					185			
3	1	2	8	3	17	3	1	1(38)

Chatham: 36, 47, 56, 577, 69, 79, 84, 86, 109, 110, 224, 228, 263, 272, 275, 283, 285, 286, 288, 289, 290, 291, 294, 296, 297, 301,307.   (27)
MSF 50: 271, MSF 51: 217, MSF 104: 174, MSF 118: 182, 187, 188, MSF 159: 239.
Portsmouth: 49, 220, 236, 237, 293, RNVR 233, 261   GT 79

1950

Belgium	Bombay	Bermuda	Denmark	Greece	Holland	Italy	Ind	Malta	Tky
182	154	222	833	1	231	32(1)	130	10	88
189		223	226	5	234	99(1)		32(2)	
193				46	292	100(1)		48	
				53		102(1)		99(2)	
				58		103		100(2)	
				144		104		102(2)	
				310		105		167(2)	
				313		106		185(2)	
						167(1)			
						185(1)			
3	1	2	2	8	3	10	1	8	1(33)

MSF 50: 271(1), 307, MSF 51: 271(2), MSF 104: 174, 181, MSF 159: 239   6
MSF 301: 109, 272, 288, 301, Royal Navy: 187, 188, RNVR: 233, 261, 275, 285   10
Portsmouth: 236, 237, 293.   3
Chatham: 35, 366, 59, 79, 86, 110, 135, 224, 228, 263, 283, 289, 291, 294, 2966, 297   17
GT 69

1951

Belgium	Bombay	Bermuda	Denmark	Greece	Holland	Ind	Yugo	Malta	Tky
182	154	222	83	1	231	130	174	10	88
189			226	5	234			48	
191				46	292			50	
193				53(1)				53(2)	
266				58				99	
				144				100	
				313				102	
								104	
								105	
								106	
								167	
								310	
5	1	1	2	7	3	1	1	12	1(33)

MSF 50: 217, MSF 51: 109, 217, 272, 286, 288, 301	7
MSF 104: 57, 69, 110, 181, 224, 228, 283, 290, 291, 296	10
MSF 108: 32, 34, 135, 172, 185	5
MSF 120: 36, 56, 79, 84, Royal Navy: 187, 188, Neptune: 275	7
RNVR 233 (St David), 261 (Venturer), 285 (Isis), 289 (Thames)	4
Portsmouth: 236, 237	2
Chatham: 35, 86, 263, 294	4
	GT 72

1952

Belg	Bemda	Bmby	Drmk	China	Grce	Gib	Holnd	HngK	Ind	Malta	Tky
182	222	154	83	79	1	99	231	56	130	10	88
189			234	84	5	100	292	286		48	
191				36		102		297		50	
193						103				167	
266						104				34	
						105				313	
						106					
5	1	1	2	3	2	7	2	3	1	6	1(34)

MSF 51: 109, 236, 301, MSF 104: 69, 110, 181, 228, 283, 290, 291	10
MSF 108: 79(1), 135, 172, 185, 32, MSF 120: 79(2), 297	6
Royal Navy: 187, 188, Neptune: 275, RNVR: 233, 261, 285, 289	7
Portsmouth: 86, 237, 263, Rosyth: 2711, Portland: 307	5
Chatham: 35, 46, 53, 217, 224, 272, 294, 296, 310	9
	GT 71

1953

Belg	Bmda	China	Dnmk	Greece	Gib	Hlnd	HnKg	Ind	Malta	Tky
182	222	36	83	1	104	237	286	130	10	88
189		79		5	105	231	297		34	
191		84				239	56		48	
193						292			50	
266									135	
									167	
									313	
5	1	3	1	2	2	4	3	1	7	1(30)

MSF 51: 109, 236, 301, MSF 104: 69, 181, 228, MSF 108: 32, 172   8
RNVR: 233, 261, 285, 289, Royal Navy: 187, 188, Neptune: 275   7
Portsmouth: 57, 100, 102, 263, Portland: 307, Rosyth: 217, 271   7
Chatham: 355, 46, 53, 58, 86, 99, 103, 106, 110, 144, 224, 261, 272, 283, 290, 291,
    296, 310   18

GT 70

1954

Belg	Bmda	China	Dnmk	Greece	Gib	Hlnd	HnKg	Malta	Tky
182	222	36	83	1	53	231	56	10	88
189			292	5	104	237	79	34	
266					261		84	48	
					272		286	135	
							297	167	
								313	
3	1	1	2	2	4	2	5	6	1(27)

MSF 51: 236(1), MSF 104: 69, 181, MSF 108, 32, 172   5
RNVR: 58 (Thames), 228 (Curzon), 233 (St. David), 285 (Isis)   4
Royal Navy: 187, 188, Neptune: 275   3
Sheerness: 236(2), Portland: 307, Rosyth: 109, 217, 271, 301   5
Portsmouth: 100, 263, Pembroke: 102   3
Chatham: 35, 46, 50, 86, 99, 103, 106, 110, 144, 185, 191, 193, 224, 233, 283, 289,
    290, 291, 296, 310 (Reserve)   20

GT67

1953

Belg	China	Dnmk	Greece	Gib	Hlnd	HnKg	Malta	Tky
182	36	83	1	53	231	56	10	88
189		292	5	57	237	79	34	
266				261		84	135	
				272		286	167	
						297	313	
3	1	2	2	4	2	5	5	1(25)

MSF 104: 181, MSF 108: 32, 172, Royal Navy: 187, 188, Npetune: 275   6
Chatham: 35, 46, 50, 86, 99, 100, 103, 106, 110, 191, 193, 233, 185, 283, 289,
    290, 291, 307, 310, Rosyth: 109, 217, 2711, 301   23
Portsmouth: 263: Pembroke: 102, Sheerness: 236   3

GT 57

1956

China	Dnmk	Grce	Gib	Hlld	HnKg	Mlta	Tky	Rus	Ros	RNVR	Shns	MSF104
36	83	5	53	231	56	10	88	90	271	228	236	181
	292		57	237	79			203				
	301		261		84			212				
			272		286							
					297							
1	3	1	4	2	5	1	1	3	1	1	1	1(25)

Chatham: 46, 50, 86, 103, 106, 109, 110, 144, 185, 193, 233, 283, 291, 307GT   39

1957

China	Gib	HnKg	Tky	Ros	MSF104	Rus	Chat
36	57	56	88	271	181	90	50
	272	79				203	86
		84				212	144
		286					193
		297					233
							289
1	2	5	1	1	1	3	6(20)

GT   20

1958

China	HnKg	Chatham	MSF104	Rus
36	56	86	181	9 0
	79	289		203
	84			212
	286			
	297			
1	5	2	1	3 GT 12

1959

China	HnKg	Chatham	Ind	Air Min	Rus
79	56	289	97	86	90
			98	245	203
				247	212
				256	
1	1	1	2	4	3 GT 12

The figures in brackets denote that the vessel was moved during the course of the year either to another base abroad or returned home following her spell with the allied forces.

APPENDIX G

MINESWEEPING FLOTILLA OPERATIONAL AREAS

MSF	1941	1942	1943	1944	1945	1946	1947
101	Sheerness	Sheerness	Sheerness	Dartmouth	Dartmouth	Sheerness	Sheerness
102	Sheerness	Sheerness	Sheerness	Sheerness	Sheerness	Sheerness	Sheerness
103	Sheerness	Med. Sea	Med. Sea	Med. Sea	Med. Sea	Med. Sea	
104	Leith	Leith	Leith	N.I.F.	Nore	Nore	
105	xxxxxxxx	Liverpool	Med. Sea	Med. Sea	Med. Sea	Med. Sea	
106	N. Ireland	Newhaven	Newhaven	Newhaven	Newhaven		
107	xxxxxxxx	N. Ireland	Clyde	Clyde	Clyde		
108	Liverpool	Med. Sea	Med. Sea	Med. Sea			
109	N. Ireland	Liv/Clyde				NW Europe	NW Europe
110	Swansea	Med. Sea	Med. Sea	Sheerness	Sheerness		
111	xxxxxxxx	xxxxxxxx	Med. Sea	Med. Sea	Med. Sea		
112	Plymouth	Plymouth	Harwich	Harwich	Belfast		
113	xxxxxxxx	Swansea	Swansea	Dover	Dover		
114	Portsmouth	Med. Sea	Med. Sea	Med. Sea	Med. Sea	Med. Sea	
115	xxxxxxxx	Portsmouth	Portsmouth	Portsmouth	N.I.F.		
116	Sheerness	Sheerness	Sheerness	Scapa Flow	NW Europe	NW Europe	
117	Sheerness	Sheerness	Sheerness	Sheerness	NW Europe	NW Europe	NW Europe
118	xxxxxxxx	Harwich	N.I.F. NWE	N.I.F. NWE	N.I.F. NWE	N.I.F. NWE	N.I.F. NWE
119	xxxxxxxx	Portsmouth	Portsmouth	N.I.F.	N.I.F.		
120	xxxxxx	Med. Sea	Med. Sea	Med. Sea	Med. Sea		
121	xxxxxxxx	Med. Sea	Med. Sea	Med. Sea	Med. Sea	Med. Sea	
122	xxxxxxxx	xxxxxxxx	xxxxxxxx	E. Indies	E. Indies	E. Indies	E. Indies
	xxxxxxxx	xxxxxxxx	xxxxxxxx	xxxxxxxx	xxxxxxxx	xxxxxxxx	xxxxxxxx
130	xxxxxxxx	xxxxxxxx	Plymouth	Plymouth	Plymouth		
131	xxxxxxxx	Sheerness	Sheerness	Sheerness	Sheerness		
132	xxxxxxxx	Liverpool	Liverpool	Sheerness	Sheerness		
133	xxxxxxxx	Sheerness	Sheerness	Sheerness			
134	xxxxxxxx	Belfast	Belfast	Belfast			
135	xxxxxxxx	Scapa Flow	Scapa Flow	Portsmouth	Portsmouth		
136	xxxxxxxx	Sheerness	Sheerness	Sheerness			
137	xxxxxxxx	xxxxxxxx	Leith	Leith	Leith		
138	xxxxxxxx	xxxxxxxx	Lowestoft	Lowestoft	N.I.F.		
139	xxxxxxxx	xxxxxxxx	Harwich	Dutch Waters--------			
140	xxxxxxxx	xxxxxxxx	Sheerness	Hwrwich	Harwich		
141	xxxxxxxx	xxxxxxxx	Liverpool	Liverpool	Liverpool		
142	xxxxxxxx	xxxxxxxx	Plymouth	Plymouth	Plymouth		
143	xxxxxxxx	xxxxxxxx	Swansea	N.I.F.	N.I.F.		
144	xxxxxxxx	Grimsby	Grimsby	Grimsby	Dover		
145	xxxxxxxx	xxxxxxxx	xxxxxxxx	N. Shields	N. Shields		
146	xxxxxxxx	xxxxxxxx	xxxxxxxx	xxxxxxxx	Levant	Levant	
147	xxxxxxxx	xxxxxxxx	xxxxxxxx	N.I.F.	N.I.F.		
159	xxxxxxxx	xxxxxxxx	xxxxxxxx	N.I.F. NWE	N.I.F. NWE	N.I.F. NWE	
163	xxxxxxxx	xxxxxxxx	xxxxxxxx	Grimsby	Grimsby		
167	xxxxxxxx	xxxxxxxx	xxxxxxxx	N.I.F.	N.I.F.		
165	xxxxxxxx	xxxxxxxx	xxxxxxxx	xxxxxxxx	xxxxxxxx	Harwich	
201	xxxxxxxx	xxxxxxxx	Harwich	Harwich	Harwich		

202	xxxxxxxx	xxxxxxxx	Lowestoft	Lowestoft	Lowestoft	NW Europe
203	xxxxxxxx	xxxxxxxx	xxxxxxxx	Harwich	Harwich	
204	xxxxxxxx	xxxxxxxx	Dover	Dover	N. Shields	N. Shields
205	xxxxxxxx	xxxxxxxx	Portsmouth	Portsmouth	Portsmouth	Lowestoft
206	xxxxxxxx	xxxxxxxx	xxxxxxxx	Leith	Yarmouth	
207	xxxxxxxx	xxxxxxxx	xxxxxxxx	Grimsby	Grimsby	
208	xxxxxxxx	xxxxxxxx	xxxxxxxx	N. Shields	Dover	
209	xxxxxxxx	xxxxxxxx	xxxxxxxx	Plymouth	Plymouth	

N.I.F. Normandy Invasion Fleet   NWE North West Europe

Five Flotillas were reformed in 1950/51 and were operational until 1954

MSF	1950	1951	1952	1953	1954
50	xxxxxxxx	Pt Edgar	Pt Edgar		
51	xxxxxxxx	Pt Edgar	Pt Edgar	Pt Edgar	Pt Edgar
104	xxxxxxxx	Nore	Nore	Nore	
108	xxxxxxxx	Med Sea	Med Sea	Med Sea	
120	xxxxxxxx	xxxxxxxx	Hong Kong	Hong Kong	Hong Kong
301	Port Edgar	Port Edgar			

APPENDIX H

MOTOR MIINESWEEPERS KNOWN TO HAVE BEEN BOUGHT OUT OF SERVICE

Air Ministry	86	1
Allan and Son, Gillingham	294	1
Belzize Boat Yard	100, 263	2
Brightlingsea	21	1
Chan Wong Singapore	36, 56, 79, 84	4
Cotterham Ltd, Kent	69	1
Challis London	182, 187, 266	3
Chichester Yacht Co.	220	1
Finnis Chatham	191, 290, 296, 307, 310	5
MMS 191 being restored by MMS Trust		
Grey and Thompson	233	1
Gibraltar	5, 57, 261, 272	4
Geary Gillingham	110	1
Gasan Enterprises Malta	172	1
Renamed *Pinu*. Sold to Greek owners 1957		
Italy	3, 10	2
Itchenor	123	1
Norway	241	1
Pounds, Portsmouth	46, 50, 106, 109, 181, 185, 301	7
MMS 46 sold to Caledonian MacBrayne, Scotland		
Phoenix Steam Co, Malta	167	1
Magro, Malta	135	1
Renamed *Queen of Peace* Foundered Gulf of Sirte 1977		
Pierce, Canvey	217, 235, 289, 291	4
Otterham Ltd.	99, 224, 275, 285	4
Roger de Smelt	83, 144, 193, 283	4
Rammage J.	104	1
Rotterdam	103	1
Russie	90, 203, 213	3
San Cheong Hong Kong	84	1
Stonehaven Engineering	35	1
Storeham I.	293	1
Smith, Gibraltar	261	1
Captain Taprael London	239	1
White J.	271	1
	Total	63

Many of these ships were bought for a song, some for as little as £450, which one must suppose in the early days of the peace was quite a sum of money, but when one compares this figure with the cost of £18,000 it would seem quite a pittance for ships only a few years old, and a number almost straight off the slips. There are stories of the larger type sweepers being taken out to sea and sunk six at a time. No more or less than happens to some of our present day craft costing in the region of millions of pounds, being used for target practice.

Minesweeping Trawler

From left to right author is 4th.
Back row sitting on Carley Float.
Ship's crew MMS 46 1945–46 (Med).

Operation Mastlift – MMS 191 – 1989

The author receiving a trophy and a cheque for £1,000 from David Bellamy, for the preservation of a Minesweeper, at BBC TV Studios, Pebble Mill, Birmingham - October 1982.